Osiris, Horus and Isis.

Source: Karl Baedeker, *Egypt. Handbook for Traveling, Pt. 1 Lower Egypt, with the Fayum and the Peninsula of Sinai*, 1885.

Waters of Life

A Devotional Anthology for Isis and Serapis

Compiled by Rebecca Buchanan & Jeremy J. Baer
and the Editorial Board of
the Library of Neos Alexandria

Copyright © 2009 by Neos Alexandria

All rights reserved. No part of this book may be reproduced by any means or in any form whatsoever without written permission from the author(s), except for brief quotations embodied in literary articles or reviews. Copyright reverts to individual authors after publication.

With fainting soul athirst for Grace,
I wandered in a desert place,
And at the crossing of the ways
I saw a sixfold Seraph blaze;
He touched mine eyes with fingers light
As sleep that cometh in the night:
And like a frightened eagle's eyes,
They opened wide with prophecies.
He touched mine ears, and they were drowned
With tumult and a roaring sound:
I heard convulsion in the sky,
And flight of angel hosts on high,
And beasts that move beneath the sea,
And the sap creeping in the tree.
And bending to my mouth he wrung
From out of it my sinful tongue,
And all its lies and idle rust,
And 'twixt my lips a-perishing
A subtle serpent's forkèd sting
With right hand wet with blood he thrust.
And with his sword my breast he cleft,
My quaking heart thereout he reft,
And in the yawning of my breast
A coal of living fire he pressed.
Then in the desert I lay dead,
And God called unto me and said:
"Arise, and let My voice be heard,
Charged with My will go forth and span
The land and sea, and let My word
Lay waste with fire the heart of man."
– Alexander Pushkin

Once more let it be your morning, Gods.
We repeat. You alone are the primal source.
With you the world arises, and a fresh start gleams
On all the fragments of our failures....
– Rainier Maria Rilke

Dedication

To She of Ten Thousand Names, Great of Magic, Eye of Ra, Great Mourner, Mother of God, Mistress of Heaven, Daughter of Nut, Lady of Beer and Bread, Lady of Inheritance, Mistress of All the Stars.

To the Lord of the Everlasting, Sovereign Over the Land of Silence, Foremost Among the Westerners, Lord of Ma'at, Beautiful One, Weary-Hearted One, Divine King, Master of Eternity.

Those who wish to stand before the Hall of Two Truths with righteousness in their hearts and truth on their tongues do consecrate the following pages in your names. The best parts of the Kemetic, Greco-Roman and modern Pagan communities have come together to offer you honor.

As our devotions are sincere, may your blessings be constant. May the greater Pagan community come to know you both through this work.

Acknowledgments

What you are about to read has been the fruition of months of work compiled from many talented individuals, all of whom must be properly thanked for this endeavor.

First and most obvious, thanks to all the talented writers, scholars and devotees who heeded the call and submitted their contributions. Second, thanks to Allyson Szabo, Erik Dutton, Brontosproximo, and Kelsey Meek for proofreading the draft.

A hearty thank you to the unforgettable Sannion for founding Neos Alexandria and for providing advice and feedback. We also extend a warm thanks to Kate Winter who provided much needed technical support for the completion of this anthology.

Not least we thank you, dear reader, for purchasing this book; with your help we can rebuild the legacy of the Alexandrian pantheon. Twenty-five percent of the profits from your purchase will be directed to a worthy charity in the name of the gods.

Table of Contents

INTRODUCTION 9
A NOTE ON SPELLING AND STYLE 11
THE STORY OF ISIS AND OSIRIS 13
   BY ANNE BARING AND JULES CASHFORD
PRAYER FOR ISIS 28
   BY JEREMY J. BAER
A HYMN TO OSIRIS 29
   BY SANNION
A NEVER ENDING BATTLE 30
   BY FRATER ELEUTHEREUS
A HISTORY OF THE WORSHIP OF ISIS AND SERAPIS 33
   BY JEREMY J. BAER
TO THE VEILED ISIS 40
   BY BRANDON NEWBERG
A SERAPIS ARETOLOGY 42
   BY SANNION
TRIAD FOR SERAPIS 49
   BY P. SUFENAS VIRIUS LUPUS
REFLECTIONS ON THE LAMENTATIONS OF ISIS
   AND NEPHTHYS 53
   BY SANNION
ISIS 55
   BY BIRDSONG
MOST ANCIENT 56
   BY REBECCA BUCHANAN
TO OSIRIS 57
   BY BRANDON NEWBERG
SOME THOUGHTS ON OSIRIS AND THE DEAD 58
   BY SANNION
IN THY ORISONS 61
   BY JEREMY J. BAER
THE CROSSING OF AKH 63
   BY CHRISTA BERGERSON

WORDS FOR THE WALL (TO HELP A MAN PASS THROUGH) ... 64
   BY NORMANDI ELLIS
MR. WEST ... 66
   BY REBECCA BUCHANAN
ISIS, MISTRESS OF HEAVEN ... 71
   BY JEREMY J. BAER
THE WHITE LION QUEEN ... 75
   BY FRATER ELEUTHEREUS
HYMN UNTO ISIS ... 77
   BY SETI APOLLONIUS
THE MIGHTY BULL OF THE TWO LANDS ... 79
   BY SANNION
ON THE WINGS OF ISIS: THE INTRODUCTION OF ISIS TO
   GREECE AND ROME ... 93
   BY D. JASMINE MERCED
HER NAMES, INSCRIBED AND SUNG ... 117
   BY REBECCA BUCHANAN
FOR ISIS ... 119
   BY SANNION
EPIPHANY OF ISIS ... 120
   BY AMANDA SIOUX BLAKE
MUSINGS ON *THE METAMORPHOSES* ... 127
   BY JEREMY J. BAER
THE PROBLEMS OF USING APULEIUS' *METAMORPHOSES* AS
   A RELIABLE SOURCE FOR THE CULT OF ISIS ... 132
   BY EMMA NICHOLSON
UNTITLED ... 143
   BY REBECCA BUCHANAN
INVENTIO OSIRIDIS ... 144
   BY JEREMY J. BAER
ETERNAL LOVE ... 147
   BY JOCELYN ALMOND
FIRST SORROW OF CREATION ... 153
   BY REBECCA BUCHANAN
PICKING UP THE PIECES ... 154
   BY SUZETTE CHAN
A MODERN FESTIVAL FOR SERAPIS ... 158
   BY JEREMY J. BAER
HYMN TO SERAPIS ... 161
   BY SANNION

NAVIGIUM ISIDIS 162
    BY JEREMY J. BAER
ISIS POETIC 165
    BY RUSSELL GOODMAN
A MOTHER'S LOVE 166
    BY GRACE
THE ISIDIS NAVIGIUM: GRECO ROMAN RITUAL OF
ANTIQUITY IN A MODERN CONTEXT; PEOPLE ARE
RETURNING TO THE ANCIENT WAYS 169
    BY KAREN TATE
ISIS, NUIT, SOL AND THE OX 176
    BY PAYAM NABARZ
ISIS WORSHIP FOR HELLENIC POLYTHEISTS 178
    BY SANNION
APPROACHING THE ALTAR OF ISIS 189
    BY AMANDA SIOUX BLAKE
MY TRAVELS WITH SERAPIS (AND ANTINOUS) 191
    BY P. SUFENAS VIRIUS LUPUS
TO APIS 208
    BY SANNION
TRACING THE THREADS OF MY RELATIONSHIP WITH ISIS .. 209
    BY AMANDA SIOUX BLAKE
PRAYER TO ISIS I 214
    BY THEOKLEIA
ALONE 215
    BY JEREMY J. BAER
SEEKING WHAT IS LOST: AN ISIAN MEDITATION 216
    BY BARBARA ARDINGER, PH.D.
AVE ISIDE 223
    BY REBECCA BUCHANAN
SLEEPING IN THE DESERT 224
    BY NORMANDI ELLIS
RITUAL TO ISIS 225
    BY JEREMY J. BAER
HAIL ISIS! 229
    BY HEATHER COX
CRY TO ISIS 230
    BY AMANDA SIOUX BLAKE
THE LADY OF TEARS 232
    BY FRATER ELEUTHEREUS

ISIS 245
    BY LOGAN GORE
PRAYER TO ISIS II 247
    BY THEOKLEIA
THE MESSAGE OF OSIRIS 248
    BY SANNION
HOW ASET LEARNED RA'S NAME 250
    BY REV. TAMARA SIUDA

OUR CONTRIBUTORS 255
SELECT BIBLIOGRAPHY AND INTERNET RESOURCES 260
APPENDIX A – LIST OF DIVINITIES 264
APPENDIX B – GLOSSARY 269
APPENDIX C – HISTORICAL ERAS 276
APPENDIX D – CHRONOLOGY OF IMPORTANT EVENTS 279
ABOUT THE BIBLIOTHECA ALEXANDRINA 282

Introduction

Isis/Aset and Serapis/Osiris/Wesir, among the oldest deities worshiped by humanity, were honored in different ways in different places by many different people across four millennia. In an attempt to explore and understand the mysteries of life and death, you are hard pressed to find better guides for your journey than this divine wife and husband.

To better understand them, you can choose a specific time and place – Old Kingdom Egypt of the third millennium BCE, Pompeii during the first century CE, the shores of the Thames during the second century, Roman Alexandria during the fourth century, the island of Philae at the beginning of the Muslim Conquest, the Pacific Coast of present day Los Angeles – or study the whole sweeping arc of their worship. In this devotional, we have attempted to provide the reader with a balance of the two: a broad study which does not sacrifice detail. Thus, entries in this devotional cover the spectrum from ancient Egypt through the Hellenistic and Roman eras to the modern Pagan rebirth, from scholarly essays to original short fiction, prayers, meditations and rituals. Every one of the contributors to this devotional has experienced Isis and Osiris/Serapis in some way, which they hope to share with you.

In the editors' case, while we appreciate and accept the vast religious continuum embodied by these two deities, we know them primarily as they were experienced in the Hellenistic era. Ptolemy Soter, the most wily of Alexander the Great's successors, was forced to reconcile the Greco-Macedonian heritage of his comrades with the Egyptian culture over which he now presided. The Hellenic and the Kemetic were blended into the cults of Isis and Serapis, and a new religious phenomenon swept the classical world from the port city of Alexandria. Isis and Serapis were now not just among the oldest and most popular of Egyptian deities; they were universal saviors for humanity.

We both belong to Neos Alexandria, a group founded to uphold the legacy of Ptolemy Soter and the Alexandrian deities. In many ways Isis and Serapis stand at the forefront of that Greco-Egyptian legacy. Assembling an anthology to them was both a sublime honor and a demanding duty. It simply *had* to be done. We can only hope our efforts are pleasing to the gods and informative to the reader.

But the glories and reverence for these deities cannot be confined to one organization. We made a conscious decision to look outside Neos Alexandria and solicit anyone who could contribute their perspective. From respected authors and scholars to random denizens of MySpace communities, from established Kemetic temples to informal Neopagan lists, we spared no effort in encouraging submissions.

What we offer to you, dear reader, is a sincere exploration of the deities from many angles. It is our hope to furnish the greater Pagan community with a living testament to the majesty of Isis and Serapis. We offer scholarly essays for your edification, poems and stories for your enjoyment, and suggested rituals and meditations for your inspiration.

During the Roman era, there were two refrains commonly etched onto the sarcophagi of adherents of Isis and Osiris/Serapis. They loosely translate as "be of good courage" and "drink of the waters of life." And so we invite you to have the courage to drink deeply of the waters of life that flow here.

Rebecca Buchanan
Jeremy J. Baer

A Note on Spelling and Style

Greek and Latin renderings for the names of the Egyptian gods understandably vary from the native Egyptian. Also, due to the problems of transliteration of Egyptian hieroglyphics, there can be several renderings of an Egyptian name.

Since our authors fall within the wide spectrum of worship of the gods – from Ancient Egyptian to Greco-Roman to Neopagan – we did not wish to impose conformity of spelling upon them. They were free to use whatever name spoke best to their own understanding of the deity. However, this can cause confusion. Thus, in the interests of clarity, the editors offer a table of the most common variations of spellings. The more familiar Greco-Roman renderings are offered first, followed by the Egyptian.

Ammon: Amon, Amoun, Amen, Amun
Anubis: Anoubis, Yinepu, Anpu, Anupu
Hathor: Hethert
Horus (also "Harpokrates"): Heru-sa-Aset
Isis: Aset, Auset
Nephthys: Nebet-het, Nebt-het
Osiris: Asar, Ausar, Wesir, User
Ptah: Phtha, Peteh
Ra: Re
Set: Seth, Setekh, Setesh, Sutekh
Thoth: Djehuty, Dhwty, Tahuti, Tehuti

Serapis may also be spelled Sarapis.

We as editors did not impose strict uniformity on our contributors in terms of style. You may find non-fiction pieces documented with endnotes, in-text citations, or simply a bibliography at the end. You may find some individuals deliberately capitalize a word or punctuate a phrase in such a manner as to add emphasis. You will find British English and American English. While we have made some corrections in the interest of nominal uniformity, if an author demanded a certain format be retained from the original writing, we have adhered to his/her wishes.

Bibliotheca Alexandrina is committed to bringing you works that convey excellence and academic veracity. But at the same time, individuals must be allowed to use their own voice when they speak of the gods. Hopefully the reader will find an acceptable balance in this devotional anthology.

The Story of Isis and Osiris[1]

by Anne Baring and Jules Cashford

Now (once upon a time) Nut and Geb gave birth to Osiris, and at the hour of his birth a voice issued forth saying "The Lord of All advances to the light." On the second day was born Arueris (called the elder Horus); on the third day, Seth, but not in due season or manner, who with a blow broke through his mother's side and leapt forth; on the fourth day Isis was born in the regions that are ever moist; and on the fifth day, Nephthys. With their parents and grandparents and Atum, they were called the Ennead, the Nine Gods and Goddesses. They were born in sacred time, in the interval of five days that were left over between one year (of 360 days) and the next, which Thoth had won playing at draughts with the moon. Nephthys became the wife of Seth, but Isis and Osiris loved each other in the darkness of their mother's womb before they were born.

Osiris became the first king of Egypt and the creator of civilization, teaching his people the art of cultivation and honouring of the gods, "establishing justice throughout both banks of the Nile."[2] He taught the Egyptians how to plant wheat and barley, how to gather the fruit from the trees and to cultivate the vine, and before their time the races of the world had been but savages. When he travelled to teach other nations, Isis rules vigilantly and peacefully in his absence.

But Seth, wicked brother of Osiris, was jealous of his virtue and his fame. So he constructed a chest the size of his brother, and one night at the palace, in the midst of the feasting, he had the richly decorated chest brought into the room and promised as a jest to give it to the one it would fit exactly. When Osiris laid himself inside it, seventy-two conspirators immediately leapt forward and nailed the lid on the chest, sealed it with molten lead and flung it into the Nile. Then it floated down to the sea.

Isis, overwhelmed with grief, cut off her hair, put on mourning clothes and searched everywhere, up and down the Nile, asking everyone she met whether they had seen the chest. It so happened that some children, playing by the river, had seen which mouth of the Nile had carried it out to the sea. Isis learnt that the chest had been carried by the waves to the coast of Byblos in Phoenicia. There it had gently lodged itself in the branches of an erica tree, which had quickly grown up around it, enclosing it on every side so it was completely hidden. So beautiful and fragrant was the tree that the local king and queen had the tree felled and fashioned into a pillar at the palace.

So Isis came to Byblos and she placed herself by a well of the city, veiled and in mourning, her divinity disguised, speaking to no one. When some of the queen's maidens came to the well, she greeted them kindly and began to braid their hair, breathing on them such wondrous fragrance that when they returned to the palace Queen Astarte smelled the perfume on the braids and, sending for the stranger, took her into her house and made her the nurse of her child.[3]

Now the great goddess gave the infant her finger to suck instead of the breast, and at night she placed him in a fire to burn away all that was mortal in him. And then, transforming herself into a swallow, she flew around the pillar, mournfully singing. But it happened that one night Queen Astarte, seeing her little son lying there in the flames, shrieked dreadfully, and in that one moment deprived her child forever of the treasure of immortal life.

Isis then revealed her true nature and asked that the pillar that held up the roof be given to her. She took it down and, cutting away the wood of the tree, revealed the sarcophagus of Osiris hidden inside. When Isis saw it, she fell upon it with such a piercing cry that the younger of the Queen's sons was frightened out of his life. Then, taking the elder son with her, Isis set sail with the chest for Egypt (though, finding the river too rough and windy, she grew angry and dried up the stream). As soon as she arrived at a desert place where she was alone, she opened the chest and, laying her face on the face of her brother, she kissed him and wept. (Suddenly, though, she caught sight of the boy watching her, and gave him a look of such gravity that he died of fright on the instant.)

Now, according to some, it was when Isis fluttered round the pillar as a swallow that she conceived her son, Horus, from Osiris. But according to others, when Isis lay upon her husband in the boat she conceived their child, for, taking the form of a kite, she hovered lovingly over him, bringing him back to life with the beating of her great wings:

> It is she, Isis, the just, who protects her brother,
> Who seeks him without wearying,
> Who in mourning traverses the whole land
> Without respite before finding him,
> Who gives shade with her feathers,
> And wind with her wings.

> It is she who praises her brother,
> Who relieves the weakness of him who is tired,
> Who receives his seed and gives birth to his heir,
> Who nurtures the child in solitude,
> Without anyone knowing where she is.[4]

Isis then hid the chest enclosing the body of Osiris in the remote marshes of the delta, while she went to Buto to take care of her son, Horus.

One night Seth was hunting wild boar in the light of the full moon when he discovered the chest hidden among the reeds. He tore the body into fourteen pieces and scattered them up and down the country, each in a different place, and he may even have thrown the phallus of Osiris into the Nile. When Isis learned of this, once again she had to search for her husband, sailing through the swamps in a boat of papyrus. This time her sister Nephthys, sister-bride of their wicked brother Seth, helped her and so did Nephthys' son, Anubis, who had the head of a jackal. Anubis had been fathered by Osiris, who, one night when it was very dark, mistook Nephthys for Isis. Some people say this is why Seth bore such malice towards Osiris. Little Horus, who had the head of a hawk, was now old enough to help, too, and they were joined by Thoth, the moon god, who had the head of an ibis, and could take the form of a baboon.

So, with Thoth's powers of discrimination and Anubis' intuitive nose, together they found all the parts of Osiris except for the genital member, which had been swallowed by a fish. Wherever Isis found a piece of Osiris' body she buried it with all the ritual due to a god, rites that were to be performed in Egypt ever afterwards. She made a replica of the missing phallus to take its place, consecrating it with great ceremony. Some say that the funeral rites were only formal, and that Isis carefully brought all the parts back together again and reassembled them as a mummy, swathed tightly in linen bandages, through the transforming magic of Anubis in the role of embalming priest. Then Isis fanned the dead body again with her wings and Osiris revived to become the Ruler of Eternity. He now sits in the underworld with all power and majesty, in the Hall of Two Truths, where he judges the souls of the dead, which are weighed in a balance against the feather of truth of the goddess Ma'at, she in whose care are the laws of the universe.[5]

> Osiris! You went away, but you have returned,
> you fell asleep, but you have awakened,
> you died, but you live again.[6]

The conflict with Seth was not over, however, and the story continues with Horus growing up to take his father's place and avenge his death.

During the "Contendings of Horus and Seth" (a New Kingdom compilation of different texts, which may point to the late arrival of this part of the story) Horus lost his left eye, which Thoth healed, and Seth his testicle. Their battles took place over three days and three nights, the figure of gestation as the time of the moon's darkness, which appears in every culture when the issue of life and death hang in the balance. Horus finally overcame Seth and gave him in chains to Isis to put to death, but she released him. Horus, enraged with his mother, cut off her head but Thoth replaced it with the head of a cow.

Seth (in an abrupt but familiar politicization of the mythic dimension) then accused Horus of being illegitimate, and the issue between them changed as to which had the right of inheritance. Formerly inheritance came through the mother, which would have given Seth, as brother to Isis, precedence over Horus; but now, the council ruled, it was to be through the father. Horus was judged the rightful heir, the patrilineal principle was assured and Horus was crowned the new king. The time of the confusion past, Seth was made to serve the new order: the unregulated, chaotic powers of the universe were now mastered and, further, brought into relation with the new order by being required to help sustain it. In the festivals of Osiris along the Nile, Seth was the boat that carried his effigy, just as he carried the sun through the watery abyss of night.

> This is Horus speaking, he has ordained action for his father,
> he has shown himself master of the storm,
> he has countered the blustering of Seth,
> so that he, Seth, must bear you –
> for it is he that must carry him who is again complete.[7]

Horus then journeyed to the underworld to tell the news to Osiris and to awaken him and "set his soul in motion." He presented him with the eye that was torn out in the struggle, which restored Osiris to eternal life and became known as the Wedjat-eye, the Eye of Eternity, called the "whole one," which protected against all harm. As Osiris revived, the spirit of life and growth awakened, and the new year began.

It is strange that nowhere in Egypt was there a complete text of the story of Isis and Osiris. Over the 3000-year period in which the tale was told texts refer only to isolated episodes as though a knowledge of the whole myth was assumed as part of the culture. This may point to an oral tradition (to which originally Homer's *Odyssey* and *Iliad* belonged); for where a myth was at the center of a culture, there would have been no need to record it in writing. The drama of the death and rebirth of Osiris was enacted every year in the Mystery plays at Abydos, so the story may have been handed down, in the manner of an art or a skill, from one generation to another. The most sequential and composite story comes from Plutarch alone, a second-century-AD Greek writer, who is known to have visited Egypt at least once. Since the Egyptian sources all corroborate Plutarch's version, it may be taken as true to the original, though they also make it clear that Greek and Egyptian speak a different mythological language.

This story is, on one level, a myth of the invisible reality that underlies and makes intelligible the workings of what we would call Nature, which is also, ultimately, for the Egyptians, the drama of human nature. It is essentially a myth of immanence, for the gods and goddesses in Egypt were manifest in and as creation, with many different and also mutual spheres of manifestation. In this way the manifold dimensions of the phenomenal world were brought into relation with human feeling, and the mystic bond that unified humanity with nature could be explored.

Osiris, for instance, comes alive in the rising Nile, the growing grain, the waxing moon, and in everything that is affirmative in nature and in human beings. He dies in the falling Nile, the withering grain, the waning moon and in all that succumbs to ignorance and violence and destruction. The rising Nile was also seen as the tears of Isis; for when the goddess was mourning for the lost Osiris, the tears dropped from her eyes and swelled the waters of the Nile, giving their moisture to the parched, inert body of her brother-husband. Isis was said to make the Nile swell and overflow, "to swell in his season," and the Greek writer Pausanias explains: "The Egyptians say that Isis bewails Osiris when the river begins to rise; and when it inundates the fields they say that it is the tears of Isis."[8] She was manifest as the star Sothis, also called Sirius and the Dog Star, whose rising on the eastern horizon brought Osiris back to life and freed the inundation. The image unites the human and the natural world, for it is Isis' compassion, her continual searching for and then finding Osiris that restores him to life and swells the waters. According to Plutarch, Sothis in Egyptian signifies "pregnancy," so Isis is pregnant with the rebirth of Osiris, which is Horus, his son, the new year: "Osiris is yesterday; Horus is today."[9]

> It is Horus the intrepid that will come forth from you
> (Osiris), in his name of Horus who is within Sothis.[10]

"Thou art the Nile ... gods and men live from thy overflow," says Rameses IV in a hymn to Osiris.[11] But Osiris did not exist alone. After his death he was fundamentally passive and hidden; in his helplessness he had to be rescued by Isis, and not just once, but twice. In the myth she is always searching for him, finding him and awakening him from his sleep. The "finding" of Osiris (which was to have a striking Greek counterpart in "the finding of Kore" in the Eleusinian Mysteries) was central to the rituals that celebrated the rising of the Nile, for, even in Plutarch's time, the pouring of sweet water from the Nile into a golden casket on the occasion of the flooding was accompanied by the cry "Osiris is found."[12]

Osiris has to be distinguished from Min, god of the harvest, whose gift was the vitality of growth. The gift of Osiris is revival or resurrection, though, as the corn must die to live again, the two are obviously connected. The plants begin to grow when the soul of Osiris rises; they are the soul of Osiris "speeding upwards." Osiris is the lunar mystery, the cyclical round where darkness is followed by the resurgence of light and life; whereas Min is the solar mystery, the vital force that is there or not, often pictured as a white bull of ithyphallic man, having more in common with Horus. It was to Min that the harvest festival was dedicated, his statue drawn along the streets in procession, accompanied by a box of lettuce plants (which were later to become the plant belonging to the rites of the Greek Adonis). Similarly, Hapi, the Nile god with female breasts, who pours out his Nile water from two vases, was often identified with Osiris, but was not himself a figure through whom the cyclical drama of the Nile was reflected. Osiris, on the other hand, waxed and waned.

The helplessness of Osiris as the dead land waits to be revived is the subject of one of the most moving Coffin Texts, in which Isis and Nephthys, the two sisters who speak with one voice, call him back to life:

> Ah Helpless One!
> Ah Helpless One asleep!
> Ah Helpless One in this place
> which you know not - yet I know it!
> Behold I have found you (lying) on your side -
> the Great Listless One.
> "Ah Sister" says Isis to Nephthys,
> "This is our brother,

Come let us lift up his head,
Come, let us (rejoin) his bones,
Come, let us reassemble his limbs,
Come, let us put an end to all his woe,
that, as far as we can help, he will weary no more.
May the moisture begin to mount for this spirit!
May the canals be filled through you!
May the names of the rivers be created through you!
Osiris, live!
Osiris, let the great Listless One arise!
I am Isis."

"I am Nephthys.
It shall be that Horus will avenge you,
It shall be that Thoth will protect you
– your two sons of the Great White Crown –
It shall be that the Company will hear.
Then will your power be visible in the sky
and you will cause havoc among the (hostile) gods,
for Horus, your son, has seized the Great White Crown,
seizing it from him who acted against you.
Then will your father Atum call 'Come!'
Osiris live! ..."[13]

Isis and Nephthys become one character in this hymn, and they are usually shown helping Osiris together, one on either side of him as he lies on his bier, making the swathings for his mummy and assisting his resurrection. Symbolically, Isis is the light moon and Nephthys the dark moon, or, in a solar image, Isis is the dawn and Nephthys is the twilight, or Isis is the morning star and Nephthys the evening star; or, more widely, in Plutarch's terms, Isis is the visible part of the world and Nephthys is the invisible. Together they form a completeness, complementing the duality of Osiris and Seth, their brother-husbands. But Nephthys, though wife to Seth, invariably takes the part of Isis against him (as the face of dark perpetually turned towards the light), lamenting for Osiris and conceiving Anubis from him, he who can see in the dark. The "throne," the name of Isis and the hieroglyph she wears on her head, is the outward form of the "Lady of the House," the name of Nephthys and the hieroglyph she wears on her head, sometimes the only distinguishing feature between them. The living king became Horus and the deceased king took on the role of Osiris, or "became Osiris" (as did all the deceased from the beginning of the Middle Kingdom) and so many sarcophagi were painted and engraved with Isis and Nephthys protecting the pharaoh with their outstretched wings. Here they are seen kneeling one at each end of the sarcophagus of Ramses III, enclosing his earthly body between them, cradling him into eternity, as they had done for Osiris and as they do for the sun (Ra, Horus), also reborn from the dark each dawn.

The bond between Isis and Osiris is one of the creative forces of life, for together they are the universal soul of growth. If he is the flooding of the Nile, then she is the earth that the Nile covers, and from this union, as Plutarch said, the Egyptians make Horus to be born.[14] The new life in the grain is the child of both, Osiris renewed as Horus through Isis. Where Osiris is manifest in the grain, Isis is manifest n the crops. As the power of growth manifest in the water Osiris is called "the Great Green Thing," and as the power of growth manifest in the earth he is called "the Great Black Thing," the moisture that generates the corn. In Memphis it was said that Osiris "becomes earth,"[15] and, in consort, Isis is called "Queen of Earth," the "green Goddess, whose green colour is like unto the greenness of the earth," "Creator of green things," "Lady of bread," "Lady of beer," "Lady of abundance." In a Coffin Text, "Spell for Becoming Barley," the poet calls on Osiris as the life-force of the corn:

> I am the plant of life
> which comes forth from Osiris,
> which grows upon the ribs of Osiris,
> which allows the people to live,
> which makes the gods divine,
> which spiritualizes the spirits,
> which sustains the masters of wealth
> and the masters of substance,
> which makes the *pak* cakes for the spirits.
> which enlivens the limbs of the living.
> I live as corn, the life of the living,
> I live upon the rib of Geb (the God of Earth),
> but the love of me is in the sky, on earth,
> on the water and in the fields.
> Now Isis is content for her son Horus her god,
> she is jubilant in him, Horus her god,
> I am life appearing from Osiris.[16]

The phases in the life of the corn were also understood as the god in the grain dying and coming to life again. When the first ears of corn were cut, there was weeping and wailing, as though the body of the god in the corn were being dismembered, and the reapers invoked Isis to lament with them. "Come to thy house, beautiful one!" For as the oxen threshed the barley, so Osiris was "beaten" by Seth, "hacked to pieces." In the New Kingdom, c. 1550–1070 BC, models of Osiris were filled with silt and planted with barley, and placed in the burial chambers of royal tombs. These "Osiris-beds," as they were called, sprouting with barley, implied that the deceased would be resurrected in the same way that Osiris was reborn in the grain. The same custom reappears in the Greek rituals of Adonis when shallow beds of fast-growing plants are thrown into the sea long with his effigy.

Late Classical writers tell of an ancient custom in which Isis collected the scattered limbs of Osiris in a winnowing basket, and certainly in Roman times throughout the empire a basket was carried in processions of Isis. A Pyramid Text compares the king to Osiris as the grain that flies to heaven in the clouds of chaff that rise when the grain is winnowed:

> Osiris is Unas in the mounting chaff ...
> He has not entered Geb to perish.
> He is not sleeping in his house upon earth
> So that his bones may be broken ...
> Unas is up and away to heaven
> With the wind, with the wind![17]

The loss and finding of Osiris were also manifest in the waning and waxing of the moon. Plutarch writes that the years of Osiris' life were twenty-eight, and in "the dismemberment of Osiris into fourteen parts they refer allegorically to the days of the waning of that satellite from the time of the full moon to the new moon."[18] Osiris is also found in the star Orion, with Isis as Sothis nearby. On a Ptolemaic text Isis addresses Osiris: "Thy sacred image, Orion in heaven, rises and sets every day; I am Sothis following after him, and I will not forsake him."[19] Plutarch adds that the Apis Bull, which was the animate image of Osiris in his visible form, comes into being when a "fructifying lights thrusts forth from the moon and falls upon a cow in her breeding season."[20] But when the moon is swallowed up by the sun, then Seth has shut Osiris up in his coffin.

Seth is the opposing principle to Osiris; he is the perpetual antagonist. Where Osiris is moisture, Seth is aridity and dryness; where

Osiris is the Nile, Seth is the desert that threatens to cover it over, or the winds that scatter the burning sand, or the scorching heat of the sun that evaporates the waters. Seth is the salt sea into which the Nile waters are dissipated and lost, he is the drought that parches the crops and bakes the ground hard, he is the darkness that engulfs the sun each night. He is the one "great of strength," and he even has red hair like the desert, the "Red Land." His animals are the ass, the crocodile and the hippopotamus. He is the earthquake, the storm, thunder, death; he is blind force, unregulated, unpredictable, ungovernable; in humans he is, as Plutarch puts it, a truculence of soul.[21] He is, in short, everything harmful and destructive that threatens to diminish life or take it away.

Yet Seth is not so much evil as the inevitably opposing element in the universe that has to be mastered, continually brought into the rule of the good. When he carries the coffin of Osiris and bears the boat of the sun god, Ra (just as the ass, Seth's animal, carries Christ in his journey from Bethany to Jerusalem), he is an image transformed through awareness, a model of how to relate to whatever is antagonistic in life. At first, Osiris did not know his brother's nature and so fell into his trap (as, in *King Lear*, Edgar did not know Edmund). When Horus revived Osiris, he gave him the power of knowing Seth and so creating a right relation to him:

> Horus has seized Seth, he has put him beneath you so that he can lift you up. He will groan beneath you as an earthquake ...
> Horus has made you recognize him in his real nature,
> let him not escape you;
> he has made you hold him by your hand,
> let him not get away from you.[22]

In this drama of conflict Isis plays the role of mediator. Without her, it is implied, in the first contest Seth would win: Osiris would be vanquished and anarchy would prevail. Yet in the resumption of the contest, when Horus is winning, she lets Seth go. Thoth also keeps the dynamic of opposites alive, assisting the side that is losing so that a creative equilibrium will be maintained. Campbell comments: "Mythologically representing the inevitable dialectic of temporality, where all things appear in pairs, Horus and Seth are forever in conflict; where as in the sphere of eternity, beyond the veil of time and space, where there is no duality, they are at one."[23]

Isis here reconciles the opposites without dissolving their opposition. But, earlier, when the story dramatizes the universal sorrow for Osiris and the falling, this side of the veil, of all things into their dissolution, then

Isis personifies the loving power of the universe, which resurrects life from death, and the act of loving in human nature, which bestows beauty upon the lover and the beloved alike:

> Behold now, Isis speaketh, –
> Come to thy house, oh An! [sun god as risen Osiris]
> Come to thy house for thine enemies are not!
> Behold the excellent sistrum-bearer – come to thy house!
> Lo, I thy sister, love thee – do not thou depart from me!
> Behold Hunnu [name of the sun god], the beautiful one!
> Come to thy house immediately – come to thy temple immediately!
> Behold thou my heart, which grieveth for thee;
> Behold me seeking for thee – I am searching for thee to behold thee
> Lo, I am prevented from beholding thee –
> I am prevented from beholding thee, oh An! ...
> I love thee more than all the earth –
> And thou lovest not another as thou dost thy sister!
>
> Behold now, Nephthys speaketh, –
> Behold the excellent sistrum-bearer! Come to thy house!
> Cause thy heart to rejoice, for thy enemies are not!
> All thy sister-goddesses are at thy side and behind thy couch,
> calling upon thee with weeping – yet thou art prostrate upon thy bed!
> Hearken unto the beautiful words uttered by us
> and by every noble one among us!
> Subdue thou every sorrow which is in the hearts of us thy sisters,
> Oh thou strong one among the gods, – strong among men who behold thee!
> We come before thee, oh prince, our lord;
> Turn thou not away thy face before us;
> Sweeten our hearts when we behold thee, oh prince!
> Beautify our hearts when he behold thee!
> I, Nephthys, thy sister, I love thee:
> Thy foes are subdued, there is no one remaining.
> Lo, I am with thee; I shall protect thy limbs for ever, eternally.[24]

Because Isis loves Osiris she searches for him, and because of her power she brings him back to life, becoming thereby, mythologically, his mother. In one of the Pyramid Texts she says:

> Thy mother has come to thee, that thou mayst not perish away,
> The great modeler she is come, that thou mayst not perish away.
> She sets thy head in place for thee,
> She puts together thy limbs for thee;
> What she brings to thee is thy heart, is thy body.
> So dost thou become he who presides over his forerunners,
> Thou givest command to thy ancestors
> And also thou makest thy house to prosper after thee,
> Thou dost defend thy children from affliction.[25]

So the pattern of the myth of the mother goddess and the son-lover becomes visible through the symbolism of the story, as a variation on the universal theme. The boar, which slays Tammuz (in one version), Adonis and Attis, as an image of the dark moon, the abyss of death, turns up here, as though incidentally, in Seth's hunting at the full moon, signifying at the point where the moon is about to wane. The fourteen pieces into which Osiris' body is dismembered are, of course, an image of the dismembered light of the moon, which Isis reassembles as the crescent moon, the day of resurrection, symbolized by the raising of the Djed column. Here again she is the essential "mother" of his rebirth, taking her place, symbolically, as the perpetual cycle of the moon and the everlasting source of the forms of life, zoe, while the role of the living and dying phases of manifestation of the source, bios, is shared in the Egyptian myth by Osiris and Horus as two aspects of the same principle. Osiris, like all the gods of myth of the goddess and son-lover, is incarnate in the bull, as is his son Horus, who, in an "adjacent" myth, is called the "bull of his mother."

The raising of the Djed pillar or column from the supine horizontal to the upright vertical position was the culmination of the rites of Osiris celebrated on the day before the new year began, which was also the day of the Sed festival when the periodic rites of kingship were renewed and the king "became Horus." The word Djed meant "stable" or "durable," and as a symbol of Osiris its uplifting meant that the god, the life-force, had endured over the inert forces of decay that lie lifeless on the ground. Seth had "laid the Djed on its side,"[26] but Osiris had prevailed; his backbone, another meaning of the pillar, had stood up again. Isis calls:

> "Come to thy house, come to thy house, thou pillar! Come to thy house, beautiful bull, Lord of men, Beloved, Lord of women."[27]

In relation to the harvest, the raising of the pillar meant that the spirit of the corn had not been killed in the cutting down of the corn. For Osiris, as the animating principle of all vegetation, is everlasting, and because of this the corn would grow upwards towards the light again. Sometimes the pillar is drawn as a tree with lopped off branches (as later is the Christian cross), recalling the erica tree that enclosed Osiris' coffin at Byblos and signifying the Tree of Life as the Axis of the World. Certainly the pillar was as heavy and difficult to erect as an actual tree would have been. The four horizontal lines, which may originally have been the uppermost branches of the tree, refer to the four quarters of the horizon, which the goddesses Hathor and Nut also encompass. After the Djed column was raised, a knot of cloth or leather, called a Tit, was tied around it, and the column was clothed in the manner of a statue in a ceremony called "the Offering of Clothes." The Tit was an emblem of Isis, and so the combination of the Djed and the Tit meant the union of Osiris and Isis, a restoration of harmony as it was in the beginning. The image of the rising up also recapitulates the first time when the High Hill (Atum) rose up out of the waters of Nun as the first "island" of consciousness, and this original event, enacted every day the sun (Ra) rises up out of the night (Atum-Ra), can be represented as coming out of the pillar itself.

[In the Papyrus of Ani] the sun rests between arms forming the sign of the Ka ~ the divine embrace in which each thing, person and god is held ~ coming from the ankh of imperishable life, itself coming from and generated by the Djed pillar, whose life-force is nurtured into being by the guardian presences of Isis and Nephthys, themselves making the Ka gesture of epiphany, embracing the rising of the sun. The baboons, more simply, greet the sun as it comes up, as they still do, chattering excitedly in the African bush. In a characteristic Egyptian merging of characters and identities the sun was Ra or Re, the sun god, the visible manifestation of Atum (often known as Atum-Ra), and Horus, the sunlight, piercing the sky like a falcon, was sometimes elided as Horus-Ra, and so the sunrise was also the resurrection of Osiris. The Book of the Dead, as it is translated, meant, more exactly, "The Chapters of Coming Forth by Day":[28]

> Yesterday is Osiris and Today is Ra on the day when he shall destroy the enemies of Osiris and when he shall establish as prince and ruler his son Horus.[29]

Consequently, when Isis and Nephthys stand with their outstretched wings across the shrine [of Tutankhamun], they are not only protecting Tutankhamun's mummy, they are nurturing his resurrection as the reborn sun – helping him to come forth by day – in the same way that they do for Osiris and the sun at dawn, and for all those who become Osiris and are "found" by Isis and Nephthys; and image of the soul's transformation.

In one of the old Pyramid Texts this stanza is addressed to the deceased king who now takes part in the order of the universe:

> Thou risest and settest; thou goest down with Re,
> sinking in the dust with Nedy.
> Thou risest and settest; thou risest up with Re
> and ascendest with the Great Reed Float.
> Thou risest and settest; thou goest down with Nephthys,
> sinking in the dust with the Evening Boat of the Sun.
> Thou risest and settest; thou risest up with Isis,
> ascending with the Morning Boat of the Sun.[30]

Notes

[1] Excerpted with permission from Anne Baring and Jules Cashford, *The Myth of the Goddess: Evolution of an Image* (Arkana/Penguin 1991), pp. 228-44.

[2] New Kingdom hymn, quoted in R. T. Rundle Clark, *Myth and Symbol in Ancient Egypt*, p. 103.

[3] The parallels between this part of Isis' story and Demeter's in the Homeric "Hymn to Demeter" are testament to a direct continuity of tradition.

[4] The Paris Stele, the Louvre, C.286; quoted in Georges Nagel, 'The Mysteries of Osiris in Ancient Egypt,' The Mysteries, Eranos Yearbooks, 2, p.122.

[5] The sources of this myth are Plutarch, 'Isis and Osiris,' in *Moralia*, Book 5, pp. 31-49; and Joseph Campbell (after Frazer), *Primitive Mythology*, pp. 424-7.

[6] Pyramid Text; quoted in Rundle Clark, op.cit. p113.

[7] Pyramid Text, ibid., p. 111.

[8] Pausanias, De Phocis, x, p.323; quoted in Henri Frankfort, *Kingship and the Gods*, p. 192.

[9] Rundle Clark, op.cit., p. 157.

[10] Pyramid Text 1636 b; ibid., p. 188.
[11] Quoted in Frankfort, op. cit., p. 190.
[12] Plutarch, op. cit., 366-7, p. 97.
[13] Quoted in Rundle Clark, pp. 125-8.
[14] Plutarch, op. cit, p. 93.
[15] Quoted in Frankfort, op. cit., p. 195.
[16] Quoted in Rundle Clark, op. cit., p. 119.
[17] Quoted in Frankfort, op. cit., pp. 186-7.
[18] Plutarch, op. cit., 367-8, p. 103.
[19] Quoted in Frankfort, op. cit., pp. 195-6.
[20] Plutarch, op. cit., 368, p. 105.
[21] Ibid., p. 121.
[22] Quoted in Rundle Clark, op. cit., p. 115.
[23] Joseph Campbell, Oriental Mythology, p. 51.
[24] Extracts from "The Lamentations of Isis and Nephthys" (Berlin Papyrus 1425), after the translation by James Teackle Dennis, *The Burden of Isis*, London, John Murray, 1910, pp. 21-7. Compare the translation by E. A. Wallis Budge, *Osiris and the Egyptian Resurrection*, Vol. 2, pp. 222-40 (quoted in Chapter 14, pp. 585-6). See also Harold Bayley, *The Lost Language of Symbolism*, who points out the similarities between this and the Song of Songs.
[25] Pyramid Text, 834; quoted in Erich Neumann, *The Origins and History of Consciousness*, p. 222.
[26] Quoted in Manfred Lurker, The Gods and Symbols of Ancient Egypt, p. 47.
[27] From Dennis, op. cit., p.25.
[28] E. A. Wallis Budge, *The Book of the Dead*, London, Routledge and Kegan Paul, 1974, p. xvii.
[29] From E. A. Wallis Budge, *The Papyrus of Ani*, New York, Metropolitan Museum of Art and Alfred A, Knopf Inc., 1976, p. 94.
[30] Pyramid Text 207-12, quoted in Frankfort, op. cit., p. 121.

Prayer for Isis

by Jeremy J. Baer

Isis of the Many Names,
Hear my prayer.
Queen of Heaven, Lady of the Gods,
Hear my prayer.
Daughter of Nut and Geb, Mother of God,
Hear my prayer.
Sister-wife of Serapis, she who suckles Harpocrates,
Hear my prayer.
Great of Magic, Seat of Egypt,
Hear my prayer.
She who knows Ra's real name,
She who protects the weary-hearted,
Hear my prayer.
She who resurrected her brother-husband,
Mighty Bull of the Two Lands, Lord of Eternity.
Hear my Prayer.
The One Who is All,
The One in Whom are Many,
Hear my prayer.
Look safe to my family, oh goddess, and give wealth unto them.
Defend me from Tyche,
Protect me from evil.
Shield me from mine enemies.
Deliver me from the cruel ministrations of Fate.
Grant that I may live justly and honorably for long days
under thine merciful star.
Guide my soul to the Duat.
Illumine the Stygian Depths
Let me live forever.
Isis of the Many Names,
Hear my prayer.

A Hymn to Osiris

by Sannion

While I live may I always kiss the earth before thee
and sing thy praises, O great Ancestral King,
whose face is beautiful in the land of shadows,
whose soul is radiant in the house of the gods,
whose spirit is life-giving to the fruit trees in the orchard.
My heart longs for thee, O Good Brother,
like the barren earth yearns for the floodwaters of the Nile,
like the cow in the field aches to be mounted by the virile bull,
like the poor man desires the coming of a righteous judge who will set
    things straight.
My mind is inflamed with the memory of thy presence, O Noblest of the
    Noble Ones,
how thy breath smells of pine and cedar and sweet acacia wood,
how thy eyes are silver, like the moon's reflection in a still pool,
how thy flesh is green like ivy clinging to a wall.
I am overcome with the thought of thee:
it makes my heart tremble in my breast.
For thou art the Lord of the Double Horns,
mightier and more potent than ten thousand bulls.
For thou art the Chief among those in the West
whom even death could not destroy.
For thou art the One whose Word is True,
who gives laws to gods and whose counsels all must obey.
O Osiris, may these words be pleasing to thy heart
so that when I come before thee thou wilt give me cool water to drink
and permit me to take my bread from the offering table of eternity.

A Never Ending Battle

by Frater Eleuthereus

With blow after blow, the Universe cried
The Moon was ripped from the sky and the stars themselves shook
The silted depths of the Nile cascaded and frothed
> Neither side came up for air
> The World's bowels shivered and quaked
> No quarter given, none asked for in return

It was a battle for dominion over the Sun and World
Brother versus brother, uncle versus nephew
Either way, It would never End.
> Storm versus Hawk
> Force versus Wonder
> Seething anger versus iron will.

Champion and Sorceress,
The Thousands-Named Isis stood and watched
 Transfixed as kin fought kin.
> She held her ground,
> A Word of Power ready on her lips,
> Enchanted harpoon in hand

And in those turbid depths, where not even the gods could quite clearly peer
Barely noticeable, a slithery presence hovering on the river mist grins back at her.
Poised and ready to strike, Isis pauses; Forcing herself to turn from the hypnotic Dragon,
> Squinting into the Nile's thrashing liquid as the Sun reflected its warmth & light
> Her face turned white, stifling back a choke, Isis winced and froze;.

> *Isis saw another sight even more disturbing than Her husband's grisly corpse.*

Victim became ravisher, attacker became conquered- Who was who?
They blended in a horrid mockery of Ma'at-
Her one eyed Heru raped & bruised jars her back to now... begging and pleading,
    "Kill him Mother! You have your chance! Avenge me!"
    Even as her brother cries to her meekly, "Sister! Blood of my blood, mercy!"
    All the while, the sea monster chuckles at his despised now gelded foe.

At some point, even Gods have limits and certainly faults
For the first and only time in Her history
The Mother gave way to the Sister and family Matriarch
    Neither death nor "justice" would be enough,
    It would never End.
    And so, Isis ended it, laying down her mystic weapon

Jetting out of the primal waters her shining Heru bellows,
"How could YOU?! WHY?!
"How could you let *HIM* get away!?"
    In a fury of traumatic rage
    Riding high a tornado of justified grief,
    The Son does the unthinkable, beheading his Mother, standing before a tragedy.

Silence, stillness.
Isis the Green took upon herself the anger and venom
Of Husband slain, Brother tricked, and the Son's wounds
    A wall of coppery blood inundates the waters and lands
    Nourishing the soil with moisture, vegetation, flowers...
    Redemption, rebirth.

Emerging from the River's depths,
Both combatants force themselves to maintain composure
Neither Nephew nor Uncle conceding a hair of ground
    Isis, the Mourner now Hathor Ascended, stares gravely.
    She has no more tears,
    Life and its preservation are her priority

For she knows what her transmuted Son has not yet realized.
And she glares at her strong and brash, manipulated brother Seth.
Realizing the lesson he had not deigned to learn.
> Victory in a battle won with savagery or trickery
> Is nothing worth celebrating
> It is ash in the mouth of a feast

As falcon black eyes stare him down, Seth refuses to flinch and a Queen sighs;

> It would never End.

A HISTORY OF THE WORSHIP OF ISIS AND SERAPIS

by Jeremy J. Baer

Pharaonic Egypt

Isis (usually transliterated as "Aset" in the native language) had her start as a comparatively minor deity of Egypt. She was a protector of the throne of Egypt, perhaps in some ways the personification of royal power. But she had been subordinate in the official Egyptian pantheon to deities more intimately connected with the great king, like Ra and Horus.

The collapse of the Old Kingdom around 2181 BCE brought about several sweeping changes in Egyptian religion. Eternal life, which had once been viewed as the sole province of the King, came to be seen as the reward for all those willing to submit to the proper cults. In this new paradigm Isis took center stage and became the central goddess in the popular religion of the Egyptian people.

Myth tells how Osiris, the first god-king of Egypt, introduced laws and agriculture to humankind. He was then deceived and murdered by his scheming brother Seth, god of chaos. Seth hacked Osiris' body into pieces and scattered them across Egypt, intending to rule Egypt himself. Isis collected the pieces and magically revived her brother-husband Osiris, who became King of the Underworld. She also magically conceived a son, Horus. Isis and her supporters warred against Seth for the throne of Egypt. A council of gods eventually decided that Horus, as son of Osiris, was the rightful ruler, and Seth was demoted to fighting nocturnal demons. A new paradigm emerged in which Osiris ruled the underworld, Horus ruled Egypt (the Pharaohs were considered the incarnation of Horus), and Ra the sun god ruled the heavens.

But Isis as mistress of magic resurrected Osiris, and thus was superior to him. She conceived her son Horus magically and was superior to him. With her magic, she even had power over Ra, the sun god. In short, she was the real power behind the universe, which led her cult adherents to proclaim her as Mistress of Heaven. More importantly, she had the power over life and death and could resurrect her followers in the same manner that saved her husband from oblivion. As the myth of Isis and Osiris grew, Isis began displacing other deities in the loyalties of the population.

Ptolemaic Egypt

The conquest of Egypt by Alexander the Great in 332 BCE opened a new era for the cult. In trying to find a religious cult that would unite both Egyptian and Hellenic subjects, Ptolemy Soter, Alexander's successor in Egypt, crafted the Isis cult as it would be introduced into Greco-Roman society. But first he had to deal with the cult of Osiris, and its related cult of the Apis Bull.

In Memphis, the Apis Bull was the most sacred of animals and something of a national mascot for all Egypt. In life the animal was considered a manifestation of the creator deity, Ptah. But in death the creature was considered an embodiment of Osiris. When the animal died it was treated as if Osiris himself had died. This Osir-Apis was given lavish funeral rites due its station.

Accustomed as they were to Homeric deities and beautiful anthropomorphic depictions of said gods in art, what the Greeks (and later Romans) objected to most in Egyptian religion was its inherent animal fetish. The Greeks who theoretically were in awe of Egypt's ancient and mysterious legacy were most often in practice derisive of its animal-headed deities. Thus if Ptolemy were to promote an Egyptian cult to his Greco-Macedonian companions, iconographically the deity had to be rendered more aesthetically pleasing to Hellenic sensibilities.

Osiris was renamed Serapis and identified theologically with a variety of Egyptian and Hellenic gods (Osiris, Apis, Dionysus, Hades). Serapis was portrayed in art as a benign Hades, with elements of the other aforementioned deities. He became a god of healing and the underworld. Under Ptolemy III, a Serapeum was built in Alexandria that quickly became one of the largest and most prestigious sanctuaries in Antiquity. In this large complex of buildings, which included an annex to the famous Library of Alexandria, the cult practiced incubation – sleeping to obtain divinely inspired dreams, usually a prophecy as to how to cure an illness.

We therefore cannot repeat an old and now demonstrably false adage that Ptolemy Soter invented the god Serapis, for the conflation of Osiris with the Apis bull was an ancient Egyptian tradition. However, we might be able to say with somewhat more truth that Ptolemy Soter reinvented the cult, or at least gave it new marketing for a new audience.

Meanwhile, Isis was linked with the Greek Demeter and Aphrodite. Isis became the protector of the family (especially women), the protector of newborns, the goddess of fertility and good fortune, and the goddess of afterlife mysteries. She was also thought to be a matron of sailors.

Isis and Osiris, along with their child Horus, were honored by Greeks and by Egyptian emigrants as a kind of trinity, but usually it was Isis who was the dominant member of the trio. Sailors traveling from the great port of Alexandria took the cult all over the Mediterranean. In those days when the provincial city-states of the Hellenic world fell to Alexander's universal empire, the traditional gods of the city-state often no longer sufficed. Gods like Isis and Serapis were not connected with any specific town and were truly universal in scope. More importantly, their mysticism could offer the Greeks of the Hellenistic age something most of their own gods could not – a way to cheat fate and death.

Journey to Rome

Backed by the Ptolemaic regime, the new cult spread throughout the Hellenistic Kingdoms. We find cults of Isis and Serapis formed as private associations throughout many major port towns of the Mediterranean, with official temple cults erected not long thereafter. Egyptian slaves sold in foreign markets often carried the cult with them to new lands. Interestingly enough, foreign merchants and slave traders were just as likely to adopt the cult, for they found in Isis and Serapis universal deities with the power to grant great boons.

Serapis made a home fairly early at Delos, one of Apollo's island sanctuaries. It seems there was even some rivalry between these two gods of healing, not least because the cult of Serapis was linked with Ptolemaic imperialism.

From the slave trade at Delos, Serapis and Isis spread to the Italian ports. In importance and prestige Isis always seemed to eclipse her consort.

The Roman Senate was not amused with Ptolemy's attempt to craft a universal religion. When the cult of Isis and Serapis swept into Rome via Hellenistic sailors and Egyptian emigrants, it became outstandingly popular with women and the lower classes, including slaves. Fearing a religious unification of the lower strata of Roman society, and fearing the loss of piety in the traditional Roman gods of the state, the Senate repeatedly placed restrictions on the new cult. Private chapels dedicated to Isis were ordered destroyed. In 50 BCE when a Roman Consul found that the demolition team assigned to him were all members or sympathizers of the cult and refused to destroy their chapel, he had to remove his toga of state and do the deed himself.

Augustus found the cult "pornographic," though the cult was known to prescribe periods of sexual abstinence to its adherents. The real reason for Augustus' wrath was that the cult was linked to Egypt and thus the power base of his rival, Antony. Cleopatra had even gone so far as to declare herself Isis reincarnated. Nonetheless, Augustus' scorn did little to stem popular opinion. Officials and servants of the imperial household were members of the cult. It seems even his own infamous daughter, Julia, was a member; whether her belief was genuine or merely another aspect of her defiance against her father cannot be determined.

Tiberius, upon hearing of a sexual scandal involving the cult, had the offenders crucified and images of Isis cast into the Tiber sometime during his reign of 14 BCE-37 CE. But much like with Christianity, periodic and sporadic persecution did nothing to stem the tide. What was death when one's deity promised salvation and resurrection?

As part of undoing the policies of Tiberius, Caligula legitimized the religion during his reign of 37-41 CE. Caligula was descended from Marc Antony, and perhaps it is not surprising that a touch of Alexandrian devotions remained with the family. Temples to Isis were permitted to be constructed. Aspects of the Isiac festivals became public and part of the civil calendar (though there were still mysteries celebrated in private). It is also known that Caligula had an Egyptian chamberlain who exerted influence on the emperor and helped him progress in the mysteries of the goddess. Perhaps this even helped play a role in Caligula's infamous promotion of himself as an autocratic, Hellenistic-like ruler. Whatever the truth, Isis was now part of Roman paganism for good.

The emperor Vespasian became acquainted with the cult while serving in the Eastern legions before 69 CE, and seems to have adopted Isis and Serapis as his personal savior deities. Vespasian claims to have been proclaimed emperor by an oracle from Serapis, and with the deity's help performed a healing "miracle." His son Domitian owed his life to fleeing opponents in the garb of Isiac cultists, and continued the family's association with the cult.

Hadrian and Marcus Aurelius were friendly to the cult, but most likely not initiates. Commodus, who ruled from 180-192 CE, shaved his head bald like the priests of Serapis. He used to beat those around him with a mask of Anubis that was common in the processions of the cult.

Septimus Severus was fascinated with the cult. But it was not until the reign of his son, Caracalla, that Serapis finally moved out from under an Isiac shadow. Caracalla erected a special cult to Serapis as god of healing and issued coins with his likeness. After a retreat to the Serapaeum at Alexandria, he was bestowed with the title *philosarapis*, or beloved of Serapis. The zenith came when Caracalla constructed a gigantic temple to Serapis around 212 CE which seems to have dwarfed that to Capitoline Jupiter, who had for centuries been officially the patron god of Rome. The Serapia of April 25th may have been to celebrate the commemoration of this temple. The gods of the East that had once been maligned by the ruling classes of the Republic were now on equal footing with the traditional gods of the State. Among the common people, perhaps they were more important.

By Caracalla's reign, Serapis was increasingly equated with such other deities as Mithras and Helios, and became a solar and sky deity. Mithraeum in Caracalla's baths show such syncretic inscriptions. The number of Egyptian slaves serving in the imperial household seems to have been large.

From Emperor to slave, the related cults of Isis and Serapis would remain a major religious force in the Roman Empire until their outlaw by Christian emperors. In many ways, the destruction of the Serapeum in 391 CE at Alexandria signified the death of paganism in Antiquity, though some temples to Isis survived until the fifth century.

Characteristics of the Cult

The cult of Isis and Serapis was, thanks to Ptolemy, Hellenized to a degree that the Roman and Greek mind could understand it, and yet still retained enough native traces to be exotic and alien.

Unlike most religious structures in the Roman world, an Iseum or Serapeum did not open to the streets or forum where public spectators could view the proceedings inside. They were walled off from the surrounding world, suggesting a space of inner sanctity. Even within their walls, there was a "sanctuary" much like modern monasteries where only clergy and the initiated could enter. In there rituals involving fire, water and incense were conducted in front of sacred statuary of the deities concerned. This secret religious life that was set apart from the community and the State is what helped arouse the suspicions of the conservatives back in the days of the Republic.

Not much is known about the details of the inner workings of the mysteries, as they were by definition secret. Prospective initiates were called to the goddess by dreams and visions. Intense preparations of purification and meditation (and abstinence) were followed by exotic rites designed to recreate the myth of Isis and the resurrection of Osiris. By enduring these rituals, the adherent was reconciled to the gods' magic and effectively granted a favorable afterlife. He or she was spiritually reborn in a manner common to Greco-Oriental savior religions.

But there were also more public festivals that didn't require initiation. The first was the Navigium Isidis, conducted on March 5th. In honor of Isis sailing the seas to find pieces of her lost husband, a colorful procession of costumed people, including especially sailors, marched to port and ritually blessed a boat. The second festival, the Inventio Osiridis, was held October 28th to November 3rd. This was an ancient passion play. Again, costumed actors took to the streets, this time to reenact the death and resurrection of Serapis. Roman conservatives complained the festival was too loud and colorful. People also had private shrines to Isis and Serapis in their homes, as revealed by the archaeological remains in Pompeii and surrounding towns.

The subject of the ethics of the cult is a complicated one. We know that Egyptian culture as a whole was free with sexuality compared to Roman culture. Isis was, in fact, rather popular with courtesans and other such professions, and there are speculations that Isiac cults may have promoted a kind of "positive sexuality" among a more conservative Roman population. Augustus and Tiberius took this as proof of a "pornographic" cult. Yet the Isiac cult also demanded regular periods of sexual abstinence from its adherents for purposes of ritual purification, and even apparently courtesans readily submitted to these observances. Curiously enough, the early Christians who were quick to complain about the degeneracy of pagan cults could not offer as much criticism about Isis as they could about some other cults in the Empire.

Stoic and Neoplatonic intellectuals tried to reinterpret the cult in terms of their own highbrow philosophies, with the deities of the cult serving as metaphors for great cosmic principles. While this may have held some influence in the literate classes, it's doubtful it had any impact on the vast majority of followers. To the average person Isis was not a metaphor or concept; she was as real to her followers as the Virgin Mary, Mother of God, is to billions of Christians around the world today. More to the point, she performed much the same function.

Unlike Mithraism which was confined to a small percentage of "middle class" Roman males, the Isis and Serapis cult was truly universal. Unlike Mithraism it could be practiced by both men and women, and it was women who perhaps took it up most enthusiastically. Unlike Mithraism it appealed to all classes; the lower classes and slaves were the mainstay of the cult, but as we have seen even those at the very top of the social strata were also adherents. Unlike Mithraism which was mostly confined to the Latin West, Isis and Serapis were honored in both halves of the empire. They were long honored in the Greek East, and penetrated into the Latin West in even barely Romanized areas such as Britain or northwest Gaul. They were, however, a cult of city dwellers; we see little evidence of the cults in rural areas outside of their native Egypt.

There was little danger of the small cult of Mithras, influential though it was, stemming the tide of Christianity and taking over the world. However, the cult of Isis and Serapis had the numbers and the appeal to mount a serious threat to Christianity. Some scholars assert that the Holy Trinity of Isis, Serapis and Horus were not really defeated – they were merely absorbed into the new Holy Trinity of Christianity. The reverence for Mary among high Christian churches is similar to faith in Isis. We should consider at the very least that many chapels to the Virgin were built purposely on the remains of temples to Isis (such as the temple of Isis at Philae, Egypt) and that furthermore, the iconography of the Madonna and Christ is quite similar to Isis and Horus.

Today, Isiac religion is undergoing something of a revival. Among New Age crowds, Isis is a popular symbol among those seeking an alternative to "patriarchal" religions. In fact, Isis worship is part of the "goddess spirituality" movement promoted by feminist and other postmodern identity groups, such as the Fellowship of Isis founded in 1976. However, New Age understandings and practices related to Isis are sometimes more conditioned by revisionist politics than by anything resembling history or archeology. Serapis, in contrast to Isis, remains virtually unknown to modern pagans. Nonetheless, alternative religious movements have coincided with periodic bursts of "Egyptomania" to open the door for a second look at the cult.

Bibliography

Apuleius. *The Golden Ass*. Translated by P.G. Walsh. Oxford University Press. Oxford, England. 1994.
David, Rosalie. *Handbook to Life in Ancient Egypt*. Oxford University Press. Oxford, England. 1998.
Hornblower, Simon & Spawforth, Antony. *The Oxford Classical Dictionary*. 3rd Edition. Oxford University Press. Oxford, England. 1999.
Pinch, Geraldine. *Egyptian Mythology: A Guide to Gods, Goddesses and Traditions of Ancient Egypt*. Oxford University Press. Oxford, England. 2002.
Turcan, Robert. *The Cults of the Roman Empire*. Translated by Antonia Nevill. Blackwell Publishing. Oxford, England. 1996.
Witt, R.E. *Isis in the Ancient World*. Johns Hopkins University Press. Baltimore, Maryland & London, England. 1971.

To the Veiled Isis*

by Brandon Newberg

O Great Goddess,
You who have been with me,
You who have not abandoned me,
I have known you as Isis.
Now I know you as Aset.
Yet still I know you not.
What is it you desire of me?
Is it worship and devotion that you desire?

You came to me in a Greek chiton and veil,
Glowing from within, surrounded by darkness,
Shining through your diaphanous robe
Like a star in the night sky.
Your veil, lifted by the wind,
Revealed but more darkness beneath.

So it was when I met you.
I felt you, but I knew you not.
And I could not stand before you.
I knew respect instinctively,
And I fell on my knees,
For it was a cold, dark, and terrible abode where I met you,
And yours was an awesome figure.
What could I do but fall on my knees?
But you bade me rise,
And I became ever after your devotee.

Even at times when I could not believe in you,
Still somehow I remained yours in my heart.
Now after more than two years,
I am still yours.
Indeed I am yours more than ever.
You are my first, foremost, and forever goddess.

You are my mother, my lady, my protector.
But I have also lain with you.
It was natural, and you did not resist,
And you have not withheld your blessings.
You opened yourself to me, and I entered.
What it meant I know not, but it matters not.
Let meaning be for you.
I will content myself with experience.
Here I am, my lady.
Here I am, great mother,
Deep lady of the veil,
Dweller in darkness,
Light within,
Hearth within my breast,
Star in my heart,
Holder of my heart strings.
I praise you now and forever.

*Inscription on a temple at Sais: "Never yet has any mortal lifted my veil."

A Serapis Aretology

by Sannion

I am Serapis, great among the gods, whose name is known by all people in every land. Egyptians kiss the earth at my appearance; Greeks sing the paean to please me; Romans erect monuments in my honor; even the barbarian is not ignorant of my glory.[1]

I am the one whose temple stood on Rhakotis before the Greeks built their city in Egypt.[2]

I am the one who balances the Two Lands, and thus I make my dwelling in Memphis.[3]

I am he who rules from Sinope;[4] the sea-loving Delians built a temple to me;[5] nor have the war-making Germans neglected my rites.[6]

I hear the prayers of every man and whatever I please - this too shall come to pass. For I am greater than Fate; my will is destiny and I may change my mind as I see fit.[7]

I make the blind to see, and cause the lame man to walk again. The dumb through me find speech; the mad-man is made sane.[8]

There is no illness that I cannot heal, for I hold in my right hand the staff of life,[9] and in my left the keys to Haides;[10] and no soul shall depart from this world unless I permit it.

I am the lord of the Nile[11] and pour its bounty upon the earth, bringing forth abundant fruit in due season. When I smile, the granaries of Egypt become swollen and no man's belly is empty.

I am the one who causes the planets to circle in their orbits and the seasons to progress in their natural cycles.[12] It is I who made order to be beautiful.[13]

I am in the rays of the sun; my brilliance is such that no man has beheld me directly.[14]

I reveal the future in dreams; I speak my oracles to those who will hear.[15]

My throne is in the underworld; I give the souls of the dead cool water to drink and they find peace at my feet.[16]

I am the lord of daimones; hosts uncountable hearken to my every word.[17]

I revealed mysteries unto men. I taught men to honor the beautiful images of the gods and care for the sacred animals of Egypt. I consecrated the holy sanctuaries of the gods and heroes, and instructed every nation in its proper ancestral customs.[18]

I delight in festal banquets, in fragrant garlands and musicians; nothing pleases my heart more than dancing-girls and the singers of choral songs.[19]

I established justice everywhere. I made an end to murder and cannibalism. I ordained that the true should be thought good, and the right of more worth than silver and gold. I taught men that nothing should be more feared than an oath. I am always at the side of litigants that nothing unjust may be done; I put wisdom and righteousness into the hearts of all judges, and taught men the art of speaking well in court.[20]

I am the one who appoints rulers; it is I who gives the King power to govern and sets fear of him throughout the land. I established laws and the proper system of government by which cities are run in an orderly fashion.[21]

I provide the needy with sustenance. I give wealth to the poor man. I protect the widow and ensure that suppliants are granted hospitality. I ordained that parents should be loved by children, and that people should set down their lives to protect their precious homeland.[22]

I protect the stranger abroad; I stand by the sailor and calm the waves of the fearful ocean when he calls out my name. I give peace to the weary, and banish sorrow from their hearts.[23]

I do all of this. I, Serapis, great among the gods.

No man knows when I came to be; I am the primordial one, old as time and yet continually made new.[24]

I am the moon-born bull and the bennu-bird reborn in flame.[25]

I am the one who came from the two; within me are multitudes.[26]

My crown is the modius, full of grain. My scepter is the lightning-bolt that drives all things. At my feet sits the fearsome dog of the underworld; around my shoulders hangs the serpent of healing. These are my tokens; by them you shall know me.[27]

I, Serapis, have proclaimed that for those who inscribe my virtues on a stele, whether in holy writing or demotic script, and set it up beside their doorway, and remember what is written there daily; I shall protect them and let no evil enter their home forever.[28]

Notes

[1] Serapis is a truly cosmopolitan, trans-cultural deity; hence each nation uses its characteristic method to worship him. Henu or proskynesis for the Egyptians, which consisted of bowing and kissing the earth before a deity or its cult statue; the paean for the Greeks, which was a cultic hymn recited for Apollon, a healing deity that Serapis was equated with; and Roman monument building, the accomplishment they were most famous for. According to Valerius Maximus (*Famous Words and Deeds* 1.3.4) Serapis had a temple in Rome already in the Republican period.

[2] A small settlement had existed on the site that would become Alexandria for some centuries, though it was used primarily for fishing and protection against pirates during the Pharaonic period. When Alexandria was built Rhakotis became the native Egyptian district, and the famous Serapeion of the Ptolemies was located here. According to the *Alexander Romance* of Pseudo-Kallisthenes Alexander consulted an oracle of Serapis about the foundation of his city and the god prophesied that it would become the greatest city in the world and feed multitudes.

[3] Memphis in ancient times was known as Mekhat Tawy "the Balance of the Two Lands" since it was located at the juncture between Upper and Lower Egypt and served periodically as the capital of the unified

kingdom. The mummified Apis bull was buried here in a huge temple which archaeologists refer to as the Memphite Serapeion. On one level this line can be understood as a reference to that – however the worship of Serapis was intended to unify the diverse elements under the Ptolemaic Dynasty, and thus the Two Lands that Serapis balances can also be interpreted as Egypt and Greece respectively.

[4] According to Tacitus (*History* 4. 82-84) the cult statue of Serapis was brought from Sinope on the Black Sea to Egypt by Ptolemy Soter.

[5] In the 3rd century BCE a sanctuary to Serapis was built on Delos by Egyptian traders.

[6] Numerous inscriptions mentioning Serapis have been found in Cologne (*SIRIS* 720), Dalmatia (*SIRIS* 676) and other parts of Roman Germania.

[7] Adapted from LI 379ff. The motif of a deity with super-cosmic powers over fate (Moira) and chance (Tykhe) was a prominent one in the Hellenistic era. After centuries of constant political upheaval, warfare, and strife many felt powerless to control their lives and uncertain about what lay in store for them. Everything seemed subject to sinister incomprehensible forces deaf and blind to man's pleading. Thus it is not surprising to find that the most popular gods in the later Roman Empire - Isis, Kybele, Mithras, Dionysos and Jesus Christ – are precisely those deities who laid claim to the ability to overcome fate and change a man's terrible lot in life.

[8] For healing miracles by Serapis see The Orations of Aelius Aristides and Tacitus (*Histories* 4.81) among others.

[9] Serapis was often depicted with the snake-twined staff of Asklepios

[10] See Plutarch, *On Isis and Osiris* 361 F – 362 E for Serapis' equation with Haides, lord of the underworld.

[11] Serapis was originally that form of Apis which is united with Osiris in the underworld; Apis is the personification of the fertilizing and life-giving power of the Nile. See Suda s.v. Serapis

[12] So claims Plutarch (*On Isis and Osiris* 362 c) deriving his name from *sairein* "to sweep; to cause motion".

[13] This is a pun, since in Greek kosmos means both "ordered arrangement" and "beautiful adornment".

[14] Macrobius (*Saturnalia* I.20.13) argues at length that Serapis is to be understood as the sun.

[15] For instance, the dream of Zoilos when Serapis commanded him to build a shrine (*PEL* 4.435) or the visitation to Ptolemy Soter when the god ordered his cult statue removed to Alexandria. (Plutarch, *Moralia* 984 A – B) Serapis also gave out much humbler oracles and dream-visitations. His devotees practiced dream incubation in the great Serapeion at Memphis (*UPZ* 1.59)

[16] Cool water is the traditional offering to the deceased in Egyptian funerary religion.

[17] Porphyry, *On Abstinence from Animal Food*, ii. 38

[18] Adapted from *LI* 379ff and A. D. Knock Gnomon XXI, 1944

[19] We have many invitations to the deipnon of Serapis, a festal banquet at which the god was the guest of honor.

[20] Again, adapted from *LI* 379ff and A. D. Knock Gnomon XXI, 1944

[21] Osiris was the prototype of the King of Egypt; the Pharaoh was the embodiment of his son Horus on earth, and in death he was hailed as an Osiris in the underworld. In patronizing the cult of Osiris-Apis, the Ptolemies continued this tradition. Beyond that, Serapis was also deeply concerned with the legal system. He urged Lucius to seek a career as a lawyer in Rome (Apuleius' *Metamorphoses*) and helped Aristides compose his speeches at court, as he recalls in numerous places throughout his Orations.

[22] Standard material in most extant aretalogies; however given Serapis' close relationship with Isis and Harpokrates this seems quite appropriate.

[23] Serapis was invoked especially as a protective deity for sailors, perhaps because of the instrumental role they had in the spreading of his cult, first from maritime Alexandria to the trading centers of Delos and Athens and thence to Rome itself.

²⁴ Although it is occasionally claimed that Ptolemy Soter "invented" the god Serapis for his own political ends, archaeology has proven this to be quite incorrect. The cult of Osar-Apis is attested already in Egypt's 18th Dynasty, making the god at least 1300 years old by the time that Ptolemy had his cult statue brought from Sinope and installed in Alexandria. Both Osiris and Apis as separate deities stretch back to the earliest predynastic period in Egypt's history. While that doesn't exactly make him old as time, it certainly makes him pretty old! This line, however, is indebted to Pseudo-Kallisthenes' account of the meeting of Alexander and Serapis. There the god is hailed as Aion Plutonios, aion signifying an eternal expanse of time.

²⁵ Apis, the physical incarnation of the Nile's abundance in the form of a bull, was said to be generated spontaneously from the light of the moon shining on a virgin calf. The bennu bird is the Egyptian phoenix and linked in numerous accounts with Osiris the lord of resurrection. As Serapis is the combination of Apis and Osiris their animal forms are transferred to him.

²⁶ This cryptic line can be understood in a number of different ways. On one level it can be seen as an expression of Serapis' nature as the syncretic deity par excellence. After all, Serapis is the fusion of Osiris and Apis. But he was also connected with Haides, Zeus, Helios, Dionysos, and numerous other deities. (*Diodorus Siculus* 1.25) For those given to Pythagorean number speculation, it can have a totally different meaning. The two signifies duality, an imperfect division. Out of this, however, arises perfection and unity – but not the sterile unity of the monad; instead a unity that encompasses the totality of all pluralistic existence. Serapis is thus the One and the Many simultaneously.

²⁷ These are the traditional iconographic attributes of the deity, borrowed from his equation with other gods. The reference to the lightning-bolt of Zeus adapts a line from Herakleitos; the underworld dog can be either Kerberos or Anubis; the serpent of healing either the snake of Asklepios or the Agathos Daimon, who was the patron of Alexandria alongside Serapis. Serapis could be depicted in this form, with a serpent body surmounted by his recognizable bearded head. Every statue of Serapis contained the modius-crown, which was constructed to resemble the vessel used for storing and measuring grain as well as the kiste or basket of the mysteries.

[28] The virtues mentioned in this last line are the text of the aretalogy itself, a genre of ancient literature in which the arete (virtues) of a deity are recited, often by having the god address the listener in his own words. The holy writing is of course the hieroglyphs; demotic signifies the common language of the people (demos) whether Egyptian, Greek, or in this case English. The admonition to remember him daily hearkens back to the proskynema that was performed each day for the Lord Serapis in one's home (P. Mich. 15.751) – an exceptional level of domestic piety inspired by the god and found in very few other ancient cults. Although Serapis was a great god, favored by Kings and given lavish state rites – he also held a dear place in the hearts of the common man, since he healed them, gave them guidance, protected them abroad, and guarded their homes.

Triad for Serapis

by P. Sufenas Virius Lupus

1. Beginning

I have felt the stirrings of myself
since the first inundation of the Nile.
I have seen the roots of my being
in the rough rutting of a bull in Memphis.
I was coming into existence
while Osiris' parts were scattered.
I was inching out of obscurity
when Hades opened the earth for Kore.
I was present when the Argive Apis
came to Memphis, curing, dying.
My name was whispered in Babylon
to Alexander as "King of the Deep."
Asklepios of the Egyptians — Imouthes —
was my hand as he healed and measured.
I was a savior when I took
the thyrsus from Dionysos' hand.
And in the mud and flood of the Nile
in the dreams of Ptolemy I took shape.
My wife is Isis, from whom was born
Hermanubis and Harpokrates.
The trident, the thunderbolt, the Nemean lion's skin
were given to me as wedding gifts.
The modius crown the grateful present
of the gods of Egypt at my birth.
Sothis descended into the underworld
to lie a moment with Echidna's whelp;
Her pup, fiery Sarpyros, given to me
with snake tail, with lion, wolf, and dog heads.
I will be sung to in Germania's Coloniae,
and from India to Iberian Hispania.
In Memphis and Alexandria,
Thebae, Ostia, Aelia Capitolina,
and at Tibur's pleasant hills

Hadrian's honors will be my glory.
Ammon and Pan, Helios, Aion,
Agathos Daimon and Mithras —
even all of these will come
under the heavy burden of my locks.
Those in white robes with purple stripes
will know, by this beard, my godliness.

2. Eboracum

To the Holy God Serapis
this Temple was Made, solely,
by Claudius Hieronymianus,
Legate of VI Victrix Legion.

*****

In this city of the legions
far north in Britannia
mere bowshots from Caledonia's wastes
I have set down these stones.
The rain and hail have not ceased
their equal trade of day and night watches
for weeks, as Maia's feast draws near.
Sons of Dis, I would cross Styx sooner!
I remember the times in Campagna
when summer sun ripened
the fragrant groves of olive trees
as I lounged eating figs and bread.
I made offerings in your temple, Great God
when I survived the fever that beset
my final ephebic years, and in dreams
you came to me and comforted.
For my life and every good thing
I vowed to repay you one day;
I have been promoted now,
and thus I give you this temple.
May it remind travelers here
of warmer climes far away,
of helpful and hospitable gods
who only hear rumors of hail and snow.
I hear tales from generations passed
that the Iceni had a god

like you, O Great God, holy,
bearded, benevolent, called "The Good."
I have seen your image adorning
the Mithraeum of Londinium,
white-faced, marble, noble, living...
a Serapeum of your own you deserve!
I know not what will happen here,
whether the Emperor Septimius Severus
will be pleased with this temple
when he comes to campaign.
So much of Hadrian's limit
on the other side of the vallum
was laid waste by the Maeatae,
temples razed to the ground in fire.
A century from now, my bones
may be dust, my soul choking on dirt,
but, with your grace, O Holy One,
may I be in pleasant fields instead.
A century from now, in this fort,
your temple may be a grain storehouse
for warlike and impious usurpers —
may that never come to pass!
A century from now, some upstart fool
may have designs for the Empire —
may he be stopped in his tracks
by all the gods of Rome!
And long after his images are tossed
into the Tiber's sewers and forgotten,
will roaming spirits, loyal and disloyal
besiege this fort forever unquiet?

I, Claudius Hieronymianus,
by Jupiter and Isis, Mithras and Serapis —
the Great and Holy Good God —
do dedicate this temple to you!

3. Endings

Atheists have come to destroy my temple.
They have pillaged my coffers.
They have killed my philosophers and priests.

They have desecrated the daughter library.
They have hacked my statue to rubble.
How unfortunate for them — their blindness!
They destroy images of the gods
thinking their imageless "God" is the "True God"
when no image is still an image
and their insistence makes its senselessness plain.
But this is a teaching too subtle for most,
and even now an image takes shape
in the minds of thousands begetting millions.
Their father god, just judge on his throne,
benevolent and bearded and all-being:
who is he but myself renamed?
That "God"'s son, prodigious child —
who is he but my own Harpokrates?
Who is this "Mother of God" but Isis?
Their sainted Christopher, bearer, way-opener
is none other than my son Hermanubis.
How unfortunate for them — their blindness!
Their saint Anthony of the desert
was my own since before his birth.
There is no god I have yet encountered
who has not given of himself to me.
Iao Sabaoth, he who speaks in winds
has thrown up his cleansed hands in frustration.
"I have been with you from the start,
even though my people were not.
They are loyal to me, I must remain loyal.
But these 'Christ-followers'? — no,
I will not have such among my people.
Do with them as you wish, they are not mine."
Their prayers will have no power, calling no holy name
but "God" — deified noun without gravity —
but I will go with them at a distance.
For centuries, I will conceal my truth in their lie
until men are prepared again to see it.
By destroying my image, they have freed me,
by sacrilege they have liberated me —
now I am freer in form
than the wind which was their god before.

Reflections on the Lamentations of Isis and Nephthys

by Sannion

All night I've been in the grip of an intense melancholy. It started while I was reading the Lamentations of Isis and Nephthys – and then at one point this intense image just seized me, and it was as if I was there, as if I was going through it and feeling everything myself.

After days of endless, frustrating searching, Isis finally discovers Osiris, fallen on his side, his face in the mud. She pulls him up out of the water, clutching him to her breast, holding his lifeless body in her arms, aching to feel his vibrancy and strength return and have him move against her, take her in his arms and kiss her, telling her it was all an accident, a joke, that none of it really happened - and instead feeling only the dead, empty weight of a corpse. The hot tears falling uncontrollably from her eyes, spilling onto his cheeks, etching lines in the mud caked on his flesh, those same lines appearing in her heart as it splinters into a million pieces.

Remembering how beautiful he was, how his whole face would light up when he smiled, how the earth shook when he walked and the green grass sprang up beneath his feet and how he made everything come alive, especially her when they made love at night. And now, all of it gone. Empty. Dark. And he'd never be coming back to her. She was alone. Completely alone. And she rocks back and forth with him in her arms, like the waves washing against the shore, keening in lament, a horrible, agonized sound beyond words, beyond comprehension of anything but the all-consuming pain. And she wants to join him, more than anything, thinks about throwing herself into the water and becoming a pale, bloated dead thing like him to stop the pain. And then she feels the hand of Nephthys on her shoulder. And at first she is filled with rage, a sharp anger that cuts through the pain. How dare that whore intrude, the one who tricked her way into her husband's bed and ultimately caused his death. And then she looks up into her eyes and sees the mirror of her own pain, and she knows that Nephthys loved him too, that her loss is just as great. And she reaches a hand out to touch her sister's hand, and Nephthys sinks down beside her, her pale hand touching the cold body of Osiris, and together they weep.

And this image just won't go away. It haunts me, heavy and dark like a shroud settling over my soul, and I feel as if I have lost my beloved, and I want to cry. And I just can't shake it. For almost an hour I lay in the dark, on the verge of tears, and nothing is going to make it go away because Osiris is dead, and he's never coming back. Even when they bring him back to life, he's going to remain in the underworld, a king of dead things. Something important was lost from the world with his passing. Only his shadow remains above ground, causing the vegetation to grow, life to quicken, time to pass – but that is only a dim reflection of the potency he once had, and which is now forever lost.

Isis

by Birdsong

She searches
    and searches,
Travels over
deserts and mountains,
Tricks the sun
    into giving her
        his crown,
Finds each piece
    of her lover's puzzle,
Pastes them together
    with her tears,
Then, when sorrow
    breaks her heart,
She makes love
    to death
And bears
    a bird.

Most Ancient

by Rebecca Buchanan

I who am Most Ancient
    Queen of the Underworld
    Star of the Sea
    Heavenly One

I who am Most Ancient
    Lady of Life
    Tree of Life
    Green One

I who am Most Ancient
    Mistress of Joy
    Lady of Charm
    Golden One

I who am Most Ancient
    Call upon me
    I am kind
    I come

To Osiris

by Brandon Newberg

O Great Father,
Hitherto I have known you little.
You have been to me as a foreign spectacle or curiosity,
Or else an adjunct to my love for Isis.
But now I reach out to you.
I call to you and entreat you,
That you enter into my life.
Show me your way and your wisdom.
Teach me of the masculine and the paternal.
Give me respect for balance and union.
I have known your wife as mother,
Now let me know you as father.
O Great God Wesir,
Lord of the waters,
Lord of the corn and barley,
Lord of the mysteries of life and death,
And wise sage of the circle of life,
I give you praise.

Some Thoughts on Osiris and the Dead

by Sannion

One of the cardinal tenets of the ancient Egyptian faith was the identification of the deceased with Osiris. The story of Osiris is an ancient and complicated one, and there are many conflicting accounts. (For instance, some mention only that he was lost and hesitate to provide any further information since mentioning his death explicitly fell under religious prohibitions or taboos. From other accounts we learn that Osiris fell on his side, that he was drowned, or that he was cut up into 14 pieces and his remains scattered throughout the land. The Greeks, somewhat uncomfortable with this ambiguity, sought to reconcile the different traditions and thus we have the elaborate harmony produced by Plutarch which records that Osiris was first drowned, then revived, and finally hacked into pieces.)

The death of Osiris was a powerful event that changed the course of the world forever. Before that time everything had existed in perfect harmony. Nothing died, or suffered, or was any different from one day to the next. But when Set slew his brother he radically altered the cosmos by inserting that element of mutability into it. Although Horus, Isis, and Thoth found Osiris, put him back together again, and restored his power to him - he could not return to life in this world. Change of that magnitude simply cannot be undone. So Osiris, the first to have undertaken the journey West, established a new kingdom there, the land of the dead, which he ruled justly as he had once ruled here on earth. (This is a fundamental way in which Osiris differs from both Dionysos and Christ, however similar they may be in other respects. While all died and were restored, Osiris remains a dead god in the underworld and does not return to the world above - though his potency does rise up to fertilize the earth at certain times.)

And all who die follow in his footsteps. The same things that happened to him happen to each of us. At first we fall on our sides, immobile, powerless, and asleep. Then, through the elaborate funerary rituals, which were first performed by Isis, Horus, and Thoth on Osiris, we are restored so that we can make the journey into Amenti and stand before the Judgment Seat. It is only a temporary restoration, however (one that can be reversed), and there are many obstacles and opponents that we have to overcome before we get there. Once we stand in the Halls of Judgment our life and soul are weighed. Our good deeds are measured against our evil ones, and if our heart is found to be heavier than the feather of Ma'at (truth, justice, balance) then we are either consigned to oblivion (our soul consumed by the monster Ammit) or we are punished for an indeterminate period until we have worked off our sin. (This notion of purgation appears relatively late in Egyptian history, and may be indebted to Greek ideas about the underworld, e.g., the stories of Sisyphus and Tantalus, which we find replicated in the late period papyrus containing the story of Setna Khamwas.)

Those who come out balanced, however, are hailed as *Maa-Kharu*, "Justified and Pure Ones." Part of them goes on to take their place in the Field of Rushes – a place of plenty and eternal joy – while another part of them ascends into heaven (the body of Nuit or Hathor) and shines eternally with the ancestral spirits or Akhu whom you see as the nocturnal stars. The Egyptian afterlife was not ethereal and otherworldly. It was very much about the continuation of life and everything that made life worth living beyond the grave. Thus people are depicted working in the fields (especially the vineyard), hunting, playing games, making offerings to the gods, performing or listening to music, dancing, eating, drinking, making love, and spending time in the company of their friends and family. Death was only sorrowful for those of us left behind – for the spirits of the deceased, it was an overwhelmingly positive and joyous experience. People say the Egyptians were death-obsessed, since they spent so much time preparing for the next world. In reality they were so life-obsessed that they could not conceive of it ending as we know it, but longed for its eternal continuance.

The dead become Osiris. Every step of the way they have followed in his footsteps - they have shared in his trials and tribulations, his reconstitution, and finally his complete restoration and eternal life. Every dead person who has successfully completed the journey is Osiris. There's a very lovely passage from the Coffin Texts (330) that captures this idea:

> "Whether I live or die I am Osiris, I enter in and reappear through you, I decay in you, I grow in you, I fall down in you, I fall upon my side. The Gods are living in me for I live and grow in the corn that sustains the Honored Ones. I cover the earth, whether I live or die I am Barley."

King and commoner, rich and poor, man or woman – all are Osiris in death (or alternately Hathor, at least in the Ptolemaic period). Originally that was the prerogative of the Pharaoh: in life he had been Horus, in death he became Osiris. But as time went on and Egypt underwent rapid transformation and periods of destabilization, things became more democratized and wealthy people started having their own mortuary temples built with the elaborate ceremonial texts detailing the passage through the underworld and what awaited them, as well as spells, amulets, and assorted magical phrases inscribed on the walls. Eventually even commoners had these texts written out and buried with them – sometimes even the very poor managed to take a few scraps inscribed with the most important spells into the next world with them.

IN THY ORISONS

by Jeremy J. Baer

O Osiris! O Osiris! Brother. Husband. King. Snatched from my love. Stolen from life. Never again to feel your tender caress in the marriage bed. You now reign in the Land of Silence, where my voice cannot bespeak my affection for you. Never to embrace me again with warm flesh, never to cast living eyes on your own son. O Weary of Heart, banished to the Western realm, I grieve for thee. Remember me. In your prayers, remember me.

O Thoth. Great of Magic. Teacher, counselor and friend. Ever shall I and humanity below have a sagacious magician to guard our counsel. Speak your heart, O god of scribes, and let your words of power ring justice from earth to sky.

O Seth. Voice of the Northern Sky. Treacherous brother. Mighty you are, but without the wisdom to guide it. Strength you have, but not the heart to make the best use of it. Power alone does not make a king to uphold Ma'at.

O Ra! Brilliant in the Sky. You glide through your heavens in your solar barque and care nothing for the travesties of earth. What good is a sun that shines no mercy or warmth on those below? You are old and distant, and give over your reign to the violence of Seth. Do you wonder why I tricked you into revealing your true Name to me? Do you wonder why I would see my child wear the Crown of the Two Lands? Humanity needs justice - and so do the gods.

O gods! I am a royal daughter of the heavenly court. I am god, queen and woman.

And I have suffered.

Nothing suffers as a woman suffers. Neither man, nor beast. Not even a god.

No one feels the scorn of a father like a cast away daughter. No one remembers the death blow to a man as she who shared his bed. No one suffers every fear and every failing of a child as does a mother.

And no one falls from grace as wretchedly as a queen overthrown – or a goddess betrayed.

People pray to gods to protect them. I had no one to protect me in the festering marsh. The hunger, the damp, the threat from animals. Always constant. I turned not to gods but to people. A crust of bread, a bite of fruit. Old, discarded cloth to swaddle my infant. It was enough to keep us alive. It was to men – and especially to women – in whom I turned my faith. Perhaps they understood my pains.

I now understood theirs.

Man, woman and child. Tears of Ra! Hunger, disease and pain are your constant companions. But I hear your cries. I, who lived as one of you while hiding in the marshes, know your grievances.

Behold! I who lost a husband am the defender of matrons.
Behold! I who raised a child in hiding am the refuge for mothers.
Behold! I who took to the seas to find my brother's corpse am the matron of sailors.
Behold! I who begged for food am the nourishment of the Nile and the bringer of seasons.
Behold! I whose son was stung by a scorpion am the healer of ills.
Behold! I am Isis. I am deliverer and savior, guide and guardian. I hear your cries as they rise to heaven. Let man and woman, Egyptian and foreigner, peasant and noble seek solace in my ministrations. Let them find comfort and justice in my embracing wings.

Man, woman and child. Tears of Ra! Remember me. In your prayers, remember me.

The Crossing of Akh

by Christa Bergerson

Sarcophagus
like some celestial vessel
of one microcosm hurtling
through nightmare moonscapes
blinding starshine shattering
ego gratification empty
hearted fists of lapis, turquoise
and gold encrusted
ornaments glittering
in the dewy dreamfield

When he awakes
there will be no more
sleep

Words for the Wall (To Help a Man Pass Through)

by Normandi Ellis

These words an old song
Some ancient water
Words veiled and unveiling
Sequences of stars, bird, hand, serpent
Palimpsest bearing the scribe's mistake eternally
Needing the rest of his life to amend.
How long did Ptah search his heart and
Hold his tongue before he pronounced
      The Light?

Text and tongue simultaneous
The goddess appears at the sound of the voice.
There are eyes observing
From these chinks in old stone
The whole world behind the words
Gazing out at you
      Standing in the dark
      Holding your little candle
      With pick axe and Open Sesame

Begin to read from left or right
Depending on where you want to go
All words are a door
Hands and feet do nothing
It is the Mind
That opens, a trick accomplished
Without thinking.
I dreamed some hieroglyphic world
      Zep Tepi – The First Time

And I saw how, at least for myself
I've grown meat around the stone
Myself for better or worse
With each utterance.

They are all words of power:
The pebble on the banks of the river
The cat blinking slowly beneath the chair
A knock at the door.
The ache we feel staring at a silent language
(Begging to be understood
As if it were plain enough
But our own hearts indecipherable)
Begins the work of true translation.
Never mind what it means.
What is it insisting?

Mr. West

by Rebecca Buchanan

"....assure you, Mrs. Dubois, all of the arrangements will be taken care of. The casket will be monogrammed and engraved, as you requested. I have already been in touch with Ted Norman over at Our Lady of Orleans Cemetery, and they are preparing the space beside your husband's parents. I'll get some roses from the garden first thing in the morning, and start work on the wreath. Everything will be ready." He patted her arm, leading her gently towards the door. "Your husband is in good hands." He smiled at Mrs. Dubois and her daughter, a middle-aged woman with pretty brown eyes and laugh lines around her mouth.

The older woman stopped and grasped his hand firmly. "Thank you so much, Mr. Chapman. You've been so gracious. I was such a wreck when Anthony - well, I didn't know what to do, and you... Well," she squeezed his hand, "thank you."

"You're very welcome, ma'am." He smiled and nodded as the two ladies exited through the door and down the steps, the porch light illuminating their path. They brushed against the great lilac and white rose bushes that threatened to overwhelm the front entry. He breathed in the sweet scent, deeply. He should really get those trimmed back. They probably looked unprofessional and messy. He shrugged to himself, waving and watching as Mrs. Dubois' daughter helped her mother into their car, then climbed in herself and drove off. The flower bushes had been his grandmother's idea, something to soften and warm the hard stone of the funeral home. She had ripped up the whole back parking lot and planted a garden of apple trees and lilac shrubs, and even developed her own breed of roses, the Chapman White.

He closed the front door and carefully locked it. Turned off the front porch light, the entry hall light, and headed back to his office. His back and legs hurt after sitting so long with the Duboises. He sighed, pressing a hand to the small of his back. Anthony Dubois. A schoolmate a few years behind him. Graduated top of his class, West Point, distinguished military career, Mayor, State Senator, then off to Congress.

He sighed again and shook his head. What an amazing life. The chapel would be packed full for the funeral. Maybe he should make more than one wreath, make sure there were enough roses to go around.

He winced as his stiff legs finally began to loosen, stinging. Stepping between his coat stand and his desk, he looked out through the glass doors, over his grandmother's garden. He remembered playing in that garden as a boy, long summer games of hide and seek and cowboys and Indians. His father yelling at him when he tripped over and mangled a baby shrub. Helping his mother set up the arch and the benches. Plucking a rose for Susan after they'd had dinner with his parents for the first time.

He shivered, trying to remember how she had looked that night, a rose tucked into her hair, and not how she had looked at the hospital –

What was that?

He squinted, scowled slightly. Better not be vandals.

There it was again. A sleek streak of black against the white flowers. It ripped around a bush, leaping, so fast, sliding to an abrupt halt to sniff at a rabbit hole.

"A dog," he said aloud to himself. "Hnh."

Gingerly unlocking the door, he flipped on the light and stepped onto the back porch. The dog's head shot up. He stopped in surprise on the top step. It was a large animal, quite large for a dog. Solid black, but for the sparkle at its throat. Muscled, but sleek, with deep golden eyes and a pointed muzzle and great pointed ears. The ears had swiveled in his direction.

"Well," he said softly, "I don't think I've ever seen anything quite like you, before."

The dog barked, once, a deep-throated *whrumph* of sound that made his blood tingle. Then the dog sat, tail thump-thump-thumping against the ground.

He winced again as he limped down the steps. His legs really did hurt tonight. The dog didn't move as he walked closer, just tilted its head curiously. He leaned down, one hand braced against his leg, and lifted up the dog's collar. It was an odd piece of jewelry; kind of like that symbol for woman that was on all the restroom doors, but the top loop was more oblong than circular; or maybe it was a cross with an open top. He flipped it over. No name, no address. Not even a phone number.

"Well, boy." He dropped the collar and rubbed the dog's head. It whined in happiness, tail thumping even louder. "I hope you got one of those fancy new chips in you, otherwise I got no way to find your family."

The dog *whrumph*ed again, a full-chested bark that he could feel in his bones.

"Ah, there you are," said a voice over his shoulder.

He turned, grunting slightly in surprise and pain. A man was striding towards him, walking stick in one hand; his pace was strong, but leisurely. His skin was as dark as the dog's hide, his suit entirely green; a dozen different shades of green, from pine to new grass to baby lettuce. Even his old-fashioned fedora was green, but for the single stripe of its white hat band.

The man doffed that fedora now, revealing a completely bald, shining head. He bowed slightly and smiled warmly. "Mr. West, sir, at your service."

He held out his hand, only then realizing that the man wore black gloves. "Harold Chapman."

Mr. West nodded. "Indeed you are," he said with certainty.

"Uh," Harold frowned, cleared his throat. "This is your dog, then."

"He is my companion, yes, my loyal friend. I'm afraid that sometimes he gets over-excited and runs ahead. I hope he didn't startle you."

"Oh, no, no. Very friendly." Harold shook his head. "I must say, though, I've never seen a dog quite like this before."

The dog trotted over and Mr. West rubbed its head. "His is a very old species, very old. From Africa, originally. They were very common once. They could be found all over. Not so common now." Mr. West smiled suddenly, white teeth a bright flash against his mahogany skin. "Your father made the same comment."

Harold blinked, puzzled. Mr. West didn't look old enough to have known his father.

"I have been watching you for some time, Harold, as I have been watching your whole family. You are a good man, Harold Chapman. You treat the grief-stricken with compassion. You treat the dead with dignity."

"Oh, I ... I'm sorry, do you need my services? For a loved one?"

Mr. West laughed, then, great guffaws that puffed out his chest and cheeks. It was a delighted, amused sound. It made Harold want to laugh, too. Even the dog seemed to be laughing, lips pulled back to reveal sharp teeth, golden eyes crinkled.

Mr. West finally stopped, hiccupping a bit, leaning on his walking stick. "Not at all, Harold." Again, the warm smile. "I am here for you."

Harold swallowed.

"All these years of faithful, selfless service to others. Of kindness. Of treating the dead with respect, not like lumps of meat as so many others do." The dog growled unhappily. Mr. West leaned forward, one large hand settling on Harold's shoulder. "Time for you to rest, Harold."

"I – I don't ...." He shook his head. "I still have work to do. The Dubois funeral. I have to arrange the flowers. And there will be others."

Mr. West shook his head. "The Duboises will be well taken care of. And so will the others who come after them. There is a woman, you see, named Mari, who lives east of here. She has been having dreams, and tomorrow, those dreams will lead her here. She will care for this place, for this community – " Mr. West waved his stick " – just as you have all these years."

"But... I...." Harold looked around, eyes taking in the stone building, his home for his entire life. And the garden of Chapman White rose bushes and the odd lilac bush and the benches in the shade of blossoming apple trees. In his mind, he saw children playing games, and his family picnicking, and quiet memorials. His grandmother's funeral, and his father's and his mother's – and Susan's, taken from him less than a year after that first dinner."

"Susan loved this garden," he blurted.

"Indeed." Mr. West's response was soft as he scratched the dog's head. "She loves the new garden your grandmother has planted almost as much. She says only you are missing."

Harold stared at Mr. West for a very long moment, fear and uncertainty slowly fading. A smile spread across his face and he drew a deep breath. "Just give me a moment to lock up, yes?"

Mr. West inclined his head, waving his fedora towards the porch. "Of course."

His legs didn't hurt anymore, he realized, as he practically skipped up the steps and through the glass doors. On the stand he found his hat and light summer jacket. Pulling them on, he caught a dark shape from the corner of his eye. He turned his head slowly, reluctant to see what he knew was there. Himself, in the chair behind his desk. He looked like he was asleep, slouched down slightly, hands clasped in his lap. He was smiling.

Shifting his shoulders, settling his hat more firmly on his head, Harold stepped around the desk, around himself, and out the glass doors. The key stuck in the lock and he had to jiggle it a bit, but eventually it caught. He paused at the top step, one hand shoved deep into his pocket.

Mr. West looked up expectantly, and the dog tilted its head.

Harold straightened his back. Nothing hurt. "All right, then."

Mr. West held out his hand. Great dog at his side, Harold walked into the west.

*****

" ....expressed their appreciation today when it was announced that the Chapman Funeral Home, which has been in operation for five generations, would remain open. After long-time director Harold Chapman was found dead last week, community leaders expressed concern that there would be no one to provide end-of-life services for the city and surrounding area. New director Mari Robinson has promised to continue the Chapman Funeral Home's tradition of affordable and compassionate care as we quote journey to our ancestors end quote. In other news..."

Isis, Mistress of Heaven

by Jeremy J. Baer

The spirituality of the Western world could use a strong feminine presence which nonetheless nurtures the masculine as well. I find this in Isis. Let me tell you how I got there, and where I want to go from here.

Overview

Religiously I had been some version or another of a Greco-Roman polytheist for some time. My views had changed somewhat as the years stretched by, but broadly I was interested in the cults of Classical Athens through the Hellenistic world to imperial Rome.

My problem was with the goddesses of Olympus. While I encountered goddesses worthy of respect, I found none who truly spoke to me on a deep and satisfying level.

Hestia is the hearth goddess, but in a broader sense a goddess of an individual's relation to home and community. Hera is the protector of married women, and stately goddess of sovereignty. Demeter is goddess of motherhood and agriculture; in relation to her daughter Kore she is matron of the afterlife mysteries. Aphrodite is the goddess of love and sexuality, but also matron of seafarers. Artemis is goddess of the moon and wildlife, of young women and childbirth. Hekate is a goddess of magic, and something of a guide and guardian. Athene, the goddess of wisdom, presides over civilization, and taught men useful arts such as weaving.

Historically speaking, certain goddesses were very popular in certain cities (Athene in Athens, Hera in Argos) while others appealed to certain classes of people (Athene to craftsmen, Hera to married women). But goddesses in normative Greco-Roman religion generally do not, by their nature, lend themselves to a universal appeal. One has to look elsewhere.

If I had trouble relating to Olympian goddesses because they seemed underdeveloped, Isis was a deity so developed she was identified with virtually every major goddess in Antiquity. In the classical age Isis was equated with Demeter, in the Hellenistic age with Aphrodite. But her mystery adherents saw her as the embodiment of all, the One of Many

Names. Isis combines all the above mentioned roles of the Greek goddesses in one divine personage.

Few goddesses command such a wide array of benevolent powers. More to the point, she is disposed to use them. She listens. Even at the earliest epochs of Egyptian myth, Isis was considered the most compassionate of the divinities. She hears the lamentations and prayers of humanity. She is the dutiful wife and mother who, because she suffered, understands humanity's suffering. While it is wrong to read myth too literally, few other divinities are portrayed as so willing to intervene in the lives of people outside their chosen elect.

With Isis comes a divine entourage of considerable majesty. Her husband Osiris is judge of the dead and Lord of Eternity; the Greeks knew him as Serapis, additionally a friendly god of healing and agriculture. Her son by Osiris is Harpocrates, a warrior god with healing attributes, and the embodiment of royal power. Isis, Osiris and Harpocrates were a Holy Trinity that long preceded Christianity. Thoth and Anubis attended to Isis in her time of need – Thoth as the god of magic and wisdom, and Anubis as a guide and guardian of the dead. Once important deities in their own right, these powerful and kindly beings become, in myth and cult, ministers to Isis and a boon to her cultic adherents.

Thus I found myself erecting a small shrine to Isis in my bedroom with regular devotions. The more I learned about Isis, the more I wanted to learn about her and Serapis. I felt nurtured and inspired by the Mistress of Heaven. My religious life came to possess a focus it had been lacking. Theologically I found a goddess with whom I could relate. In cultural terms, I did not have to choose between the legacies of Rome, Greece or Egypt; the Isiac cult admits to all of them. Rapidly taking everything to its logical conclusion, I decided to devote myself to Isis.

But how do I honor her?

Levels of Worship

In Antiquity, Isis could be honored on a variety of fronts. Domestic worship was the most accessible level of religion. The poorer sorts could erect a small household shrine and make daily offerings of incense and food stuffs. In Roman Pompeii, figurines of Isis on lararia (domestic shrines) seem to have been common. Wealthy individuals or corporations of individuals might build private chapels dedicated to the goddess.

Cultic festivals were enacted throughout the year. There were two high festivals in particular that attracted attention: The Navigium Isidis, a joyous procession in early March, and a somber occasion in late October and early November called the Inventio Osirides. One did not have to be a duly initiated member of the cult to participate, and it seems these colorful events attracted large segments of the city population.

A temple of Isis, or Iseum, was a focal point of cultic activity. Clergy led adherents in prayers and song in the morning and early afternoon. In the evening the temple doors were shut and only the initiated were allowed into the inner sanctuary.

Finally there were the Mysteries, a process of secret initiation into the deeper levels of the cult. Initiation involved much preparation and esoteric rituals. Those who underwent the rites achieved a higher understanding of the goddess which conferred upon them her highest blessings and protection from fate.

The Mysteries were by definition secret, and thus many of the details are lost to history. The temples and city-wide festivals are obviously beyond us at this stage due to the low number of adherents. But in our homes and in small gatherings we can dutifully honor the goddess. All we need is a flat space, an image or statue of the goddess, a candle, some incense or other scented offering, and offering bowls for water and food. Prayers, meditations and offerings are how we will commune with this Mistress of Heaven. It is time we bring back her religion for the modern age.

The Future

Many agnostics and skeptics today may consider the worship of Isis as a foolish or even profane anachronism, a religion that was consigned long ago to the forgotten winds of history. A few others disposed to Jungian psychology and the study of psychological archetypes might accept Isis only on a purely psychological level, one culture's symbol of divine femininity.

Those who have experienced her know her as an active and conscious entity possessed with incredible power and maternal warmth. In some respects modern cult adherents might draw an analogy to the Virgin Mary, for Isis presaged Mary's role as Mother of God and great intercessor. But Isis, unlike Mary, is ultimately more important than the god to whom she gave birth, and more powerful as well. Another difference, and not the least one either, is that Isis as patron of courtesans is not linked with perpetual virginity. Isis is a wife, not just a mother, and embodies a positive sexuality in contrast to some religions' dim view of sexuality.

How Isis manifested herself to the Ancients, and how they knew and cherished the goddess, will offer us valuable insights for developing a living, breathing cult in contemporary times. But while history is an excellent beginning, it is not the end. As the world, and our understanding of it, has changed considerably in the last two thousand years, resurrecting the cult of Isis exactly as it existed in pre-Christian times does not seem possible. In our homes and in small gatherings we can honor Isis still. If and when our numbers swell, greater things will be possible, and we will honor the goddess as she manifests to us.

Simple yet steadfast devotion will carry us into the future.

Bibliography

David, Rosalie. *Handbook to Life in Ancient Egypt*. Oxford University Press. Oxford, England. 1998.

Pinch, Geraldine. *Egyptian Mythology: A Guide to Gods, Goddesses and Traditions of Ancient Egypt*. Oxford University Press. Oxford, England. 2002.

Turcan, Robert. *The Cults of the Roman Empire*. Translated by Antonia Nevill. Blackwell Publishing. Oxford, England. 1996.

Witt, R.E. *Isis in the Ancient World*. Johns Hopkins University Press. Baltimore, Maryland & London, England. 1971.

THE WHITE LION QUEEN

by Frater Eleuthereus

The Veil of Planets shatters before the Queen of Alchemy
Salt spills and dances about
Coagulating and redefining itself
Amongst the putrid the Red the congealed

The remnants of a War fought just as much with words, intrigue and vice.
A War She wanted no part of
Not in Her World.
She takes to the Sky, Her favored realm

A harpoon glimmers in the distance
And the Sun, her Father and Son,
With Whom She shares Her Power glistens on her wing
She gathers helm, sword and shield.

No more sulphur
No more dross
The time has come to end this
So vows the White Queen,

Lady of Hawks,
Master of the Rivers and the Soot
She lands, and weeps and screams!
An undulating bellow that soars to the stars

Ma'at, Where are you?!
Amidst this tomb of filth and sludge?
I lay a feather in honor of your Incalculable Truth
And it bristles away in the wind of an angry missionary

Isis, the White Queen
Comes and dances with sword and spear upon the land
No bolt may touch her, no siren song may allure her

She is Victory and Truth in MOTION

Slashing away the darkness of the Red
And bringing down the Star of Evening
in a bellowing of tears and grief
She stands amidst corpses, arrows, and shafts

The Master of Purity
Walks amidst the broken hall of Conflict
Maiden of Lions who suckles on her foes' marrow
Stands victorious amongst the lascivious and wicked.

So heaving, and panting, the day is won by the General of Generals Queen Isis.

Hymn unto Isis

by Seti Apollonius

Praise flows unto thee, Isis
Born of Nut
Lady of Heaven
Great of Heka
Goddess of Goddesses.
Thee who did overcome
Mighty Ra
weaving poison
by cunning & earth
Isis, Holder of Ra's silent name.

Isis, wife of Asar
sister of Set the Strong
Bearer of Heru-sa-Aset
sister of Nepthys
who, though bound to Set,
shared thy grief
married to the joy
born of resurrected desires
upon the rising of Osiris.

Praise flows to thee. Isis
who is as Hathor, Mother of Beauty,
Isis, I praise thee with meager offerings
and a sea of myrrh aflame
Bringing forth Horus anew
To dance war against Set
Both of thy blood
who are at last reconciled
to peace.

Praise flows anew to thee
even as your ancient temples
are married to naught

& wrapped in dust.
Goddess of Life-Giving Waters
Let these your new temples
be built
as many as your names
erected in our hearts & minds
raised in the Septian sky.

THE MIGHTY BULL OF THE TWO LANDS

by Sannion

There is a startling array of evidence which suggests some kind of link between the Egyptian Osiris and the Greek Dionysos. What I have done with this article is to collect as much of that evidence as I could, so that the reader can determine what sort of connection there may be between the two. Although I have my own personal theories, I have tried to keep these out as much as possible, for I do not feel that it is my place to dictate such an important matter for the reader. I have simply provided the information for you to draw your own conclusions – and would recommend that if this is a pressing issue for you, that you go directly to the Gods and ask them themselves. I think the answers you receive will be most interesting indeed.

The Testimony of Ancient Authors

There are numerous ancient authors who assert the essential unity of these two Gods.

> "There is only the difference in names between the festivals of Bacchus and those of Osiris, between the Mysteries of Isis and those of Demeter." – Diodorus Siculus, *The Library of History*, 1.13

> "It is proper to identify Osiris with Dionysos." – Plutarch, *On Isis and Osiris*, 28

> "Osiris is he who is called Dionysos in the Greek tongue." – Herodotus 2.144

Cicero included Osiris among the many Gods equated with Dionysos by the Greeks (*De Natura Deorum* 3.21).

Whether as a result of this equation, or on his own and through his own name, Dionysos has long been associated with Egypt and her neighbors. For instance, Hesychius located Nysa, the mythical birthplace of Dionysos, variously in Egypt, Ethiopia, or Arabia (*Lexicon* 742). Hesiod locates the mysterious city of Nysa "near the streams of Aegyptus" (*Frag.* 287) as do the author of the first *Homeric Hymn to Dionysos* and Apollonius Rhodius (*Argonautica* 2.1214). Herodotus placed Nysa alternately in Egypt (3.97) or Arabia (3.111) with which Diodorus Siculus was in agreement (1.15).

According to Apollodorus (*Library* 1.6.3), Ovid (*Metamorphoses* 5.319ff), and Hyginus (*Fabulae* 152) among others, during the battle of Zeus and Typhon, the Gods were forced to flee Mount Olympos and take up residence in Egypt, where they took on the shapes of animals in order to conceal themselves. Hermes became an ibis, Aphrodite a dove, Apollo a hawk, and Dionysos a goat. This myth was, in all likelihood, an attempt by the Greeks to explain the predominance of zoomorphic Gods in Egypt, as the ancient author Lucian shrewdly perceived (*On Sacrifices*, 14).

After the Ptolemies came to power in Egypt, Dionysos was one of the most popular Gods. He was the tutelary deity of their Dynasty – Ptolemy IV even adopted the title "Neos Dionysos" (*Oxyrhynchus*, ii No. 236b) – and under their reign, numerous temples and theaters were erected to him, including a few that are still standing, despite the best efforts of Christians and Moslems over the centuries. It was the destruction of Dionysos' temple in Alexandria by a mob of insane, violent Christians instigated by the Bishop Theophilus which inspired the remaining Pagans of the city to rise to the defense of the Serapeum (Gibbon's *The Decline and Fall of the Roman Empire*, XXVIII). Under Ptolemy IV Philopator, Egypt became a center of Dionysian mysteries. This King sent out an edict decreeing that "those who perform initiations for Dionysos" should travel to Alexandria and register there, declaring "from whom they have received the sacred things, up to three generations, and to hand in the hieros logos in a sealed exemplar" (3 *Maccabees* 2.30).

Culture Bringer

Concerning Osiris, Diodorus Siculus wrote, "Osiris was the first, they record, to make mankind give up cannibalism; for after Isis had discovered the fruit of both wheat and barley which grew wild over the land along with the other plants but was still unknown to man, and Osiris had also devised the cultivation of these fruits, all men were glad to change their food, both because of the pleasing nature of the newly-discovered grains and because it seemed to their advantage to refrain from their butchery of one another" (1.14).

Tieresias, in Euripides' *Bacchae*, says Dionysos "discovered and bestowed on humankind the service of drink, the juice that streams from the vine clusters; humans have but to take their fill of wine, and the sufferings of an unhappy race are banished" (279-82).

And there are numerous references - too many to recount here – to Dionysos instituting the cultivation of the vine in various localities within the Greek world. (Apollodorus and Pausanias recount most of these in a fairly coherent order.)

Peaceful Conquest of the World

"Of Osiris they say that, being of a beneficent turn of mind, and eager for glory, he gathered together a great army, with the intention of visiting all the inhabited earth and teaching the race of men how to cultivate the vine and sow wheat and barley; for he supposed that if he made men give up their savagery and adopt a gentle manner of life he would receive immortal honours because of the magnitude of his benefactions. And this did in fact take place, since not only the men of his time who received this gift, but all succeeding generations as well, because of the delight which they take in the foods which were discovered, have honoured those who introduced them as Gods most illustrious." – Diodorus Siculus I.17

Dionysos also gathered together a great army, comprised of his Nurses, Satyrs, Panes, Seilenoi, Mainades, Nymphs, and mortals who came to join him (Nonnos' *Dionysiaca*). They set out to "visit men in order to demonstrate the sweetness and pleasantness of his fruit... he gave a skin full of wine as a gift and bade them spread the use of it in all the other lands" (Hyginus *Fabulae* 130), and also to spread the worship of the Meter Kybele which included mysteries, nocturnal orgies, ecstatic trances, and wild dances. Dionysos "traveled over the whole earth civilizing it without the slightest need of arms, but most of the peoples he won over to his way by the charm of his persuasive discourse combined with song and all manner of music" (Plutarch, *On Isis and Osiris*, 13). When confronted by the Indian army, the Goat-God Pan who traveled in Dionysos' train gave a great shout, filling them with panic, and the army dropped their weapons and fled, thus allowing Dionysos to conquer India without even having to shed a drop of blood. (Nonnos, however, tells a different story, and glories in the bloodthirstiness of Dionysos' battle with the Indians.)

Wine

Diodorus Siculus wrote, "And the discovery of the vine, they say, was made by Osiris and that, having further devised the proper treatment of its fruit, he was the first to drink wine and taught mankind at large the culture of the vine and the use of wine, as well as the way to harvest the grape and to store the wine" (1.15).

Wine is so intimately linked with Dionysos that scarcely anyone speaks of the God without mentioning it. It shares his nature, for like the God it is "fiery" (Euripides *Alkestis* 757), "wild" (Aeschylus *Persians* 614), and "madness-inspiring" (Plato *Laws* 7.773 d), and yet it brings "great joy to mankind" (Homer *Iliad* 14.325). Perhaps the best description of the powers of wine are to be found in a hymn of the Roman poet Horace, "You move with soft compulsion the mind that is so often dull; you restore hope to hearts distressed, give strength and horns to the poor man. Filled with you he trembles not at the truculence of kings or the soldiers' weapons" (3.21). Like the God, it is not complete without a second birth, and suffers immeasurably before it attains its final form. Achilles Tatius called wine "the blood of the God" (*The Adventures of Leucippe and Clitophon* 2.2) and Nonnos compared it to the tears of the God (7.367). Wine was said to spring up miraculously whenever the God approached (*Homeric Hymn* 7) and the female followers of Dionysos caused "the earth to flow with milk, with wine, with the nectar of bees" (Euripides' *Bacchae* 708). Wine was poured out in libations to the Gods, drunk at symposia, and used by initiates to attain a mystical union with Dionysos. Euripides equated Dionysos with wine itself, saying, "As a God Dionysos himself is poured out to the Gods" (*Bacchae*, 284).

The Ivied Rod

The thyrsos is the supreme symbol of Dionysos, carried by all of his devotees. It is a stalk of fennel or other wood, topped by a pine-cone, and wreathed with ivy. It is a powerful tool, through which the God's coursing, vibrant, ecstatic sexuality manifests. "The maenads, followers of Dionysos, pound the ground with the thyrsos, which drips honey and causes milk and wine to gush up from the earth; a phenomenon into which it is not difficult to read sexual symbolism" (Delia Morgan, *Ivied Rod: Gender and the Phallus in Dionysian Religion*).

The thyrsos, also, is found in possession of Osiris. Before Lucius is initiated into the mysteries of Osiris, the God visits him in a dream, prefaced by an encounter with one of the God's devotees. He was "clad in linen and bearing an ivied thyrsos and other objects, which I may not name" (Apuleius' *Metamorphoses*, 27).

Trees and Vegetation in General

Robert Graves observed that the character of Osiris as a tree-spirit was represented very graphically in a ceremony described by Firmicus Maternus. A pine-tree having been cut down, the center was hollowed out, and with the wood thus excavated an image of Osiris was made, which was then buried like a corpse in the hollow of the tree.

The body of Osiris becomes enclosed in the trunk of a tree and is associated with the Djed pillar in Utterance 574. Similarly, Dionysos was connected with all vegetation and green growth, not just the vine and its alcohol-producing fruit.

A fragment of Pindar's [writings] preserved in Plutarch reads, "May gladsome Dionysos swell the fruit upon the trees, the hallowed splendor of harvest-time." Plutarch also informs us that Dionysos is worshipped "almost everywhere in Greece" as Dendrites, "Tree God" (*On Isis and Osiris*, 34). Dionysos' image was found inside of a plane tree which had been split asunder in Magnesia, and the Corinthians were given an oracle by Apollo at Delphi to worship the pine tree "as the God" whereupon they had a statue of Dionysos carved out of its wood (Pausanias 2.27). Dionysos was called Sykites, "Fig-God," the wood from which phalloi were carved. The scholiast to Aristophanes' *Frogs* mentions that the myrtle was sacred to Dionysos, and Ovid says that "Bacchus loves flowers" (*Fasti* 5.345), specifically roses and violets, according to Pindar (*Frag.* 75). This is not surprising considering his epithets Anthios "Blossoming," and Euanthes, "He Who Makes Grow" or his festival the Anthesteria which celebrated the return of life to the earth.

Bull

In Egypt, there were a number of sacred bulls who were associated with Osiris. Perhaps the most famous of all of these was the bull God known to the Egyptians as Hapi and to the Greeks as Apis.

According to Herodotus, the Apis bull was conceived by lightning and was recognized by the following signs: "it is black, and has a square spot of white on its forehead, and on the back the figure of an eagle, and in the tail double hairs, and on the tongue a beetle" (3.28). Plutarch said that "on account of the great resemblance which the Egyptians imagine between Osiris and the moon, its more bright and shining parts being shadowed and obscured by those that are of darker hue, they call the Apis the living image of Osiris" (*On Isis and Osiris*, 43). The bull, Herodotus says, was "a fair and beautiful image of the soul of Osiris." Diodorus similarly states that Osiris manifested himself to men through successive ages as Apis. "The soul of Osiris migrated into this animal," he explains.

Dionysos was represented as having bull horns (Sophocles *Fragment* 959) and Ion of Chios refers to him as the "indomitable bull-faced boy" (*Athenaios* 2.35 d-e) like the author of Orphic Hymn 45 who invokes Dionysos as the "bull-faced God conceived in fire." The women of Elis sought Dionysos to come "storming on [his] bull's foot" and hailed him as the Axie Taure, "Worthy Bull." In Euripides' *Bacchae*, the Theban maenads ask him to appear as a bull (1017) and Pentheus discovers that in place of the effeminate stranger he had thought he'd imprisoned in the palace, there is a mighty and ferocious bull in his place. At Pergamon and elsewhere, priests of Dionysos were called boukoloi and arkhiboukoloi (*IPergamon* nos. 485-88) and the sacred marriage of Dionysos and the Basillina was celebrated in the boukoleion or sacred cow-shed at Athens (Aristotle *Constitution of the Athenians* 3.5).

Sexuality

Sex saturates the Dionysian world-view. The Samians worshipped Dionysos Enorkes, "the Betesticled" or "In the Balls" (Hesychius s.v. *Enorkes*). And at Sicyon the God's lustiness was honored by the title Dionysos Khoiropsalas, "Cunt-Plucker" (Polemon *Historicus*, FHG 3.135.42).

The phallus is ubiquitous in the worship of Dionysos. According to Plutarch, the things carried in the earliest rites of Dionysos were: "A wine jar, a vine, a basket of figs, and then the phallus" (*Moralia* 527D). According to Aristophanes, Phales, the phallus personified, was the "friend and constant companion" of Dionysos, and accompanied him in processions and sacred dances (*Acharnians* 263). Herodotus says that Melampos, who supposedly introduced Dionysos' worship into Greece, instituted phallic processions in his honor (2.49). At Methymna on Lesbos there was a cult of Dionysos *Phallen* in which a wooden trunk with a face on it was carried in procession (Pausanias 10.19.3). Each colony sent a phallus regularly to the Athenian Dionysia, and at Delos large wooden phalloi were carried in processions. And Herakleitos speaks of the phallic songs which would be shameful if they were not sung in honor of Dionysos (*Fragment* 15). We even have a fragment of one of those songs from the Delian poet Semos, who sings of Dionysos, "Give way, make room for the God! For it is his will to stride exuberantly erect through the middle."

Sexuality is just as important in the realm of Osiris. He is called "the Lord of the Phallus and the ravisher of women" (*The Book of the Dead*, CLXVIII, 15) and "the mummy with a long member," in which form he is frequently depicted in funerary art. The phallus was even carried in processions to honor Osiris, according to Plutarch. "Moreover, when they celebrate the festival of the Pamylia which, as has been said, is of a phallic nature, they expose and carry about a statue of which the male member is triple; for the God is the Source, and every source, by its fecundity, multiplies what proceeds from it" (*On Isis and Osiris*, 36). In the *Pyramid Texts*, it is said, "Your sister Isis comes to you rejoicing for love of you. You have placed her on your phallus and your seed issues into her" (Utt. 366, sect 632). Nor was it just Isis with whom Osiris was said to have erotic encounters. Plutarch recounts a secret liaison that Osiris had with his sister Nephthys, "Isis found that Osiris had loved and been intimate with her sister while mistaking her for herself, and saw a proof of this in the garland of melilot which he had left with Nephthys" (*On Isis and Osiris*). This scene is hinted at in the *Great Magical Papyrus* of Paris, where we find the following line, "I have discovered a secret: Yes, Nephthys is having intercourse with Osiris" (PGM 4.100-02). It is often suggested that this myth was a later invention, perhaps inspired by Greek stories of infidelities among the Gods - however, in the 183rd Chapter of the *Book of the Dead* a quarrel between Nephthys and Isis is recorded, which clearly predates the Greek presence in Egypt, and for which there is no other mythological explanation.

God of Joy

Firmicus Maternus records the symbolon of Osiris' Roman initiates (mystai) as "Be of good cheer, O mystai, for the God is saved, and we shall have salvation from our woes" (*The Error of the Pagan Religions*, 2.21). According to Plutarch, Osiris is "laughter-loving" (*On Isis and Osiris*, 18), and in *The Great Hymn to Osiris*, the following is proclaimed: "There is joy everywhere, all hearts are glad, every face is happy, and everyone adoreth his beauty."

According to Nonnos, the God Aion complained to Zeus about the laborious, care-ridden life of mortals. Zeus declared that he would beget a son who was to dispel the cares of the human race, and bring them a message of joy (*Dionysiaca* 7:7). This was Dionysos, who, according to Euripides in the Bacchae, "ends our worries" (450), "keeps the household safe and whole though the other Gods dwell far off in the air of heaven" (466-67) and is a "lover of peace" (500). For, as Horace said, "Who prates of war or want after taking wine?" (*Carmina* 1). Wine is the tangible symbol and fluid vehicle of the God. When people wish to speak of his blessings, they use wine to symbolize it. Hence we have "Wine is mighty to inspire new hopes and wash away bitter tears of care" (Horace, *Carmina* 4). "Wine frees the soul of subservience, fear, and insincerity; it teaches men how to be truthful and candid with one another" (Plutarch's *Symposia* 7.10.2). And, as Aristophanes adds, "When men drink wine they are rich, they are busy, they push lawsuits, they are happy, they help their friends" (*The Knights*). Dionysos' blessing is for everyone – male and female, young and old (Euripides' *Bacchae* 205). And it is very important – for "where Dionysos is not, love perishes, and everything else that is pleasant to man" (*Bacchae* 769).

Drama

> "[Osiris] was the subject of what was known as the Abydos passion play, a yearly ritual performed during the period of the Old Kingdom and until about AD 400. The Abydos passion play depicts the slaying of Osiris and his followers by his brother Seth, the enactment of which apparently resulted in many real deaths. The figure of Osiris, symbolically represented in the play, is then torn to pieces by Seth, after which his remains are gathered by his wife Isis and son Horus, who subsequently restore him to life. The play thus follows the pattern of birth, death, and resurrection, and it also echoes the cycle of the seasons." – *Encyclopedia Britannica*.

> "The world's earliest report of a dramatic production comes from the banks of the Nile. It is in the form of a stone tablet preserved in a German museum and contains the sketchy description of one, I-kher-nefert (or Ikhernofret), a representative of the Egyptian king, of the parts he played in a performance of the world's first recorded 'Passion' Play somewhere around the year 2000 B.C.E." – Alice B. Fort & Herbert S. Kates, *Minute History of the Drama*, p. 4

Similarly, drama in Greece was thought to have developed out of early rituals commemorating the death and dismemberment of Dionysos. Long after the plays enacted ceased to be about Dionysos directly, the theater was still considered sacred to him, new productions were debuted at the Dionysias, and his priests were always given the choicest of seats.

John M. Allegro notes, "At the beginning of the fifth century BC tragedy formed part of the Great Dionysia, the Spring festival of Dionysos Eleuthereus. Three poets competed, each contributing three tragedies and one satyric play. The latter was performed by choruses of fifty singers in a circle, dressed as satyrs, part human, part bestial, and bearing before them huge replicas of the erect penis, as they sang dithyrambs" (*The Sacred Mushroom and the Cross*).

Mysteries and Initiation

John M. Allegro in *The Sacred Mushroom and the Cross* writes, "The female votaries of the phallus god Bacchus were known as the Bacchants...They were characterized by extreme forms of religious excitement interspersed with periods of intense depression. At one moment whirling in a frenzied dance, tossing their heads, driving one another on with screaming and the wild clamor of musical instruments, at another sunk into the deepest lethargy, and a silence so intense as to become proverbial. The Bacchants both possessed the god and were possessed by him; theirs was a religious enthusiasm in the proper sense of the term, that is, 'god-filled'. Having eaten the Bacchus or Dionysos, they took on his power and character..."

The great center for Osirian mysteries in Egypt was Abydos, which was said to hold the tomb of the God, and to which people made annual pilgrimages to take part in the great celebrations. Craig M. Lyons writes about the mysteries as they were celebrated at Abydos: "We know that at all the temples of Osiris his Passion was re-enacted at his annual festivals. On a stele at Abydos erected in the XIIth Dynasty by one I-Kher-Nefert, a priest of Osiris during the reign of Usertsen III (Pharaoh Sesostris), about 1875 B.C.E., we find a description of the principal scenes in the Osiris mystery-drama. I-Kher-Nefert himself played the key role of Horus. In the first scene, Osiris is treacherously slain, and no one knows what has become of his body; thereupon all the onlookers weep, rend their hair, and beat their breasts. Isis and Nephthys recover the remnants, reconstitute the body, and return it to the temple. The next scene, in which Thoth, Horus, and Isis accomplish the revivification, undoubtedly occurs within the sacred precincts, and is therefore not witnessed by the populace. However, in due course the resurrected Osiris emerges at the head of his train; at this glorious consummation, the anguish and sorrow of the people are turned into uncontrollable rejoicing. Horus thereupon places his father in the solar boat so that he may, since he has already been born a second time, proceed as a living god into the eternal regions. This was the great "coming forth by day" of which we read so often in *The Book of the Dead*. The climax of the play was the great battle in which Horus defeated Set and which is described so vividly by Herodotus (*History*, II, 63)."

The mysteries of Isis and Osiris spread beyond the fertile Nile valley, and found great success in the Roman west. During the reign of Ptolemy Soter, Isis became so popular in Greece that a great temple was built for her at the foot of the Acropolis; and in the ensuing centuries, as we learn from Pausanias, almost every Greek city and village had its Isis-temple. Under the Emperor Caligula, Isis was admitted into Rome, and her worship became so popular that only Christianity and Mithraism rivaled her in number of adherents. Central to her worship was the celebration of the mysteries concerning the death and revivification of her husband, Osiris. The Christian author Firmicus Maternus describes the Roman mysteries of Osiris as follows: "In the sanctuaries of Osiris, his murder and dismemberment are annually commemorated with great lamentations. His worshipers beat their breasts and gash their shoulders. When they pretend that the mutilated remains of the god have been found and rejoined they turn from mourning to rejoicing" (*Error of the Pagan Religions*, 22.1).

Death and Dismemberment

"When he was away Typhon conspired in no way against him since Isis was well on guard and kept careful watch, but on his return he devised a plot against him, making seventy-two men his fellow-conspirators and having as helper a queen who had come from Ethiopia, whom they name Aso. Typhon secretly measured the body of Osiris and got made to the corresponding size a beautiful chest which was exquisitely decorated. This he brought to the banqueting-hall, and when the guests showed pleasure and admiration at the sight of it, Typhon promised playfully that whoever would lie down in it and show that he fitted it, should have the chest as a gift. They all tried one by one, and since no one fitted into it, Osiris went in and lay down. Then the conspirators ran and slammed the lid on, and after securing it with bolts from the outside and also with molten lead poured on, they took it out to the river and let it go to the sea by way of the Tanitic mouth.... Having journeyed to her son Horus who was being brought up in Buto, Isis put the box aside, and Typhon, when he was hunting by night in the moonlight, came upon it. He recognized the body, and having cut it into fourteen parts, he scattered them." – Plutarch, *On Isis and Osiris*, 13-18).

"The Titans, who are the Sons of Gaia, tore to pieces Dionysos-Zagreus, the child of Zeus and Persephone, and boiled him, but his members were brought together again by Demeter and he experienced a new birth as if for the first time. And with these stories, the teachings agree which are set forth in the Orphic poems and are introduced into their rites, but it is not lawful to recount them in detail to the uninitiated." – Diodorus Siculus 3.62)

Lord of the Underworld

The Lamentations of Isis and Nephthys hail Osiris as "Thou Lord of the Underworld," and Plutarch wrote, "There is a doctrine which modern priests hint at, but only in veiled terms and with caution: namely that this god (Osiris) rules and reigns over the dead, being none other than he whom the Greeks call Hades and Pluto" (*On Isis and Osiris*, 78).

As Walter Otto observed, tradition has much to say about Dionysos the God who visits or even lives in the world of the dead. Horace described how the fearsome Kerberos, guardian of the Underworld quietly watched as Dionysos entered with his golden horn, and even licked his feet as he left (*Carmine* 2.19). Numerous authors tell the story of how Dionysos descended into the underworld to bring his mother, Semele, back to the world of the living. In Aristophanes' *The Frogs*, Dionysos goes down to the Underworld and joins the Eleusinian mystai in their sacred songs and dances. According to *Orphic Hymn 46*, he himself grew up in Persephone's home, and *Hymn 53* says that he sleeps in the house of Persephone during the long intervals before his reappearance. Clement of Alexandria (*Protreptikos* 2.16) cites the ancient myth whereby Persephone is the mother of the first Dionysos, the Horned Child Zagreus, and there are hints in the *Homeric Hymn to Demeter* that the God who ravishes Kore and steals her away to his underworld realm is actually Dionysos. (The abduction occurs at Nysa, and later when Demeter in her wandering is offered a drink of wine she angrily refuses.) Both Hades and Dionysos share a number of epithets.

Dionysos is called Khthonios or "Underworld" as well as Nyktelios, "The Nocturnal One," Melanaigis, "Of the Black Goat Skin," and Polygethes, "Giver of Riches" – all titles traditionally belonging to Hades. Euripides speaks of "Bacchantes of Hades" (*Hecuba* 1077) and Aeschylus calls the Erinyes "Maenads" (*Eumenides*, 500). Euripides compared the maenads to ghosts, calling them both nyktipoloi, "night-stalkers," since both became active only after sunset. (*Ion* 717, 10458-49) And when we turn to actual cult and funerary practices, we see that this connection remains just as strong.

Revivification

Although both Dionysos and Osiris were said to have been murdered, they both were able to regain their power and life.

An inscription from Thasos describes Dionysos as a God who renews himself and returns each year rejuvenated (Susan Guettel Cole, *Dionysos and the Dead*, pg. 280 in *Masks of Dionysos*). The Christian author Justin Martyr, in his *Dialogue with Trypho the Jew*, grudgingly observed that, "Bacchus, son of Jupiter, being torn in pieces, and having died, rose again." Plutarch informs us that the "Phrygians believe that the God sleeps in winter and is awake in summer, and with Bacchic frenzy they celebrate in the one season the festival of his being lulled to sleep *Kateunasmous* and in the other his being aroused or awakened *Anegerseis*. The Paphlagonians declare that he is fettered and imprisoned during the winter, but that in the spring he moves and is freed again" (*On Isis and Osiris* 69). Diodorus Siculus says that after being torn apart by the Titans, Dionysos was pieced back together again by Demeter, and "he experienced a new birth as if for the first time." (3.62) Macrobius in the *Saturnalia* observed that, "In their Mystery-tradition Dionysos is represented as being torn limb from limb by the fury of the Titans, and after the pieces have been buried, as coming together again and whole and one. By offering itself for division from its undivided state, and by returning to the undivided from the divided, this Dionysian process both fulfills the duties of the cosmos and also performs the mysteries of its own nature."

While it is true that Osiris, unlike Dionysos, did not return bodily to the earth, but remained a powerful being in the Underworld, he regained his power, strength, and vitality through the ministrations of his sisters Isis and Nephthys, as we see in *Coffin Text 74:*

"Ah Helpless One! Ah Helpless One Asleep! Ah Helpless One in this place which you know not-yet I know it! Behold, I have found you [lying] on your side the great Listless One. 'Ah, Sister!' says Isis to Nephthys, 'This is our brother, Come, let us lift up his head, Come, let us [rejoin] his bones, Come, let us reassemble his limbs, Come, let us put an end to all his woe, that, as far as we can help, he will weary no more. May the moisture begin to mount for this spirit! May the canals be filled through you! May the names of the rivers be created through you! Osiris, live! Osiris, let the great Listless One arise! I am Isis.' 'I am Nephthys. It shall be that Horus will avenge you, It shall be that Thoth will protect you - your two sons of the Great White Crown - It shall be that you will act against him who acted against you, It shall be that Geb will see, It shall be that the Company will hear. Then will your power be visible in the sky. And you will cause havoc among the [hostile] Gods, for Horus, your son, has seized the Great White Crown, seizing it from him who acted against you. Then will your father Atum call 'Come!' Osiris, live! Osiris, let the great Listless One arise!'"

Worshipers Become Identified with the God

According to Euripides, "He who leads the throng becomes Bacchus" (*Bacchae* 115). and Plato wrote that during the Dionysian initiations, the initiates "search eagerly within themselves to find the nature of their God, they are successful, because they have been compelled to keep their eyes fixed upon the God... they are inspired and receive from him character and habits, so far as it is possible for a man to have part in God." Uniting with God was also an idea shared by the Stoics of that era. Seneca wrote, "God is near you, he is with you, he is within you." We know from the Inscriptions of the Iobacchoi that certain members held the title of Bakkhos, and we find a female devotee who was addressed as a Bakkhes. The Neoplatonic philosopher Olympiodoros wrote, "Our body is Dionysian, we are a part of him, since we sprang from the soot of the Titans who ate his flesh" (*In Platonis Phaedonem Comentarii* 61C).

E. A. Wallis Budge in *The Legend of Osiris* writes, "Osiris was the God through whose sufferings and death the Egyptian hoped that his body might rise again in some transformed or glorified shape, and to him who had conquered death and had become the king of the other world the Egyptian appealed in prayer for eternal life through his victory and power. In every funeral inscription known to us, from the Pyramid Texts down to the roughly written prayers upon coffins of the Roman period, what is done for Osiris is done also for the deceased, the state and condition of Osiris are the state and condition of the deceased; in a word, the deceased is identified with Osiris. If Osiris lives forever, the deceased will live forever; if Osiris dies, then will the deceased perish."

Judgment in the Afterlife

Chapter 125 of the *Book of the Dead* is entitled, "What is to be said when one reaches this Hall of Truth." This spell was intended to prepare the deceased for his trial in the Hall of Judgment in the Underworld. In the vignette that accompanies the spell, the deceased stands at the far right facing Ma`at, the goddess embodying Truth and Order, as his heart is weighed against the feather of Ma`at by Horus and Anubis. Sitting above the scene are the 42 Gods who judge the dead. Thoth, the ibis-headed scribe of the Gods, records the verdict as Osiris, seated on the throne at left, watches. The creature Amamet, facing the King of the Dead, would devour the deceased if he were found to be unworthy.

Pindar wrote, "From whom Persephone will accept atonement for ancient grief, their souls she will send forth again into the upper sun in the ninth year" (*Frag.* 133). This "ancient grief" felt by Persephone likely refers to the death and dismemberment of her child, the first Dionysos who was called by the ancient Orphic poets Zagreus.

An Orphic lamella from Thurii reads:

"Pure I come from the pure, Queen of those below the earth, and Eukles and Eubouleus and the other gods and daimons; For I boast that I am of your blessed race. I have paid the penalty on account of deeds not just; Either Fate mastered me or the Thunderer, striking with his lightning. Now I come, a suppliant, to holy Phersephoneia, that she, gracious, may send me to the seats of the blessed."

On the Wings of Isis:
The Introduction of Isis to Greece and Rome*

by D. Jasmine Merced

Though modern societies perceive Isis as one of the most prominent goddesses of Egyptian antiquity, prior to Ptolemaic rule she was only one of many gods, with her primary distinctions being the sister-wife of Osiris (king of the gods) and mother of Horus (legitimate successor to the king). From Isis' first excursion outside of Egypt to Greece, and subsequently to Rome, her temple and her statuary forms evolved, resulting in the not-quite-Egyptian worship of a not-quite-Egyptian deity, and with the tenacity of a chameleon, she gradually blended into her new surroundings while maintaining just enough exoticism to conserve interest and permit recognition of origin. This article details the social and political environments surrounding the emigration of Isis from Egypt to the Greco-Roman world while concurrently elucidating how her worship adapted to reflect regional norms and religious expectations.

Isis in Greece

From as early as the 3rd – 2nd millennium BCE, some Aegean peoples had a history of amicable relations with Egypt prior to Greek sovereignty. Frescoes discovered in the Nile Delta suggest that Egypt and the early Minoan cultures had relations as early as the late 3rd or early 2nd millennia BCE (Biers 48, Bourriau 215). An 11th – 10th century necklace depicting Horus seated on Isis' lap was discovered in Lefkandi, near Eretria, and was imported from Egypt (probably) via Cyprus. Even Homer (c. 8th century BCE) hints at friendship ties between the Mycenaean Greeks and Egyptians in Book 4 of *The Odyssey*, in which he describes the homeward journey of Menelaus and Helen. They amassed wealth during that voyage from various countries, including Egypt (Homer 4.85-7); Helen had received gifts of a slave from an Egyptian (4.130-2), "a golden spindle and a silver basket with gold-rimmed wheels" (4.137-9), and Menelaus was given "two silver baths, two tripods, ten bars of gold" (4.134-5). Homer also wrote that "Men [in Egypt] know more about medicines than any other people on earth, for they are of the race of

Paeon, the Healer" (4.256-8), alluding to a Greek admiration of Egyptian knowledge and education.

An alternate version of Helen's whereabouts during the legendary Trojan War was later given by Euripides (c. 480-406 BCE) in *Helen*, in which Helen was secreted to the shores of Egypt by the Greek gods, and was held safe in the court of Egyptian king Proteus, "the man [Zeus] had judged to be the most virtuous of all mortals, so that I [Helen] could keep my marriage with Menelaos undefiled" (Euripides *Helen* 47-50) by Paris, Trojan prince. After the Trojan War, Menelaos retrieves Helen, safe and unsullied, from Egypt. Both the Homeric version and this version of the story relate a cooperative atmosphere between the Greeks and Egyptians. Dates for the Mycenaean period of Greece vary among scholars, but we can tentatively place them within a range of 1600-1100 BCE.

Cultural ties between Greece and Egypt continued to increase during the 1st millennium BCE. Greece expanded its territories by colonizing southern portions of the Italian peninsula and Sicily (collectively called *Magna Graecia*) in the 8th century BCE. Thence, "*nel corso di quel periodo Orientalizzante nel quale la penisola italiana fu investita e trasformata profondamente nella struttura sociale delle sue comunità dall'ondata della colonizzazione greca e, insieme a essa, del commercio fenicio*" (Ministerio 13).[1] Egyptian religion (including Isis) had influenced Phoenician culture, and the spread of Phoenician culture, albeit less directly, helped spread awareness of Egyptian culture and Isis. Therefore, the combined Greek and Phoenician influences in Italy facilitated the introduction, awareness, and eventual settlement of Egypt's culture into the west with its continuing ties.

Back in Egypt, Pharaoh Psammetichus I (664-610 BCE) granted land settlements astride the Nile to the Greek mercenaries who had helped him secure his throne. Later, pharaoh Amasis (570-526 BCE) moved them to Memphis (Lloyd 372), where he used them as his personal bodyguards. These mercenaries "were the first foreigners to live in Egypt, and it is thanks to their residence there that we Greeks have had some connection with the country" (Herodotus 2.154). Herodotus' statement suggests that there was a period where the connection between the two countries had dissipated or disappeared. Whether he refers to a connection beyond trade or to dwindling trade in the preceding centuries is unknown. Egypt had experienced a time of civil wars, hence Psammetichus I's need for Greek mercenaries, which may suggest an Egyptian preoccupation that resulted in less contact between the two countries.

In the later 7th and 6th centuries BCE, Greek and Egyptian ties grew stronger "through various interrelated media of exchange and communication: commerce, mercenaries, and elite level guest friendship and gift exchange" (Tanner 126). These ties resulted in what might be called low-levels of cultural exchange, in which increased presences of Egyptians in Greece (and vice versa) introduced facets of Egyptian culture into the eyes and minds of local Greeks on a daily basis, particularly in port towns, where cultural barriers were most permeable due to constant exchange of Mediterranean trade goods and the ongoing presence of foreign merchants and travelers.[2]

The Egyptian gods first took up residence in Piraeus, the port city of Athens, by the early 5th century BCE.[3] Though the earliest evidence for an Egyptian god in Piraeus is Ammon and his syncretized counterpart Zeus-Ammon in 400–350 BCE (Von Reden, chart 31), Isis arrived shortly thereafter in the mid-4th century, when "on the very eve of the Hellenistic period, before 332/1, the Athenians allowed Egyptians, probably merchants, to purchase land for Isis in Piraeus, a sanctuary intended only for Egyptian worshippers" (Mikalson 201). Hence, Isis, despite having a least one sanctuary in Greece, was worshipped predominantly by Egyptians, though we cannot discount the possibility of her worship by Greeks. This needs to be qualified, however. In order for Isis to have been accepted by local Greeks, aspects of her cult must have adapted to appear not so outside the realm of Greek religious expectations, particularly the worship of gods-as-animals and the practice of mummification. There was little or no Greek animosity towards the Egyptians, though one's culture was quite different from the other's; there were only curiosities that were acknowledged with hardly any condescension due to the immemorial antiquity of Egyptian civilization.[4]

During the period prior to Hellenistic rule over Egypt, Isis had already taken flight across the Mediterranean. Herodotus identified Isis with the Greek goddess Demeter (Herodotus 2.59), which "facilitated the popularity and expansion of her cult and enhanced her role as wife and mother […] By the mid-4th century, inscriptions of Isis were found in Athens and other parts of Greece" (Tripolitis 27). We must be cautious, however, to not overestimate her popularity in Greece at this time. Though she was one of the most appealing imported gods, she was still a very minor player in the Greek pantheon. It cannot be said with any amount of authority that she was worshipped by any more than a small percentage of the Greek population during the 4th century BCE.

The most significant changes to the worship of Isis in the Mediterranean occurred in the decades after Alexander the Great had liberated Egypt from Persian rule (332 BCE) and assumed pharaonic rule. His rule was short-lived, as his victory over the Persians was followed by his death less than a decade later, in 323 BCE while on a campaign in Babylon (Lloyd 396) to eradicate the Persian threat once and for all.

Prior to his death, however, he founded Alexandria in 331 BCE (Lloyd 404), a new city 20 miles west of the Nile delta, which soon became "the most spectacular city in the Hellenistic world" (ibid). Alexander planned this city to be a union of Greek and Egyptian cultures, a center of learning, and a trade hub of the Mediterranean and beyond: *"un fulcro comerciale di vitale importanza nei traffici non solo dei prodotti dell'Egitto, ma anche di quelli che vi giungevano dall'interno dell'Africa e, lungo le coste del mar Rosso, dall'Arabia e dall'India"* (Ministero 14).[5] Alexander's plans for the city were successfully implemented, and his successors ruled Egypt from Alexandria until the conquest of Rome.

After his death in 323 BCE, the fabric of the empire Alexander had woven threatened to unravel, as he had not named an heir. His half-brother, Arrhidaeus, was named king, and Perdiccas, a commander of Alexander's battalion (Hornblower 1138), was named regent. Perdiccas allocated significant sections of the empire to Alexander's generals, and Ptolemy, later called Ptolemy *Soter* ("Savior"), was given Egypt, though his rule was not deemed official until 305 BCE. The allocations were not satisfactory to the other generals, and the War of the Successors ensued. These battles were fought by the Antigonids (the 'unitarians' who wished to keep the empire intact) and the 'separatists' (the Ptolemies, Seleucids, and Lysimachos), all of whom "were determined to carve out their own kingdoms" (Lloyd 396), and all of whom were either Alexander's kin or generals.

The War of the Successors resulted in a tripartite division of Alexander's empire: the Antigonids ruled Macedon and assumed control over neighboring cities on the Greek mainland[6]; the Seleucids governed large sections of Asia Minor; the Ptolemies ruled Egypt, Cyrene, Cyprus (a Ptolemaic province), and the Levant up to the Syrian border. Egypt's influence greatly increased after these large kingdoms were carved out and became a threat to the other kingdoms, which resulted in intermittent and tenuous alliances between the Macedonian and Seleucid kingdoms. Battles to wrest Egypt from Ptolemy were met with failure "by Egypt's geography rather than by Ptolemy himself" (Lloyd 396), but constant fighting between the kingdoms did not cease until Rome's rise to power and ultimate subjugation of Greece.[7]

Ptolemy I, perhaps as a continuation of the Egyptian late pharaonic tradition, adopted and Hellenized the Egyptian triad: Isis, Osiris (renamed Serapis)[8], and Horus (renamed Harpocrates), thereby modifying the Egyptian version of these deities "in order to bring together Egyptian and Greek beliefs and practices" (Jeffers 97). It is important to note, however, that evidence indicates that the Hellenized trinity "won only limited popularity with the Egyptian population in the third century [BCE], and that it was to the *upper classes* of the Greek population that it mainly appealed" (Fraser 260, emphasis added). Recognizing the social class of the Greeks who worshipped these Hellenized deities will be critical when we turn our attention to the dissemination of the trinity in the Roman Republic.

Of the numerous deities in the Egyptian pantheon, Ptolemy I's choice to Hellenize Isis, Osiris and Horus, was the most logical, both culturally and politically. Not only did Isis already have a presence on mainland Greece, thereby making her less of a shocking introduction to the Greeks, but also the Egyptians held these gods to be legitimizers of the throne. Thus the Ptolemaic Dynasty arrogated the pharaonic tradition of rule by divine right by conjoining familiar social and spiritual themes, one of which included the divine Egyptian and Greek traditions of brother-sister marriages (like Isis and Osiris, and Zeus and Hera, respectively); the Egyptian version went further by securing divine succession for their children (like Horus) and applying these divine ideals to mortal rulers.

Osiris (hereinafter Serapis) also acquired a significant following among the Greeks; he was not only Isis' husband, but he ruled the underworld, and healed "much like Asclepius, the sick and injured through incubation and dreams in his sanctuaries" (Mikalson 201).[9] Culturally, his "cult statue was Greek, not Egyptian, in form" (ibid), and politically, he "was made the patron of [the Ptolemaic] dynasty" (ibid). The modified dual cultural and political aspects enabled Serapis, and other gods similarly Hellenized, to travel throughout Greece, despite regional political animosities between the bickering factions of Alexander's successors.

At this point, temples to Isis and Serapis appeared throughout Greece and "in Athens Serapis first appeared in 215/4, worshipped by non-Athenians, but by 158/7 an Athenian was serving as his priest on Delos" (Mikalson 201).[10] This shows that Greeks had not only taken up their worship, but that the clergy was no longer exclusively Egyptian. Temples to Isis and statuary of Egyptian deities had been iconographically and ideologically transformed into an amalgamation of Egyptian and Greek, concurrently making them somewhat familiar and beguilingly exotic.

Traditional Greek gods were tied by epithet and location; the Poseidon who was worshipped in Sounion was distinct but not completely different from the Poseidon who was worshipped in Athens (Mikalson 33). In addition to being tied by epithet and location, they most often represented specific emotions or facets of human existence, such as love, war, occupations, etc., yet the Egyptian deities enjoyed flexibility in their divine roles, which facilitated their multifaceted appeal. Isis was originally associated with Demeter by Herodotus, and continued to be syncretized with other Greek goddesses (Aphrodite, Hera, Tyche, etc.) and their divine attributes, eventually resulting in the evolution of Isis into a more "universal" goddess.

Despite the inseparable integration of religion into Greek (and later, Roman) politics, it can hardly be said that the acceptance or rejection of new deities into the pantheon happened exclusively due to political seesawing. In addition to the Hellenized elements of Isis discussed so far, she was also considered patroness of sailors, agriculture, both domestic and commercial arts, and much more.[11] Such attributes added considerably more attraction for Isis, resulting in more adherents, despite the political attempts to suppress the religion at the time.

Mikalson sums up how Isis was accepted in Greece:

"By the end of the Hellenistic period, Isis, usually with Serapis, had sanctuaries and devotees in virtually all Greek cities everywhere, and her devotees were identifying her in long *aretalogies* (lists of "virtues" *aretai* in Greek) with many of the Greek goddesses and were crediting her with power over and protection of virtually all aspects of human life and even with the initial structuring of the cosmos and all elements in it. Unlike a Greek god or goddess, Isis alone, now could, for her devotees, fulfill virtually all their religious needs. Of all the gods we have encountered, Isis alone opens the way of concepts of monotheism for her worshippers – she can be thought of as the goddess who encompasses and incorporates all other deities and their powers." (Mikalson 201)

Isis on the Italian Peninsula and the Tyrrhenian Sea

At the time the Greeks assumed control of Egypt, Rome was a comparatively young republic, having been established only four centuries earlier, and was plagued both by internal patrician-plebeian conflict as well as by frequent warring with various local tribes to the north, west, and south.[12] As previously mentioned, Greece had colonized many southern portions of the Italian peninsula in the 8th century BCE, as well as several islands in the Mediterranean Sea. With them, they brought their social values, trade relations, and applied their old customs to a new landscape.

The first region to adopt the new religion of Isis and Serapis was Greek Sicily, most likely during the reign of Ptolemy I in Alexandria in the late 4th or early 3rd century BCE.[13] On the mainland, Isis and Serapis were already in Campania "in the second century BCE, when there were close economic ties between Delos and Ptolemaic Egypt" (Takas 269), which resulted in the presence of Egyptian traders who worshipped Isis in the Greek regions of Italy. Politically speaking, "Campanians and even Romans had served in the Ptolemaic forces already in the third century" (Fraser 89), which shows that in addition to Greece, the Early Republic of Rome, or at least its people as hired hands, were present in Egypt.

As Rome grew into a military power, it had gradually but certainly dominated many local tribes, such as the Sabines, the Etruscans, the Latin League, and the Samnites. Yet until the Pyrrhic War (280-275 BCE), in which Rome came directly into conflict with the Greeks (and especially the city-states of *Magna Graecia*), Rome was still a fairly small state itself. But "[b]y the end of the Pyrrhic war, the entire region [of *Magna Graecia*] was under Roman domination" (Hornblower 912). One tangential result of this war was the recognition by other Mediterranean countries of the need to develop or maintain good diplomatic relations with Rome. Egypt expressed such by the establishment of a permanent Egyptian embassy in Rome in 273 BCE (Lloyd 421).

In the late 3rd and early 2nd centuries BCE, Alexander's successors on the Greek mainland continued their trends of avarice and discontent, which led to infighting, conspiracy, and regular skirmishes between each other. The only exception was the Egyptian territory, whose weakened state and geographical distance from mainland Greece restrained it from outward hostilities. The other generals "continued their rivalries [...] and they did not hesitate to appeal to Rome against one another" (McDonald 66). Having been exhorted to aid various factions – in offense, defense, or retaliation – Rome had unknowingly been given the role of a policing agency over the Greeks, and by "167 BC no one escaped the penalty of Roman peace" (ibid).

The Antigonids, headquartered in Macedonia, increased the enmity between themselves and Rome by supporting Hannibal against the Romans in the Second Punic War with Carthage. This war coincided with Rome's First Macedonian War versus the Antigonids. Aware of the precarious nature of fighting two wars on two different fronts, Rome appealed to its Greek allies, the Aetolians, to aid in the battles. They decided that the Romans would fight by sea, the Aetolians by land, and a treaty was signed in which "the Aetolians should retain the land and buildings in any places captured in allied operations [in Macedonia] and that the Romans should seize any other kind of booty ... Rome needed slaves to serve the landowners who were members of the senate" (Adcock 111). Subsequently, the costs of maintaining the hard-fought peace and order had indebted Greece to Rome, and the final campaigns to straighten out the problems of Greece, called the Third Macedonian War, were conclusive:

> "In the course of the second century BC, Rome was drawn across the Adriatic to Greece, at first in struggles with the Macedonians under their king, Philip V. Though he was defeated in 197 BC, enmity continued off and on until Macedon was finally broken at the Battle of Pydna in 168 BC. Later, the Romans had to contend with the Achaean League, which their general, Mummius, defeated, before then sacking the League's leading city, Corinth. From this moment (146 BC) Rome ruled Greece" (Pedley 338)

From this point forward, we will contend exclusively with Roman and Egyptian relations; with Greece having been conquered and is assets assimilated into Rome's holdings, the "voice of Greece", either in the form of independent city-states, the Hellenistic kingdoms, or even the Byzantine Empire, fell mute until 1829 CE. The year after Rome subsumed Greece, its presence on the Alexandrian political, social, and economic stages increased: "From [145 BCE] onwards Alexandria was overshadowed politically by Rome, and we find that numerous Romans appear in Alexandria on political errands. From about the same time the changed economic situation in the Mediterranean increased the importance of Italy as a market for Alexandria" (Fraser 89). Egypt, though part of the Greek territories, "retained something of its power and position while its rivals had been humbled by Rome" (Charlesworth 9) until Cleopatra's death in 30 BCE. The Romans were admirers of Greek culture – if not the trade interruptions due to their internal political enmities – and offered both amnesty and limited citizenship to many who pledged loyalty to Rome.

The Late Republic

The initial phase in Roman history began at its foundation ca. 753 BCE, during which time "kings" ruled, and ended with the creation of the Republic (ca. 510-509 BCE). The Republican period is marked by increases in Roman trade, facilitated by the Tiber River and port towns, and by regional expansion. The Republic was a system in which elected officials replaced the monarchial ruler. The most prominent feature of the Republican period was its ability to conquer its regional rivals and assimilate them into a loose confederation of city-states with Rome as leader. These indigenous and settled populations had their own social cultures and religious practices. Rome allowed each region religious autonomy, and interfered only in cases of perceived danger to "national" security.

"Indeed part of the success of the Romans as imperialists was their tolerance, acceptance and even takeover of the gods of their enemies" (Blond 182) until the first decades of the 1st century BCE. This early leniency could either be ascribed to Rome's preoccupation with wars (1st, 2nd, 3rd Punic Wars; 1st, 2nd, 3rd Macedonian Wars; Social Wars; Mithridatic Wars, etc.) and a host of internal conflicts, but perhaps it is better explained by recognizing that Rome "had imposed order upon Italy under loose confederate conditions" (McDonald 151), and not more strict regulations. For example, only a Senate-declared 'state of emergency' allowed Rome to dictate instructions to its allies. Such was the case in 186 BCE when the Senate demanded the orgiastic worship of Bacchus, which was imported from Greece, to cease. Concern over the private assembly of these *foreign* worshippers rose and the Senate declared these rites the *Bacchanalian Conspiracy* - "an illegal association to subvert the Italian confederacy" (McDonald 84). The Senate chose to "proclaim an emergency, give the consuls powers of martial law, and pass detailed orders to the allies" (ibid). A little later in 139, the government "evicted the first Jewish immigrants into Italy for proselytising" (Cary 312) yet tolerated the presence of synagogues in the 1st century BCE (ibid). Hence, the Senate's desire to suppress foreign influences on Rome manifested in religious repression.

The cult of Isis "was established at Rome by Sulla's day, no doubt at first as a private and secret cult" (Scullard 207) shortly after the Social War (91-87 BCE). This was an uprising against the dominance of Rome by its allies primarily because of the Rome's refusal to give voting rights to the allies. The campaigns of Sulla, the consul of Rome, in the south and east "brought a fresh wave of Hellenism to Rome: we have to think not only of Greek models, but of the actual presence of Greek craftsmen in the city" (McDonald 139).

In the late 3rd century BCE, Rome "had a long history of giving citizenship to Italian communities, either with the vote (*optimo iure*) or without the vote (*sine suffragio*)" (Hornblower 334), but citizenship grants had dwindled by the 2nd century BCE. Though Rome had militarily won the Social Wars, and "by 89 BC all surviving cities were Roman colonies of *municipia*" (Hornblower 912), Rome had conceded to the allies' demands and instituted the *lex Iulia*, the law by which citizenship was extended to allied states "who had for the most part remained loyal" (334). Hence, the number of Roman citizens boomed, and as a result, new social, cultural, and religious diversity was injected into the constituency of the Roman population. Because the Greeks in *Magna Graecia* had already worshiped Isis for over a century by that time, this extension of citizenship not only automatically made citizens of worshippers outside of Rome, but also paved the way for Isis' gradual introduction into Rome.

The Last Gasps of the Republic

We have thus far established: 1) Isis' association with divine and secular political power developed since ancient Egyptian times and continued through the Ptolemaic period of Alexandria, 2) Rome had become a military and political force in the Mediterranean by means of conquest and dispute settlement, 3) By the beginning of the 1st century BCE, Rome's citizen, visitor, and slave populations were extremely diverse, and 4) Isis was already present in Rome by the end of the Social War (91-88 BCE).

With the exception of the singular fact that Isis was in Rome in Sulla's time, there is an echoing silence in the literary and archaeological records about Isis in Rome from the Social War until shortly after Rome became arbiter of Egyptian dispute resolution. In 80 BCE, Roman consul Lucius Cornelius Sulla settled problems of Ptolemaic succession by establishing "Ptolemy XI as joint ruler with and husband of stepmother Cleopatra Berenice" (Hornblower 1273) when "Ptolemy IX Soter II died without legitimate male issue" (Lewis 12). Even this, though, was not Rome's first intervention in Egyptian politics: the precedent was set in 168 and again in 164 BCE, when Roman assistance was sought and delivered to arbitrate succession between Ptolemy VI and VIII (Hornblower 1272). We will soon notice that the rising level of Roman assistance in Egypt runs parallel with the exertion of power over

Egyptian presences within Rome and how the political climate of Egypt bore a direct relationship to Isis' treatment in Rome.

Ptolemy XI murdered his wife and in turn was assassinated by the Alexandrians (Hornblower 1273). Ptolemy XII ("Auletes") succeeded his father in 80 BCE, and grateful for the ongoing Roman assistance in the securing and maintenance of his throne, he cultivated the friendship of the Romans. He had continued hardships due to familial contestation of his rule and also experienced severe backlashes from the Alexandrian people due to his amicable relationship with Rome. Open hostility towards Auletes began in 63 BCE, despite Egyptian concern over Rome's obvious preference to him: "Diodorus, who was in Alexandria in 60, tells us that the fear of Rome was such that every sign of respect was shown to Italians in the city for fear of giving a pretext for war" (Fraser 124). Knowing who was able to help him secure his throne, Auletes "had purchased Roman recognition of his position in Egypt by a gigantic bribe of six thousand talents (59 B.C.)" (Oost 99), gaining him the title of 'Friend of the Roman People'. Auletes also "allowed Cyprus, the last Ptolemaic possession, now held as an appendage by his brother, to fall a prey to his new protectors" (Fraser 124), a decision which did not sit well either with the remnants of his family, or with the Egyptian people. The bribe, which was paid in part by the Alexandrian people (ibid), the concession of Cyprus, which "had regularly been involved in the civil wars of the last Ptolemies during which they played musical chairs between the island and Egypt" (Oost 102), the installation of Auletes' chief creditor Gaius Rabirius Postumus as *diocetes* (Chief Treasurer)" (Smith 512), and other pro-Roman legislations quickly "led to [Auletes'] expulsion by the Alexandrians in 58 BCE" (Hornblower 1273).[14]

Auletes' forced exile must have been taken as an affront to Rome and required some demonstration of anger against Egypt, for coincidentally "in 58 B.C. altars to Isis on the Capitol were destroyed by the consuls" (Scullard 207). Once again, "they were very soon reinstated 'owing to the violence of the people's intervention' (Varr. From Tert., *Nat.*, 1, 10, 17)" (Turcan 121). This may be connected with the struggle between the *Optimates* and *Populares*, as the *Optimates* controlled the senate, but legislation was passed in the *comitia tributa*, whose agenda could be (and often was) controlled by *Popularis* tribunes. Though *comitia* were technically assemblies of Roman people who would vote on proposals put forth by magistrates, they "were far from democratic" (Hornblower 372). The *comitia plebis tributa* "discriminated against both the urban *plebs*, who were confined to only four of the 35 tribes, and the rural population, who lived too far from Rome to attend [the *comitia*] in person" (ibid).

Therefore, with a remote semblance of democracy the *Optimates* could out-vote any *Populares*. Therefore, the bipartisan animosities could be played out with the Roman landscape as the battlefield.

The reinstatement of Isis' altars, along with the rebuildings after the 65 BCE mass demolitions of Isis' temples, clearly show that the political mandates were going contrary to the wishes of a significant portion of Rome's population. This, however, can be explained in terms of the political recognition of perceived seditiousness that participation in such a cult could entice:

> "Part of the appeal of these cults and religions may have been their slightly subversive nature. The traditional cults of the Graeco-Roman cities were so much a part of the traditional power structures of those cities that to reject the cults was implicitly a political act as well as being of religious significance. Cities and citizens tended to define themselves through participation in religious events" (Alston 317).

It is crucial at this point to recall that Isis by this time had been thoroughly Hellenized; it is unlikely that Roman citizens would have adopted her had she remained totally Egyptian. Her form and temple were, for the most part, Greek with Egyptian elements, and later, Roman with Hellenistic and Egyptian elements. Only in origin was she exclusively Egyptian, for even her name "Isis" was Greek (Aset was her Egyptian name).

Auletes arrived in Rome in 57 BCE (Smith 512), "where his restoration became a mainstream political issue, and through heavy expenditure, in 55 he was restored by A. Gabinus, Roman governor of Syria" (Hornblower 1273). Gabinus subsequently "left behind him those troops who had imposed order on the Alexandrians" (Fraser 90). This did not bode well for the improvement of the Alexandrian sentiment towards Rome: "Romans and Roman influence were uniformly disliked in Alexandria [...] This hostility to Rome was essentially political and not racial in origin, and we are able to witness for the first time the emergence in Alexandria of something like a common movement against the intruder" (Fraser 90). The feeling was probably mutual, as we see increased acts of aggression against the most prominent Egyptian symbols in Rome at the time: Isis and Serapis.

The exact construction dates of the temples to Isis and Serapis are unknown, but they existed in Caesar's time, for Catullus (Roman poet, ca. 84–ca. 54 BCE) refers to the Serapeum: "'*quaeso*' inquit '*mihi, mi*

Catulle, paulum istos commoda; nam volo ad Serapim deferri'" (Catullus X, 25-27).[15] Various scholars contend that Isis shrines and statues were also destroyed by senatorial mandate in 53, 50 and 48 BCE (give or take a year in either direction for each); Turcan succinctly describes the general course of events:

> "Far from being disheartened, Isiac militants had chapels privately built, but the Senate ordered their destruction in 53 BC. Three years later, the Senate again ordered the demolition of the temples of Isis and Serapis, but no workman dared put his hand to the task. Removing his toga praetexta, the consul seized an axe and struck the sanctuary doors (Val. Max., 1,3,4). Two years later (48 BC), as prodigies had affected the Capitol, the augurs recommended razing the sacred enclosures of the Egyptian gods that had been built on the hill, where a 'priest of Isis Capitolina' perhaps officiated (CIL, 6, 2247). The fact that an exile managed to escape his would-be killers thanks to Isiac costume and the mask of Anubis is evidence of the respect shown to the Nilotic gods (Val. Max., 7,3,8; App., bc, 4, 47)" (Turcan Gods 121).

Continuing scholarly disputes about the precise dates of specific events will hinder further direct dating parallels between political actions and acts of aggression against Isis. It will suffice to say that at least three separate instances of shrine destructions occurred between 54 and 47 BCE, during periods of ongoing Ptolemaic situations, Roman civil war, and Roman political and military aid to Egypt. These acts of persecution were not inspired by Isiac dogma, nor were they concerns about the Roman population turning away from the established state religion, or resulting from direct political disputes with Egypt.[16] Rather, they represented attacks on the perceived threats of the loss of cultural identity, Rome's current political tensions, and a visible manifestation of frustrations toward yet another sequence of instabilities caused by the untamable Orient.

The politics of the Late Roman Republic were predominantly bipartisan, consisting of *populares* (liberals) and *optimates* (conservatives), whose distinctions were "one of procedure in exercising government over the people, as between dictatorial 'advisory' authority and aggressive 'executive' power" (McDonald 139). Their constant bickering and legislative roadblocks resulted in the creation of an initially secret coalition (ca. 60-59 BCE) called the First Triumvirate, which included

Gaius Julius Caesar, Gnaeus Pompey Magnus, and Marcus Licinius Crassus. This partnership was uneasy at the start, for each of the three men held different political views. Caesar was in the *Populares* camp; Pompey (at first) was an *Optimate*, as was Crassus, who was one of the wealthiest men in the period. The tendency for the *Populares* to be for the lower-class and disenfranchised masses often directly conflicted with the proposed legislations of the *Optimates*, whose primary goals were to secure the interests of the wealthy aristocracy. It can easily be inferred that many actions decreed by the *Optimate*-majority senate attempted to discredit the *Populares* with the people, including, but not limited to, acts of aggression against unsanctioned religions that were popular with them, such as that of Isis.

Caesar "wanted a freer hand than the strict senatorial procedures of the Optimates would allow" (McDonald 167). Pompey, as we have seen, had several large military triumphs in the east and was well regarded as both a military leader and politician. Crassus sought to annex Egypt, but his plan was overruled (Hornblower 857), and later he went to war against the Parthians in 53 BCE, where he was defeated and killed at the Battle of Carrhae. Crassus' death led to stronger tensions between Caesar and Pompey, as the two were then wrestling for greater rule. The First Triumvirate attempted to solidify their mutual dependence with marriages between the families, and after the death of Pompey's wife (Caesar's daughter, Julia) in 54 BCE, Crassus' death in 53 BCE, and Caesar's continued absence from Rome during his Gallic campaigns, the Triumvirate fell apart.

Due to the concern of the possibility that any individual praetor or consul could seize too much power, the situation arose in which there was "no consul or praetor or prefect of the city that had any successor, but at the beginning of the year the Romans were absolutely without a government in these branches" (Cassius Dio XL.46.3) in 52 BCE.[17] Cassius Dio notes that: "It seems to me that the decree regarding Serapis and Isis passed near the end of last year was as equal a portent as any, for the senate decided to tear down their temples which some people had built on their own account" (XL.47.3).[18] There are several interesting facets to his statement: 1) use of the plural ναοὺς ('temples') asserts that there were separate temples to Isis and Serapis, even if they were somehow conjoined and considered one sacred precinct (as they were later in the Campus Martius); 2) construction was undertaken by private citizens; 3) at a time when the predominantly *Optimates* senate needed support from the people, they opted to destroy privately-constructed temples; and 4) Cassius Dio perceived the destruction of those temples as an evil portent.

Pompey demanded that Caesar disband his army because his political term as proconsul had been completed. Caesar refused, and Pompey responded by "ram[ming] a resolution through the senate declaring Caesar a public enemy if he refused to lay down his command" (Lewis Civ 279) in 50 BCE. Caesar knew that without his armies, he would be defenseless against his enemies in Rome, so he refused the ultimatum.

Caesar's famous XIIIth Legion marched across the Rubicon in January 49 BCE and camped there until Caesar learned of the Senate's decision (Jiménez 68). The XIIIth, led by Marc Antony, was commanded to head toward Rome and secure various towns surrounding it (ibid). Caesar's movements were too swift for Pompey to muster his armies to defend the city, so Pompey "issued a declaration of civil war and abandoned Rome the same night, Cicero the next day. At the urging of Pompey, most *optimate* families and thousands of others fled south from the capital on the Appian Way into Campania and beyond" (69). Pompey had gone south to Brundisium and subsequently fled to Greece to claim his troops and raise ally support. Caesar secured Rome and made plans to defend vulnerable areas and grain shipments from Pompey's inevitable retaliation and attempts to weaken Caesar's hold and turn the people against him via empty stomachs.[19]

Ptolemy Auletes died in 51 BCE, and "his will named as his joint successors his eldest daughter, Cleopatra, then eighteen, and his eldest son, Ptolemy [XIII] then a lad of nine or ten; and Rome was named their guardian" (Lewis Life 13). In 49 BCE, Cleopatra attempted to remove her brother from rule but failed and she fled to Syria where she raised allies. Returning with armies in 48 BCE, she camped on the eastern edge of Egypt while her brother and his ministers went to oppose her near Pelusium.[20]

In the same year, Caesar decisively defeated Pompey in the Battle of Pharsalus. Pompey fled to Egypt, confident of asylum and military support because "Ptolemy XIII, a boy of 13 strongly influenced by his chief minister, a eunuch named Ponthius, had supplied him with 50 ships and 500 men just a year earlier for the war against Caesar" (Grenier 162). Pompey arrived in Egypt on 28 September 48 BCE (Hornblower 1216). Ptolemy and his advisors sought to "curry favor from Caesar, and to avoid any possible retaliation by Pompey should they simply refuse him refuge" (Jiménez 170), and assassinated Pompey. They decapitated him, took his consular ring, and presented both to Caesar when he arrived in Alexandria. Plutarch reports Caesar's response to Ptolemy's offering: he "turned away from him in loathing, as from an assassin; and when he received Pompey's signet ring on which was engraved a lion holding a sword in its paws, he burst into tears" (Plutarch 80). Lucan holds a different version of Caesar's reaction: he "squeezed out groans from his happy breast, not able to conceal his mind's conspicuous joy except by tears, and he destroys the tyrant's savage service, preferring to lament his son-in-law's torn-off head than be in debt for it" (Lucan 205). Regardless of Caesar's true feelings toward seeing the severed head of his nemesis, Pompey, he was infuriated at Ptolemy for having ordered the murder of a consul of Rome, and needing time to procure money to pay his armies, Caesar decided to remain in Alexandria to arbitrate the quarrel between Ptolemy and Cleopatra.

Cleopatra saw an opportunity to regain her throne with Caesar's help, and at great risk, she secreted herself from exile into Caesar's quarters in the Alexandria palace to meet with him. Though there is much debate about the romanticized version of Caesar's and Cleopatra's initial meeting commonly portrayed on the silver screen, it will suffice to say that they developed a relationship and that Caesar authoritatively placed Cleopatra on the throne along with her brother Ptolemy XII, so that he would "share the throne with Cleopatra in the way that their father wished" (Jiménez 173). This arrangement was obviously not suitable for Ptolemy, and a 5-month engagement known as the Alexandrian War ensued. Caesar fought against Ptolemy to uphold "Rome's" decision; he won the war, "left a substantial Roman garrison behind him" (Fraser 90) after the war, continued his relationship with Cleopatra, and in 47 BCE, became a father for the first time. Though paternity of Cleopatra's first child Caesarion has never been definitively established, the important thing is that it did not really matter: Cleopatra had asserted that her child was Caesar's, named the child after him, and those two facts were in the minds of the Roman people. Caesar remained with Cleopatra until late 47 BCE, at which time he acceded to senatorial discontent over his political decisions and his extended stay in Egypt, and returned to Rome.

Shortly thereafter, Cleopatra visited Rome with Caesarion, and the intimate ties between 'Imperator' and 'Queen' resulted in growing concerns of 'Imperator' turned 'King' – anathema to the Romans, who feared above all else the return to despotic monarchy. Cleopatra had become a symbolic vehicle through which a Roman ruler would don the diadem. She had fashioned herself as Isis incarnate, "was addressed as the New Isis" (Blond 90), and had therefore indelibly tied Isis' fate to her own. Caesar supported this Cleopatra-as-goddess image in Rome:

"Caesar ordered a gilt-bronze statue of Cleopatra placed beside that of Venus Genetrix, clearly associating her with the founder and protecting goddess of the Julian *gens*. The incident is significant in that Caesar not only implied that the Egyptian Queen was to be part of his family, but also elevated a human being, for the first time in Rome, to the level of a goddess [...] For all that was suggested, there is no surviving record of any objection to Cleopatra's statue" (Grenier 213).

Roman concern over Caesar's rise to 'King' was partially realized, as he exercised supreme power from 49 until 45 BCE while holding the consulship, and later, dictatorship, of Rome. In 44 BCE, he was named dictator for life, to which his political opponents responded with a plot to assassinate him. The conspiracy was completed on the Ides of March, and the struggle for ultimate power for Rome rejoined. Cleopatra, with expeditious stealth, returned to Alexandria to observe from a safe distance the political struggles of Rome to ascertain the fate of her own country. Caesar, the man who placed her on the throne, had been assassinated as tyrant; it would remain to be seen how the mandates of a tyrant would hold.

In his will, Caesar adopted his grand-nephew Octavian, then 18 years old, and bequeathed onto him his entire estate as well as full rights to his name. To fill the gap of leadership over Rome, Caesar's general Marc Antony, along with Octavian and Lepidus, formed the Second Triumvirate, an "official commission exercising supreme authority" (McDonald 171). This coalition began as unsteadily as the first, for Marc Antony had attempted to deprive Octavian of the monetary portion of his inheritance. Quarrels ensued, but they managed to establish an uneasy truce in order to share power instead of bringing Rome back into civil war.

Isis received a respite from persecution and was "temporarily recognized by the triumvirs in 43" (Scullard 207) and subsequently the triumvirs "promised to build a temple to Isis and Serapis to win favour with the populace" (Turcan Gods 121) at the Republic's expense. The order was never brought to fruition. Despite the broken promise, "worship of Isis in Rome was [officially] established by Antony in 43 BC" (Alston 313). So in 43 BCE we finally see the official recognition of Isis in Rome. And, not surprisingly, the context is highly political: it could be argued that this recognition was intended to dramatize the loss of power by the Senate and the *Optimates* by putting Isis' power and influence in Rome on display.

The Roman territories at this time were vast, and the triumvirs divided administration of the regions between them, with "Antony taking the East, Octavian and Lepidus taking the west" (McDonald 171). Consequently, Antony willingly and perhaps eagerly chose to oversee the Orient and associate himself with the excessive opulence of the East. To solidify political ties, Octavian gave Antony his sister Octavia in marriage in 40 BCE. The Second Triumvirate, in an increasingly complicated tale of suspicion and treachery, ended the same way as the first one – in civil war. Marc Antony went to Egypt to seek support from Cleopatra for the impending war with Octavian. Cleopatra, then 29, wooed Marc Antony; they fell in love, and "in 33, if not already in 37, he consented to become Cleopatra's Prince Consort by Greek dynastic law, although such a marriage was not valid under Roman law" (Cary 296). In 37 BCE, Octavian sent his sister Octavia (Marc Antony' wife) to Alexandria in an attempt to remind him of his obligations back in Rome; Marc Antony sent her home (295). Openly at odds with each other, Antony and Octavian prepared for battle while the Republic braced for yet another civil war.

Octavian used all of the propagandistic tools at his disposal in Rome to turn popular opinion against Antony. Antony made things easy for Octavian because his policies were clearly against the better interests of Rome:

> "[Caesarion] was now proclaimed King of Kings, and his mother Cleopatra was named Queen of Kings; together they were to rule Egypt and Cyprus. Under them the three children of Antony and Cleopatra were to govern parts of the East, whether Roman territory, client-kingdoms or even the lands of foreign kings. Alexander Helios (the Sun), aged six, received Armenia, Parthia and Media, his twin sister Cleopatra Selene (the Moon) got Cyrenaiza and Libya, while the two-year-old Ptolemy Philadelphus obtained Syria and Cilicia ... Had all these transfers of territory been carried onto effect, the result would have been to form an empire within the Roman Empire, and in all probability to disintegrate the Roman dominions into two rival states" (Cary 295).

Between these "Donations of Alexandria," Antony's affront to his good Roman wife Octavia via his divorce in 32, the publication of his will which revealed his desire to be buried in Alexandria next to Cleopatra, the rumor that he "intended to make Cleopatra the Queen of Rome and to transfer the seat of Roman government to Egypt" (Cary 296), it was not difficult to sway the opinion of those who had formerly been Antony's supporters in Rome. Back in Egypt, "Antony won the affection, if not the respect, of the Alexandrian people (particularly those with his own tastes), but this was an exception, explicable partly as due to respect for Cleopatra, and acceptance of the high rank she had bestowed on him, and partly to his own winning personality" (Fraser 90). His popularity in Alexandria, however, did not help him circumvent the storm that was heading his way from Rome, as Octavian had declared war on Cleopatra and Egypt in 31 BCE.

Antony and the Egyptian fleet were conquered by Octavian's forces led by general Agrippa in the decisive Battle of Actium. Antony and Cleopatra retreated to Alexandria with Octavian and his general Agrippa hot on their heels. They committed suicide instead of being captured by Octavian. Cleopatra's suicide led to a joy-filled poem by Horace (XXXVII 68-9), which calls all Romans to rejoice in her death while claiming her suicide more noble than being captured by Augustus for parading in his inevitable triumph.

Because Antony had previously "declared *urbi et orbi* that Caesarion (Ptolemy Caesar) was the legitimate son of Julius Caesar" (Cary 295), Octavian had the child murdered, but allowed the children of Antony and Cleopatra to live. With the last of the Ptolemaic royal line dead and the children either killed or taken into custody, Octavian "converted Egypt into a Roman province under a prefect responsible to himself, and carried off the royal treasure which Cleopatra had recently replenished by confiscations and by the seizure of hitherto untouched temple funds" (Cary 297). Thus ended the civil war, and the Roman Republic. The Roman Republic and the independence of Egypt ceased to exist at the same time, confirming the close relationship between Egyptian and Roman politics. Taken in this light, an independent Egypt was somehow a sign or gauge of the continued existence of the *Res Publica*.

Despite the conquest of Egypt and Augustus Caesar's propagandistic attempts to restore religious purity by expelling foreign influences from Rome, the popularity of Egyptian cults flourished. Isis in particular enjoyed increasing favor and patronage from the Imperial family after Tiberius, at which time shrines began to dot the Roman hills, emperors minted coins depicting the Egyptian gods and their temples, empresses were depicted as Isis, senators sought initiation into the cult, and many other examples of the political acceptance of Isis were prevalent. Rome never fully outgrew its dependency on Egypt for food; and Isis, as symbol of the fertile Nile, may have enjoyed a fortuitous revival based on the need to feed the growing population of Rome.

Alston succinctly summarized the increased favor the later Roman emperors bestowed onto Isis:

> "Caligula rebuilt the Iseum Campense and Nero introduced Isiac festivals into the Roman calendar. Domitian once more rebuilt the Iseum Campense while the Iseum at Beneventum, where his portrait as pharaoh was exhibited, may have been constructed during his reign. Rome had three large Isea: the Campense, one in Regio III and one on the Capitol; there were also smaller temples on the Caelian, Esquiline and Aventine Hills" (Alston 313)

Subsequent emperors increased Isis' visibility and prestige throughout the Roman landscape, culminating in a "Golden Age" of sorts for Isis from 208 until Constantine, whose 313 CE Edict of Milan legalized the previously-contraband Christian religion. Later emperors granted Christians increasing levels of power until the Christians, previously persecuted for their beliefs, zealously oppressed all other religions in the empire until the "pagan" religions were forced underground. The religions of Isis and Mithras (another important Eastern cult) proved to be serious contenders for religious supremacy in the empire, and as such, were specially targeted. The Theodosian Code, established in 438 CE, "aimed to shut down pagan sanctuaries in the Roman Empire" (Frankfurter 234); the last recorded Isiac festival is in this century. Scholars argue that Christianity's failure to suppress Isis in this period resulted in the elevated role of the Virgin Mary and an ensuing syncretism with Isis.

*Editors' Note: the preceding is a modified extraction from the author's Master's thesis on Isis. The full thesis can be read at: http://www.jazzhaven.com/thesis.

Notes

[1] "during the Orientalizing period in which the Italian peninsula was beset and profoundly transformed in the social structure of its communities through the waves of Greek colonization and, together with that, from Phoenician commerce". Translation by author.

² See Lloyd 372-374 for descriptions of Greek settlements around the Nile Delta in the 7th-6th centuries BCE.
³ This assumption is made based on the lack of any datable material or literary evidence confirming the presence of Egyptian gods within Greece prior to Ammon and Zeus-Ammon in 400-350 BCE, because the presence of the gods must surely have preceded extant evidence. This assumption follows from Witt's assertion that "the two big problems for the Egyptian cults (and the same is true of others) are the nature and value of the documentation and the chronological systemization [...] as so often happens with Egyptian objects on European objects on European sites [...] reliable data about find spots cannot always be provided" (Witt Review 281).
⁴ Summarized from Isaac, pp 354-359.
⁵ "a commercial fulcrum of vital importance in the traffic not only of Egyptian products, but also of those things that arrived from the African interior, the distant coasts of the Red Sea, from Arabia and from India". Translation by author.
⁶ This control was tenuous, as the cities often did not recognize Macedonia as their ruler. (Lloyd 396)
⁷ Events summarized from Lloyd 395-8, 482 and Hornblower 105, 1381.
⁸ Scholars continue to debate whether Serapis is a simple renaming of Osiris, or if he is another god from the East who syncretized with Osiris. This article will assume the former for simplicity.
⁹ From this point, we will predominantly be considering the Hellenized, and later Romanized, versions of Osiris. Therefore, we will use his new name unless the specific Egyptian version of the god is intended. Note that Egyptians continued to worship their native version of Osiris and for the most part ignored Serapis.
¹⁰ Pausanias, 2nd century CE Greek geographer, attests temples to Isis at Megara in Attica (Pausanias 1.41.3), Corinth (2.2.1), Phliasia (2.13.7), Troezen (2.32.6), Hermion - to both Isis and Serapis (2.34.10), two precincts each to Isis (Isis Pelagian and Egyptian Isis) and Serapis (Serapis and Serapis "in Canopus") in Acrocorinth (2.4.6), Laconia (3.22.13), Thebes - to both Isis and Serapis (4.32.6), Bura in Achaia (7.25.9), statuary of Pentelic marble in Achaia (port of Aegeira) (7.26.1); and Tithorea near Phocis - "the holiest of all [precincts and shrines] made by the Greeks for the Egyptian goddess" (10.32.13). His account is by far incomplete, as he fails to record known temples or shrines in several regions, including Athens, Piraeus, Delphi, and Delos.
¹¹ "Isis was known as mistress of the heavens, the earth, the sea, and even the underworld. More powerful than Fate, she was ruler of the universe, all-powerful and all-seeing. All civilization was her creation and her charge.

Isis established laws that can never be broken, and was the lawgiver and the champion of justice. She invented navigation, gave speech to mankind, introduced the art of writing, spinning and weaving, and instructed all people in the cultivation of the land. She gave to mankind all that makes life comfortable and worthwhile. Isis was both protectoress and aide. She gave safety to the sailor struggling on the high seas, protected the wanderer in a foreign land far from home. Freed the prisoner, healed those who were sick, and gave comfort to those in distress" (Tripolitis 28).

[12] The traditional date for the founding of Rome is 753 BCE.

[13] Based on the reference to Ptolemy's stepdaughter: "*La prima regione in Italia ad adottare la nuova religione fu la Sicilia greca con Atagole, probabilmente allorchè questi sposò Teoxena, la figliastra di Tolomeo I Sotèr*" (Ministerio 14): The first region in Italy to adopt the new religion was Greek Sicily with Agathocles [tyrant of Syracuse], probably when Theoxena, Ptolemy I Soter's stepdaughter, was given to him in marriage. Translation by author.

[14] Rabirius was later imprisoned for extortion by Auletes, who was seeking to placate his people lest he be exiled again. Rabirius escaped, and Cicero later defended him for extortion in Egypt under the *lex Iulia*. Unable to pay the fine, Rabirius probably was banished, but was later recalled by Julius Caesar (Smith 312).

[15] "Please, my Catullus, oblige [your litter] to me for a little while, for I want to be carried to the temple of Serapis". Translation by author.

[16] The term "'[r]eligion' may be misleading: the Romans worshipped gods as it suited them and a Roman could worship Juno one day and Isis another without conflict." (Alston 308)

[17] "οὔκον οὔθ' ὕπατος οὔτε στρατηγὸς οὔτε πολίαρχός τίς σφας διεδέξατο, ἀλλὰ ἄναρκτοι κατὰ τοῦτο παντελῶς οἱ Ῥωμαῖοι τὰ πρῶτα τοῦ ἔτους ἐγένοντο".

[18] "δοκεῖ δὲ ἔμοιγε καὶ ἐκεῖνο τὸ τῷ προτέρῳ ἔτει, ἐπ' ἐξόδῳ ατοῦ, περὶ τε τὸν Σάραπιν καὶ περὶ τὴν Ἴσιν ψηφισθὲν τέρας οὐδενὸς ἧττον γενέσθαι · τούς γὰρ ναοὺς αὐτῶν, οὓς ἰδίᾳ τινὲς ἐπεποίηντο, καθελεῖν τῇ βουλῇ ἔδοξεν".

[19] Because of Pompey's location, he was able to easily intercept grain shipments from Egypt and Africa, though at the time, Sicily and Sardinia were the most important provider of imported wheat and particularly critical during Caesar's altercation with Pompey (Jimènez 82).

[20] Summarized from Jimènez 169.

Bibliography – Primary Sources

Cassius Dio. *Roman History.* Trans: Earnest Cary. London: William Heinemann. 1914.

Euripides. *Bacchae*. Trans: Paul Woodruff. Indianapolis: Hackett Pubs. 1998.

_____. *Euripides, Medea and Other Plays*. Trans: James Morwood. Oxford: Oxford UP. 1997.

Herodotus. *The Histories*. Trans: Robin Waterfield. Oxford: Oxford UP. 1998.

Homer. *The Odyssey*. Trans: Stanley Lombardo. Indianapolis: Hackett Pubs. 2000.

Lucan. *Civil War*. Trans: Braund, Susan H. Oxford: Oxford UP. 1992.

Pausanias. *Pausanias Description of Greece with an English Translation*. Trans: W.H.S. Jones, Litt.D., and H.A. Ormerod, M.A. Cambridge: Harvard UP; London, William Heinemann Ltd. 1918.

Plutarch. "Pompey". *Fall of the Roman Republic*. Trans: Rex Warner. Harmondsworth: Penguin Books. 1958.

Tacitus. *The Annales of Imperial Rome*. London: Penguin Books. 1996.

Bibliography – Secondary Sources

Adcock, Sir Frank, D.J. Mosley. *Diplomacy in Ancient Greece*. NY. St. Martins Press. 1975.

Alston, Richard. *Aspects of Roman History AD 14- 117*. London: Routledge. 1998

Biers, William R. *The Archaeology of Greece*. 2nd Ed. Ithaca: Cornell UP. 1996.

Blond, Anthony. *A Scandalous History of the Roman Emperors*. NY: Carrol & Graff Pub. 2000.

Bourriau, Janine. *The Oxford History of Ancient Egypt*. Ed: Ian Shaw. Oxford: Oxford UP. 2000.

Burkert, Walter. *Greek Religion*. Cambridge: Harvard UP. 1985.

Cary, M., H.H. Scullard. *A History of Rome*. 3rd Ed. NY: Palgrave. 1975.

Charlesworth, M.P. "The Fear of the Orient in the Roman Empire." *Cambridge Historical Journal* 2.2. (1926): 9-16

Fraser, P.M. *Ptolemaic Alexandria*. Oxford: Clarendon Press. 1972.

Grenier, Albert. *The Roman Spirit in Religion, Thought and Art*. NY: Cooper Square Pubs. 1970.

Hornblower, Simon, Antony Spawforth. *The Oxford Classical Dictionary*. Oxford: Oxford UP. 2003.

Isaac, Benjamin. *The Invention of Racism in Classical Antiquity*. Princeton: Princeton UP. 2004.

Jeffers, James S. *The Greco-Roman World of the New Testament Era: Exploring the Background of Early Christianity*. Downers Grove: Intervarsity Press 1999

Jiménez, Ramon L. *Caesar Against the Romans*. Westport: PraegerPubs. 2000.

Lewis, Naphtali. *Life in Egypt Under Roman Rule*. Oxford: Clarendon Press. 1983.

Lewis, Naphtali and Meyer Reinhold. *Roman Civilization*. Ed. Austin P. Evans. NY: Columbia UP. 1951.

Lloyd, Alan B. *The Oxford History of Ancient Egypt*. Ed: Ian Shaw. Oxford: Oxford UP. 2000.

McDonald, A.H. *Republican Rome*. NY: Frederick A Praeger Pubs. 1966.

Mikalson, Jon D. *Ancient Greek Religion*. Malden: Blackwell Pub. 2005.

Ministerio per i Bene e le Attività Culturali. *Egitomania: Iside e il Misterio*. Napoli: Museo Archeologico Nazionale. 2006.

Oost, Stewart Irvin. "Cato Utincensis and the Annexation of Cyprus " *Classical Philology*. Vol 50, No 2. 1955: 98-112.

Pedley, John Griffiths. *Greek Art and Archaeology*. 3rd ed. Upper Saddle River: Prentice Hall. 2002.

Petersen, Lauren Hackworth. *The Freedman in Roman Art and Art History*. Cambridge: Cambridge UP. 2006.

Said, Edward W. *Orientalism*. NY: Pantheon Books. 1978.

Scullard, H.H. *From the Gracchi to Nero*. London: Routledge. 1982

Smith, William. *Dictionary of Greek and Roman Antiquities*. Boston: C. Little, and J. Brown. 1870.

Takacs, Sarolta A. "Alexandria in Rome". *Harvard Studies in Classical Philology* 97 (1995): 263-273.

Tanner, Jeremy. "Finding the Egyptian in Early Greek Art". *Ancient Perspectives on Egypt*. Ed. Roger Matthews and Cornelia Roemer. London: UCL Press. 2003.

Tripolitis, Antonia. *Religions of the Hellenistic-Roman Age*. Cambridge: Wm. B. Eerdmans Pub Co. 2002

Turcan, Robert. *The Gods of Ancient Rome*. NY: Routledge. 2000

Von Reden, Sitta. "The Piraeus – A World Apart." *Greece and Rome*. Vol. 41, No 1, Apr 1955.

Witt, R.E. Rev. of "I Culti Orientali in Sicilia." by Giulia Sfameni Gasparro. *The Classical Review*. Vol 26, No. 2. 1976: 280-281.

HER NAMES, INSCRIBED AND SUNG

by Rebecca Buchanan

Gentle (Calamisis)
Savior (Petra)
Affectionate (Carene)
Most Great (Hypsele)
Immortal Giver (Niciu)
of Favors (The Delta)
Almighty (Naukratis)
and of Beautiful Form (Hermopolis)
Abundant (Gaza)
Mistress (Raphia)
All-Seeing (Rhinocolura)
Supporter (Tripolis)
Immaculate (Pontus)
and Beloved of the Gods (Roma)
Unapproachable (Ptolemais)
yet Source of Friendship (Dora)
She, Bull-Faced (Samothrace)
Whose Name is the Sun (Tenedos)

First Ruler of the World
Who stands with glad face in the waters of Lethe.
You who hold dominion over wind, thunder, lightning and snow.
Guardian of the Seas
Who straddles the mouths of rivers.
Mistress of light and flame.
True Jewel of Creation.
You taught mortals the proper form of worship and established shrines
    for all time.
You set the year in its course and taught mortals to observe the heavens.
Mistress of War and Right Government,
Your laws are gentle but implacable,
and you bring low the tyrant with truth and might.
You fashioned words and numbers, and taught mortals speech.

You devised the loom and the spinning wheel.
By your will, women and men come together as equals.
We worship you at the rising of the stars,
You who bring decay upon the cruel, and increase upon the oppressed.
For it was you alone who brought your Divine Brother back from the
    Western Lands and made him immortal
– A gift promised all mortals who rightly honor you.

For Isis

by Sannion

Soft music suggests the sound of wings overhead,
In my hands the heft of a thick loaf of bread,
The air heavy with rose petals and jasmine scent,
Ivy creeping up the shrine wall like the pillars of a tent,
Red-gold the color of the beer poured out in the libation bowl,
And the candles' flames flickering like the mane of a foal.
Through each one of these things the presence of Isis grows stronger
Her dark eyes and gentle curves and endlessly patient smile stays in my mind longer
Until I am intoxicated by the goddess, dancing in joy before her altar.
"Hail, many-named mother, of countless gifts to mortal kind, your love never falters,
You who searched the wide earth for your beloved, and overcame the confines of death,
And taught us just laws, a kinder course of life, magical arts, and all the rest!
Accept these offerings, graciously given,
And help me to enjoy all that life has, without being too driven."

Epiphany of Isis

by Amanda Sioux Blake

Amaltheia raced through the city streets of Rome, dodging ox-carts and litters carried by bronze-skinned slaves. With one hand she hiked up her dark blue skirts, and with the other she held the precious package she carried close to her chest. She ignored the annoyed shouts of drivers and other pedestrians, for she was on an urgent mission. Her sandaled feet hit the cobblestones in a staccato beat, her breath coming in ragged gasps. She silently prayed to Diana as she navigated the labyrinthine twists and turns of Rome's back streets.

Behind the street of the cloth-merchants, she found her destination. Amaltheia skid to a sudden halt. She took a quick moment to compose herself, brushing her dark hair behind her ears and straightening her dust-covered stola. After taking a deep breath, she climbed the stairs to her family's cramped apartment.

The door swung open with a painful-sounding squeak. Surely it was an ill omen from Janus. Amaltheia stepped inside, pausing to allow her eyes to adjust to the low light. The curtains were permanently drawn these days, thanks to her father's ill health. The sickly stench of his wounds hit her nostrils at the same moment she heard him call for her.

"I'm here, Papa," she responded, picking her way through the wooden toys and other debris littering the small room, to sit at his bedside. "Where are the twins?"

"Lyadora took them for the night." Her father responded, and then collapsed into a fit of hacking and coughing.

"Easy, Papa, don't speak too much," she chided him in a voice so soft it was nearly a whisper.

"Nonsense," he insisted, "I'm perfectly fine." He continued to cough, and when he was able he added, "And its only for the night, they'll be back tomorrow."

"Of course, Papa," Amaltheia said while unwrapping the cloth package she had clutched so tightly; it contained several bags of precious healing herbs and plants. She set to work, changing her father's bloody and pus-covered bandages, cleaning his wounds, applying an herb poultice, and replacing the dressings again.

Of course, Amaltheia knew the real reason that her aunt had taken her younger brother and sister. And it would be for more than a night. When her father had returned home from the war, severely wounded, he had found that his wife had already preceded him into the Underworld. Amaltheia had only been eleven years old when Dis had taken her mother. She had been caring for her young siblings, Helios and Selene, for several years at that point.

That was only a few months prior, and every day her father seemed to get worse. Not only did his wounds refuse to heal, but it now appeared that he had contracted some lingering sickness. Likely from tramping through the mud of rain-soaked Gaul, in Amaltheia's opinion. It was truly a terrible place to be wounded or to take sick, no doubt! Amaltheia wondered if the Gauls had any healing Gods to attend to them, as surely no natural means could do the trick in those environs.

Her aunt, having lost her sister to disease already, was not about to risk her niece and nephew falling prey to the same affliction their father now dealt with. Fine, Amaltheia thought, let her take off with them. At least they would be safely out of harm's way. She, however, had no intention of abandoning her father. She would stay with him, to whatever end the Fates had laid out for them.

It was not long after she changed his dressings that her father fell into Somnus's embrace. All he seemed to do these days was sleep. While he did so, Amaltheia brewed some tea and tidied up the one-room apartment, putting away the toys the twins had left behind and sweeping out the crumbs from under the table. She cut vegetables and what little meat they had, to let them begin shimmering for tonight's stew. At least with her brother and sister gone, she could stretch out the food supplies for a while longer. Amaltheia saved a few beans and a small piece of ham to throw on the fire, an offering to Vesta. It would not do to insult the Gods at such a time.

Her household duties completed, for the time being, Amaltheia stepped out into the bright sunshine for some fresh air. She blinked in the light of Sol's rays, a sharp contrast to the gloom inside. The air was sweet with the smell of Flora's arrival, of roses and hyacinth and narcissus.

With a heavy sigh, Amaltheia sat on the top step of the stairs and watched the activity in the courtyard below. At this time of day, the men were still working, and most of the women and young children had retired to their dwellings for respite from the unrelenting sun. A few of the more hardy children chased each other back and forth in the courtyard.

Amaltheia rested her head in her hands, her mind blank. This quiet moment was a rare and welcome break from the stress of providing the constant care her father required. She closed her eyes, allowing her consciousness to sink inside itself for a brief moment.

She began to hear the beat of drums, accompanied by the sweet sound of flutes and exotic bronze sistrums. Voices were singing in a foreign tongue. It was a beautiful and haunting tune, although she did not understand the words being intoned. The music was spellbinding, calling to her was a sweet allure. Fearful that she was dreaming, Amaltheia remained in her position perched on the stairs, head in her hands, eyes closed.

The sounds become louder and clearer, as if they were approaching her house. Was it a festival day? Was it possible that caring for her father had caused her to lose all track of time?

Amaltheia cautiously opened her eyes. The enchanting music continued, and now she could hear the joyous sounds of shouting crowds, in Latin and in several languages she did not recognize. She stood, craning her neck to see the source of hubbub.

Through the buildings that stood on either side of the passage to the main street, Amaltheia saw two men – priests, no doubt – in linen robes, heads shaven, who called out "Make way for the Goddess Isis!" Her heart leapt in her breast, and before she had realized what she was doing, she was on the street, standing among the crowds watching the procession go by.

And a magnificent procession it was! Behind the two opening priests walked every manner of worshiper. There were gladiators in full armor, polished to shine in the sun, and men and women of all stations and occupations took part. Amaltheia recognized fishers and bakers and cloth dyers, and magistrates and judges and philosophers, even a few fine-looking men wearing the purple-hemmed robe of a senator! Tame bears and apes walking with their trainers took part in the procession, and everyone was dressed in the finest, most beautiful clothes they could afford. One woman was swathed head to toe in crimson silk, a layer wrapped around her head in a veil that fell in pleats to surround her arms, so that only her face was visible. And what joy was evident on her beautiful face!

Many of the processioners were in costume, dressed as figures from myth. Amaltheia laughed out loud at one man dressed as a shaggy satyr chasing the women in the procession. A heavy, horned and goat-snouted mask obscured his human face. Most of the women had garlands in their hair, some had baskets full of blossoms which they strewed along the road and tossed to onlookers. Still others sprinkled precious oils of frankincense and myrrh, gentle rose and fragrant sandalwood, making the way as beautiful to the nose as it was to the eyes and ears. Worshipers of both sexes carried lamps, candles and torches, though the sun shone in all his brightness.

Then came the long line of initiates, and the mood changed to one of intense devotion, although the joy was no less. Amaltheia was struck with awe as she watched these men, women, and even a few children pass by, walking slowly and chanting in that bewitching foreign tongue, which she now realized was Egyptian. They came from every station of life, and they were all dressed in pure white linen, the women with a light veil covering their hair and the men's heads shaved bald and polished to shine as bright as the armor of the gladiators. The children and youth were singing in Latin about the birth of Isis, of Her marriage to Her brother Serapis and her search over the whole world for the pieces of his body after he was murdered by Set. It was they, the initiates, who carried the shrill sistrums, made of brass and bronze, silver and even gold.

Scores of musicians followed behind the initiates, drummers and flute-players and men with panpipes, more curly-haired women shaking the sistrum. The officiating priests came next, their white robes trailing behind them on the ground. They carried what Amaltheia guessed were holy relics and symbols of Isis. The first priest cradled a golden lamp, the second carried a beautiful pot. The third held a palm branch in one hand and a caduceus in the other, the rod of Mercury entwined by two snakes. The fourth bore an amulet of a hand with the palm open, and he carried a vessel in the shape of a woman's breast, from which he occasionally spilled droplets of milk onto the ground. A fifth priest carried a winnowing fan, another a krator of wine, and the last a garland of roses.

Next came the sacred players, men and women chosen to represent the Deities on this day. Among them was Anubis, the dog-headed nephew of Isis, holding a palm branch and a wand in his hands. Following him was a cow walking upright, perhaps meant to be Hathor. Last of all came the bearers of an ornate golden box, carried on poles like a litter by four initiates, tightly closed as if something sacred and secret rested within it, the High Priest walking ahead of it.

Behind the official procession followed a group of enchanted Romans in everyday dress who had been swept up in the festivities. Without even thinking about it, Amaltheia found herself falling into step with them. The excitement of the crowd was infectious, and the musical atmosphere took her away from herself, until there was nothing left but the overwhelming awe in the presence of the Goddess, and the anticipation of reaching their destination.

After what seemed like a lifetime, the procession arrived at the harbor. A large and beautiful ship awaited there, painted with the name "The Isis" along the side. The ship of Isis was covered from stem to stern with colorfully painted Egyptian symbols. The looped crosses and the Eye of Ra stood out to Amaltheia's eye.

She craned her neck to watch as the ship of Isis was dedicated. An egg was broken on the hull, a torch thrown into the sea, and the prow was smeared with sulphur. Libations of milk were poured into the sea, and the priests prepared to launch the ship, setting it free on the waters.

"Beautiful, isn't it?"

Amaltheia was startled out of her trance by a lyrical voice. She turned around, coming face to face with the woman who had spoken. She was exotically beautiful, clearly Egyptian. The stranger was tall for a woman. Her dark curly hair flowed down around her shoulders in beautiful waves. White flowers and golden corn husks were woven into her thick mane. Her face was broad, and kohl was painted around her deep, snappy green eyes. Her lips were plump, and her skin the color of dark gold. Circles of pounded bronze hung from her ears, and around her neck she wore an orange stone, glimmering like a flame. Her dress was made of a fine linen in many colors – a white purer than any seen on Gaia's earth, a deep yellow brighter than corn or crocus, and a red deeper and darker than heart's blood. Her bare arms were adorned with a twining cobra of gold on either side, and her belt of palm reeds was tied with a bronze amulet in the shape of a vulture head. Her dainty bare feet were not unadorned either; she had golden rings on her toes and a chain of finely-wrought links around one ankle. A scent wafted from her body that suggested all the perfumes of Egypt and Asia, and Amaltheia was sent into a shocked stupor.

"It is a fitting gift for Isis." The woman spoke again, gazing deep into Amaltheia's soul.

"What?" was all that she could muster in response.

"The ship," the Egyptian woman explained.

"Oh. Right." Amaltheia began to turn pink, her embarrassment overcoming her addled brain. Amaltheia looked around, amazed that no one else had noticed the exotic woman, but they were all occupied by staring at the rapidly departing ship.

"Of course," the strange woman continued, "Isis accepts all offerings, no matter how small. She hears the voices of all who cry out to Her, even the lowest of people. She enfolds the slave, the widow, the orphan in Her wings."

The woman was staring intently at her. Amaltheia felt compelled to give a response, although she was at a loss as to what would be appropriate.

"That's... very nice of Her."

"Indeed" was the Egyptian woman's only response. She continued to stare, and Amaltheia began to fidget under the weight of her gaze. Why was nobody else noticing her? Surely she was royalty of some sort. But why did she have no guards to protect her? And surely Amaltheia would have heard if Kleopatra had come to the city. Unless... No, Amaltheia chided herself, don't think like a child, that's impossible.

"Isis is a merciful Goddess," the woman went on. "She is a savior, even to those who have never before honored Her. She redeems past slights and sins. Isis is the healer of the world." Now the woman paused, as if the words that were about to come out of her mouth were especially important. Amaltheia found herself holding her breath.

"She releases the pains of our fathers."

Amaltheia gasped, suddenly remembering. A wave of guilt washed over her like the frothing sea. How could she have abandoned her father, alone in the house? Surely he was awake now, and calling for her! Amaltheia turned tail and sped off without a word. Behind her, the Egyptian woman watched her retreat, the mysterious pools of her emerald eyes unreadable. No one noticed when she disappeared.

Amaltheia ran faster then she had that morning, faster then she had ever run in her life. Once again her feet beat out a rhythm on the cobblestones. Caution and hope warred within her. Even though she was running at full tilt, it seemed to take her much longer to get home than it had taken for her to leave it.

When she reached the steps leading to her apartment, she stopped. Her heart was pounding in her chest. Fearful of what she would find, she slowly and quietly crept up the stairs.

"Amaltheia?" Her father's voice, clear and sharp as a bell, with no hint of a cough, rang out. "Amaltheia!"

"Papa!" She cried, bursting through the door. What she saw stopped her dead in her tracks, amazement plain on her face. Her father was standing!

"Papa, how...?"

"I haven't the slightest idea," he responded, clearly in as much shock as she. "I heard you on the stairs, and I wanted to get up to greet you. And," he paused. "I don't know what happened. The pain disappeared. I felt new life flow into my limbs. And, and, I just stood up! Daughter, look!"

Before Amaltheia's eyes, her father peeled off the bandages surrounding his midsection. The bandages were stained with blood and pus, but there was no wound, no break in the skin, nothing to suggest that there had once been a gaping, infected hole. Amaltheia raced to her father, hugging him with all the might in her tiny body, burying her face in his neck and sobbing out her joy. They sank to the floor, embracing in a way that they hadn't since she was a small child. When she could speak again, Amaltheia pulled away from her father's arms and looked into his eyes.

"Father," Amaltheia began, still crying. "I know. I know what happened. It was Isis. Isis healed you. I *saw* her, Papa, I talked with her. I understand now. Today is the Navigium Isidis, I completely forgot. I've been so busy taking care of you and the twins, I had no idea what day it was. You were sleeping, and I was outside, and I was swept up the procession, I'm so sorry! I know it sounds crazy, but I really did speak to her, Papa. She was so beautiful, you have no idea –"

"Shush, Daughter." Her father cut off her babbling, placing a gentle finger to her lips. "I believe you. Only the Gods could bring this to pass. We will send word to your Aunt Lyadora, and she'll bring Helios and Selene back. We'll be a family again. We must thank Isis for this miracle."

Father and daughter embraced again. Far away, in Her temple, Isis smiled.

Musings on *The Metamorphoses* (P.G. Walsh Translation)

by Jeremy J. Baer

[Editors' Note: Apuleius was a second century Roman and author of the The Golden Ass, *also called* The Metamorphoses. *The eleventh book of the novel describes the main character's conversion to the cult of Isis. Historians have long used the passages there as a kind of eye witness account of the cult. Given their importance to the cult of Isis, the editors felt discussion of the novel and the author is highly relevant to the devotional. This entry provides an overview of the novel itself, while the subsequent entry analyzes to what extent the author was involved with, or had knowledge of, the cult.]*

To paraphrase Egyptologist Geraldine Pinch: all myths are sacred, but not all myths are solemn. Some myths are even laced with ribald perversions. *The Golden Ass* has not the timeless majesty of Homer, the dignified moralizing of Hesiod, or the conscious patriotism of Virgil. Its characters usually range from somewhere between agents of petty self-interest to despicable dregs of society. It is told not as an epic clash of heroes against monsters and gods, but as the absurd adventures of a hapless fool. The setting is not some archaic realm lost to history, but the Roman province of Greece.

That is precisely what makes *The Golden Ass* so interesting as a read. It is so thoroughly... modern?... compared to the classical mythographers, providing as it were a window to the daily life of second century Rome. Yet appearances are deceiving, for beneath the humorous vulgarities lay a testament to an earnestly religious and philosophical mind. Apuleius' *Golden Ass* is firmly entwined with tangible contemporary reality, and yet seeks so desperately to transcend it for the realm of the Empyrean. This is one of my favorite reads – not because it is elegant, but because it is so often crude. Not because it is popular, but because it is more esoteric. Not because I agree with it, but because it vexes me.

Apuleius was an interesting product of his time. He was born in a Roman colony in Africa, and we may assume he took in a Romano-Punic heritage with his mother's milk. His father was one of the leading municipal magistrates; on his death he willed to his son two million sesterces, twice the minimum required for the Senatorial order. Apuleius studied in Carthage, the leading city in the West after Rome. Then, as all smart upper-class Roman youths must do, he finished his schooling in the empire's university town of Athens. Apuleius became conversant in the Greek language, as well as its rich heritage of philosophy and literature. He knew something of Egypt and took a brief trip there. He then lived for a time in Rome, and finished his days in Carthage as a celebrated man of letters. His wealth thus afforded him the chance to partake of the cultural and intellectual legacy of all the best parts of the empire.

The empire of Apuleius' time was also in its heyday. He was born sometime in the reign of Hadrian. He thus lived through the golden era of the Principate: when the borders were to reach their furthest extent, when peace and wealth were plenty, and when it seemed the glories of Rome might spread to the far corners of the earth. Apuleius could know nothing of the doom awaiting the post-Severan empire, when the whole imperial edifice nearly collapsed from military anarchy. In short, few people could have lived so well as the wealthy and cultured Apuleius, immersed in the grandeur of the high empire.

Yet, *The Golden Ass* is not a happy book, dutifully extolling the Pax Romana. Therein lies the key of the book's worth.

Apuleius has taken an old and humorous Greek fable, and ennobled it through his additions of certain philosophical parables. Perhaps it is best to analyze these two parts, the Greek fable and the Roman parables, as separate entities.

The original Greek fable is called *Lucius or the Ass*, and survives today only in an abridged version. The central character, Lucius, is a businessman traveling to Thessaly, a region of Greece known for pervasive witchcraft. He lodges in a friend's house, whose wife just happens to be a mistress of the black arts. Unknown to the master of the house, the mistress uses these arts to charm young males to her will. She can also apparently transform into various animal shapes so she may attend to her nocturnal, adulterous excursions unobserved.

She has taught something of these arts to her maid. Lucius and the maid have eyes on each other, and it is not long at all before they hop into bed. Lucius is curious about magic transmogrifications, and asks his new bedmate to apply one of the forbidden potions to him. His idea is to become a bird, soaring through air, scanning further possibilities with the town's comely maidens. Only the maid applies the wrong potion and Lucius turns into an ass.

From there robbers suddenly loot the household and carry off Lucius as one of their spoils. So begins a series of adventures during which Lucius repeatedly changes masters while still an ass. The masters are invariably cruel and despicable dregs, using Lucius as the beast of burden he appears to be. He is eternally beaten and degraded, and threatened with death and castration more than once (often comically). The highpoint of his career is when he becomes something of a trick-performing circus animal for an aristocrat. His master asks him to perform tricks of another nature when an oversexed female hires out the charming ass for a bout of bestial conjugal pleasures (did I mention this tale was ribald?)

In this original Greek fable, Lucius finally attains his humanity by eating a rose, a natural balm to the witch's potion. The female who had made use of Lucius' donkey sized phallus has no use for a restored Lucius and his (presumably) normal sized human phallus. Thus closes the tale with Lucius returning home, having begun and ended his harrowing odyssey under the dangerous auspices of lustful women.

Apuleius has however changed the ending from the original. In his version, Lucius-turned-ass receives a stunning vision from Isis, Goddess of Many Names, Mistress of Heaven. It is a priest of Isis who administers to Lucius the rose which returns to him his humanity. Afterwards, Lucius dedicates his life to the cult of Isis, a goddess that promises protection in this world and the life beyond. (The ass, it must be said, was one of the symbols of Set, he whom the Greeks called Typhon, the ancient enemy of Isis who murdered her husband Osiris).

Apuleius has also inserted various passages. They are usually told as tales within tales, recollections of characters of various misadventures and misfortunes that resulted from some vice. The most famous of these is the tale of Cupid and Psyche, a myth within a myth. Told in Plato's Cave – er, excuse me, I mean the robbers' cave in which Lucius the ass finds himself – it is a story of how a maiden named Psyche fell in love with Cupid, passed through the underworld, and eventually received apotheosis and admission into heaven. As "psyche" is Greek for "soul" there are obvious allegorical connotations.

The original Greek fable is obviously meant as a comical morality play about the dangers of lust and deceitful women. Apuleius has however ennobled it into something still higher. In Apuleius' time the educated elite often subscribed to a particular philosophy, most of which claimed to reveal the ultimate nature of reality (however defined). In Apuleius' time there were also a variety of cults promising salvation from the capricious whims of Fate in exchange for submission, and Isis was the most successful of these deities. In an intellectual epoch now known as Middle Platonism, these two trends merged. The empyrean savior goddess of Isis and her promise to deliver men from the ravaging effects of Fate was reinterpreted in Platonic terms of escaping the world and achieving the ultimate source of reality.

All of the characters in *The Golden Ass* suffer from their attachments to a corporeal world. Quite often sex is the vice, but money, food and envy for material possessions are also culprits. Those that seek them suffer and bring suffering to others. In Lucius' case, his troubles began when he contracted into cheap sex with a serving girl, and then attempted to use debased magic to see what other lustful encounters it might give him. He is turned into an ass – the symbol of the enemy of Isis, a metaphor for a human soul disfigured into a beastly nature by sensual attachments. Lucius suffers the ministrations of cruel masters who are ignorant to his true nature – just as Fate is blind to humanity and doles out its tragedies thoughtlessly. Lucius is saved only when he realizes the true spiritual nature of reality as a way of avoiding the vagaries of corporeal fate. The rose, as a symbol of life and beauty, transforms Lucius from an ass into a man. For the soul that realizes its true nature can finally ascend into the empyrean.

For those that think of paganism as drunken, sexual debauchery, this is quite enlightening. Middle Platonism has the beginnings of what Christianity might call the Seven Deadly Sins. And Isis, the great intercessor, pioneered a path later adopted by the Virgin Mary.

I myself have never subscribed to Platonism and its quest to transcend corporeal manifestation. It seems to me like a negation of reality rather than a search for reality. It comes across as a passionless existence. Given that educated men like Apuleius were immensely wealthy and enjoyed great material comfort, and were part and parcel of an earthly empire like Rome, the whole enterprise to abandon the glories of the world seems rather hypocritical. However, I do sometimes look at modern America, plagued as it is by over consumption, obesity, substance abuse, sexual crimes and mindless entertainment, and at such times I begin to think the Platonists may have had a point.

Regardless, *The Golden Ass* is one of the great literary works of antiquity. A man of Punic origins turns a Greek fable into an apology for an Egyptian goddess, and all this written for a Latin speaking audience? Such was the multi-cultural nature of the Roman Empire. The Pax Romana did not make the world safe from the vicissitudes of blind fate, but it did make the world safe for the transmission of universal savior cults.

I am sadly incapable of reading the origin Latin, but the translation by P.G. Walsh is lively, and his introduction offers more detail on Apuleius and his life than I can give above. Whether you read it as a comical adventure tale set in second century Roman Greece, or as a timeless spiritual manifesto, you probably will not find another work quite like it.

The Problems of Using Apuleius' *Metamorphoses* as a Reliable Source for the Cult of Isis*

by Emma Nicholson

Book 11 of Apuleius' *Metamorphoses* has been the cause of much scholarly debate not only concerning its relevance to the rest of the novel but also in its description of the procession and cult of Isis in the Roman world. It has been questioned whether this book can be taken seriously as an accurate depiction of the cult and whether it represents an autobiographical or semi-autobiographical account of Apuleius' own experience. We also have to consider whether Apuleius would have altered reality (if he knew it) for contextual and fictional reasons to make it more in keeping with the rest of the novel. This essay will first attempt to discuss what little we know of Apuleius' life and background and question whether he would actually have experienced the cult of Isis as an initiate, or whether his account derives from other texts and public observation and knowledge. It will then turn to the influence of various sources and genres which may have influenced his description of the cult of Isis and the purpose and meaning of Book 11 itself.

The study of Apuleius has always been full of controversy and confusion as so little is known about his life. Haight has described it as a "mystery story" or "melodrama", as he "appears as a fantastic, clad in the garb of various subtle roles."[1] As our main sources for Apuleius' life are his own works (*Metamorphoses, Apologia* and *Florida*) it is no surprise therefore that this view is taken of him; the *Metamorphoses* has such a variety of tales, written in a language so peculiar and artificial,[2] a style so cunning and witty, and at times inserting himself into the place of the primary character "...from Madaura" and thereby suggesting at least a semi-autobiographical account, that it is hard to place him as anything else other than as a mystery or a fantastic in a melodrama. However, the "colour of [his] personality"[3] is more revealed with certainty by this work than the events of his life. The *Apologia* and *Florida*, believed to be written after the *Metamorphoses*, can be seen to reveal both personality and life (the court case over his use of magic and lectures influenced by Platonism); however, the exuberance of character, so greatly demonstrated within the *Metamorphoses* as a tale of comic fiction, is more subdued here in more serious works. It has been suggested by many that the *Metamorphoses* represents an autobiographical or at least semi-autobiographical account; the evidence to which this depends is the fact that the account of the procession and cult of Isis are very detailed and that in certain places in Book 11 Apuleius seems to be referring to himself or assimilating the character of Lucius to himself. Lucius is described as coming from Madaura (xi. 27), and there has been much scholarly contention (started off by Adlington) about Lucius also being Apuleius' first name; however, other than the authorial statement that his character came from Madaura, and therefore that perhaps the account is autobiographical or semi-autobiographical, there is no evidence whatsoever for this suggestion except easy assumption. Even if Apuleius' first name was not Lucius, the detail of the text concerning the procession and cult of Isis could still suggest that he was making a connection between what the character goes through in Book 11 and what he himself had experienced.

Whether the last book of the *Metamorphoses* is semi-autobiographical or not, it is likely that Apuleius had been in some contact, in one form or another, with the cult of Isis. As the son of a duumvir of Madaura, Apuleius had the means and opportunity to acquire an elite education, not only going through the complete cycle of education in the schools of *litterator*, *grammaticus*, *rhetor* and *philosophus*, learning Greek and Latin (his native language is unknown, but it is possible that it could have been a provincial dialect of Latin), but also studying in and travelling to Carthage, Athens, Rome and the east.[4] It is unlikely that Apuleius would *not* have come across Isiac worshippers as anyone in ancient Athens, Corinth or Rome could hardly avoid seeing them and therefore being familiar with the public outlook of the cult.[5] Apuleius being a witness to the public display of the cult of Isis seems to be relatively certain considering his very detailed account of the procession down to the harbour of Kenchreai to celebrate the very public festival of *Ploiaphesia* (xi.17). Whether all the components within the account of the procession are accurate is very difficult to determine, but it is known from archaeology for example that there were lamps and lights relating to the cult of Isis surviving in Kenchreai and Apuleius himself mentions them at xi.9-10.[6] It seems that he also possessed knowledge of the harbour of Corinth, Kenchreai, as his vague description of the position of the harbour and a nearby sanctuary of Isis seems to imply. Apuleius' description is also supported by that of Pausanias in his *Guide to Greece* (2.2.3) and implied by the archaeological record.[7] It could therefore be suggested that Apuleius had been to Corinth himself and witnessed such a procession, or perhaps that he had read Pausanias' description of

Kenchreai, witnessed a similar procession elsewhere and based his narrative in Corinth.

Considering his status in society it would also be unlikely that Apuleius had not taken part in and been initiated into mystery cults himself. At this time, 'oriental' or 'mystery' cults were starting to become more popular among the Roman elite, and many would still make the journey to Eleusis to be initiated into the Eleusinian Mysteries as well as participate in other Eastern cults such as that of Bacchus, Magna Mater, Mithras and Isis. Apuleius' detail of the internal workings of the cult of Isis leads one to suggest that he himself might have been initiated into the cult. The serious tone of Book 11 in comparison to the other ten books before might also be a sign, among other things, that he held religious piety and respect for the goddess and the cult. This would suggest that the details within Book 11 would be relatively reliable. It is possible to cross-check some of the details relating to the cult of Isis with Plutarch's *Isis and Osiris*, a source available to Apuleius which would be reliable enough in most of the details, but which might then again be tainted by Platonic philosophy and moralising. For example Apuleius' opening description of the moon representing Isis (xi.1) is stated by Plutarch:

> "Thus they make the power of Osiris to be fixed in the Moon, and say that Isis, since she is generation, is associated with him. For this reason they also call the Moon the mother of the world, and they think that she has a nature both male and female..." (368E-D)

The descriptions of Isis' and Osiris' robes and the Isiac horns are also similar (xi.3-4, 24):

> "As for the robes, those of Isis are variegated in their colours; for her power is concerned with matter which becomes everything and receives everything, light and darkness, day and night, fire and water, life and death, beginning and end. But the robe of Osiris has no shading or variety in its colour, but only one single colour like to light." (382C-D)

> "Isis is none other than the Moon; for this reason it is said that the statues of Isis that bear horns are imitations of the crescent moon, and in her dark garments are shown the concealments and the obscurations in which she in her yearning pursues the Sun." (372D)

There are also similarities between Apuleius' statement that it was a hard regimen to follow the ways of the cult of Isis (xi.19), that there were sacred writings in hieroglyphs involved within the cult (xi.22), and how the final purpose and aim is to reach knowledge of the greatest of all gods – Osiris (xi.27-30). Plutarch states all this in one paragraph:

> "...the sacred writings, which the goddess collects and puts together and gives into the keeping of those that are initiated into the holy rites, since this consecration, by a strict regimen and by abstinence from many kinds of food and from the lusts of the flesh, curtails licentiousness and the love of pleasure, and induces a habit of patient submission to the stern and rigorous services in shrines, the end and aim of which is the knowledge of Him who is the First, the Lord of All, the Ideal One." (351F-352A)

There are many more connections between the description of the cult of Isis in Apuleius' *Metamorphoses* and Plutarch's *Isis and Osiris*, and it is possible that, without having been initiated into the cult of Isis and Osiris (we have no evidence that he was ever initiated into the cult, despite the enthusiasm of many scholars), he could have read Plutarch (or other sources on the cult of Isis and Osiris, such as the aretalogies and others which we no longer have access to), and taken some of the details from this treatise (and others) and positioned them in such a way that it would be believable to those familiar with mystery cults (which he probably was to some extent). It, however, must be remembered that Plutarch was not only writing about the Graeco-Roman cult of Isis but also the Egyptian practice of it, and we must beware of placing a practice out of context. From cross-checking these sources, however, it appears that these elements would have been familiar to a Roman readership in Apuleius' time, and probably present in some manifestations of the Graeco-Roman cult. There are numerous elements within the book which are similar to many other 'mystery' cults; for example the element of secrecy, the procession, purification in the sea, sacred books and various levels of initiation. Another example which may show Apuleius' familiarity with other mystery cults is that he names the priest who is the intermediary and initiator of Lucius as Mithras and also hints at the astrological aspects of Mithraism (xi.22, 25). This surely would not be a coincidence given the fact that if Apuleius knew of the cult of Isis he would probably know that of Mithras. We then also find another statement which may suggest Apuleius' reason for using Mithras as the name of the priest and possibly illustrates another connection with Plutarch's text concerning the Zoroastrian gods and daemons:

> "Oromazes may best be compared to light, and Areimanius, conversely, to darkness and ignorance, and midway between the two is Mithras: for this reason the Persians give to Mithras the name of 'Mediator.'" (369E)

Could Apuleius' naming of the priest of Isis as Mithras be a link with Plutarch's text? And Isis therefore be associated with Oromazes the god of light, and Lucius Areimanius, the daemon of darkness and ignorance? Following the next line of Plutarch's paragraph, "Zoroaster has also taught that men should make votive offerings and thank-offerings to Oromazes, and averting and mourning offerings to Areimanius," could this also be an association with Isis and Seth, which might also be connected with Lucius as an ass, one of the animals of Seth? This kind of religious fusion, also seen in Platonic philosophy which we know Apuleius was a follower and preacher of, was of course very common; the reality of which may be seen in how some of the traits of the Eleusinian Mysteries were taken over by the cult of Isis, such as the story of Demeter's/Isis' wanderings and the association of corn and civilisation.

In my opinion it seems likely that Apuleius would have had knowledge of the cult of Isis and Osiris, yet there is no evidence for Apuleius ever having been initiated into the cult. He was a celebrated public speaker and was awarded a public statue in Carthage for his lectures as a philosopher not as a pastophoros; what is more, the inscription of the statue read *Philosopho Platonico*, not *Isiaco*, and in the fourth century references appear describing Apuleius as a mage or miracle worker and not as an Egyptian devotee.[8] On account of his widespread reading he would not necessarily have needed to have experienced the cult first hand, as his elite background and education would have given him greater access to information on mystery cults. What is difficult to decipher, when taking this point of view however, is his apparent insertion of himself into the character of Lucius by "mitti sibi Madaurensem sed admodum pauperem" (xi.27). His very detailed description of the religious experience and the seemingly pious tone of the book seem to point to a semi-autobiographical account, but this need not be an account of his personal experience in this cult. If this was the case, his preference towards the cult of Isis might be the association, which comes with scholarly reading and study, of the ass and Egyptian religion (this will be discussed further below). Apuleius' knowledge of the cult and therefore his reliability, in my opinion, would therefore be one of a secondary nature without actual knowledge of the specific secrets contained within it, but also one with detailed study, experience and familiarity with other mystery cults.

We must now however discuss Apuleius' influences in writing the *Metamorphoses* and consider how these will have affected the factual aspect of Book 11.

Just as when trying to reconstruct his life, there are many problems when trying to determine Apuleius' purpose, influences and style in the *Metamorphoses*. Scobie (1978: 49) has stated the problem perfectly: "Apuleius, unlike 'Lucius of Patrae,' not only creates retrospective doubt in the reader's mind about the fictional authenticity of his hero-narrator, but the structural logic of the narrative remains uncoordinated thanks to a fluctuating combination of fact and fiction, the full extent of which cannot be determined because of our ignorance of exact details of Apuleius' own biography."

Most scholars now generally agree that 'Lucius of Patrae's' *Metamorphoses* was one of Apuleius' primary sources in regards to the general outlying story of a man turning into an ass and back again.[9] However, this does not account for religious conversion and in particular conversion to Isis at the end. Mason believes, and it seems likely, that Apuleius was also influenced by other genres, such as novella, myths, folklore, fable, drama and Greek romance.[10] We have evidence through his style and use of language that Apuleius had come across, and was influenced by, Plautus and Terence,[11] as well as Milesian tales or novellas (*Met.* 1.1). Alongside the influences of Plautus and Terence is mime, a category which Mason sees as reflected in the poison-cup scene at 10.26 and possibly in the description of the transformation of Aetaeon (*Met.* 2.4). These genres, however, do not seem to have much influence on Book 11, where the tone, detail and purpose of the book are very different. Griffiths believes there to be at least a basic Egyptian mythological and folkloric origin, and considering that Apuleius grew up in Africa this connection would not be difficult to believe.

The presence of the Egyptian gods may also possibly emphasize this origin; an insertion and an association which appears to have been instigated by Apuleius himself. The ass is one of the favourite animals of (Aesopic) fable, and it is possible that themes of the ass's stupidity, stubbornness, sexual characteristics and even curiosity derive from here. We can also find a connection with the ass and Seth/Typhon, which seems to be a feature particular to Apuleius. Greek romance, however, is deemed by many scholars as the most significant genre in regards to various features of Apuleius' ass-story, especially in terms of structure and the tale of Cupid and Psyche. It also provides an obvious literary model for the invention of a divine saviour unlike the other genres, and other contemporary authors of romance, such as Iamblichus and Achilles Tatius, also illustrate the loss of structure and numerous digressions so typical of Apuleius. It would seem therefore that his debt to Greek literature was significant: the basic plot may have derived from an already existing theme – the ass story, reshaped by Lucius of Patrae, and possibly from mime; the tone, spirit and ending from Greek romance, and other numerous features, especially the novella, from short story forms, comic, serious and paradoxical as well as fables and drama.[12]

That Apuleius had a large network of sources to influence his work is clear, and unsurprising in regards to his elite background. However, Apuleius was known not only for copying but also adaptation and originality: "in dealing with details, as with major plots, Apuleius appears to range from close dependence on his sources to almost complete alteration. Mere translation rarely continued for more than a sentence or two."[13] Considering the deficiency of the extant sources, our ability to determine what was copied and what was not is greatly reduced, and therefore our ability to determine the reliability of various facts within the work. We know that he used and adapted a large amount of Lucius of Patrae's work for the ass-story, and Walsh believes that Apuleius expanded upon features of Petronius for example techniques of presentation and the inserted story.[14] However, very little of these influences seems to be of especial significance when we consider the factuality of Book 11 of the *Metamorphoses*. The ending, as Mason suggested, could reflect the Greek romantic model of divine intervention at the end. It would therefore be an innovation when we consider how the ass-story in all previous accounts, does not end in the character learning from his past experiences and finish in religious conversion.[15] Apuleius states at the beginning that this is a story about "figures fortunasque hominum in alias imagines conversas et in se rursum mutuo nexu refectas..." (*Met.* 1.1), but in the end we find it is also about mental changes, an additional dimension to the original story. It appears therefore that Apuleius added his own feature to the ass-story, and changed it into a variety of different genres, which he expressed in the beginning, but most notably a comic-romance.[16] The increased connection with Egyptian themes, which may or may not have already been evident from mythology and folklore,[17] appears to be another innovation of Apuleius.

Winkler (1985:277-9) gives three plausible suggestions for the use of Isis as the final saviour instead of another: 1) Apuleius seems to have made the connection between the ass and the ass-god Seth or Typhon; despite other associations with the ass such as Jewish worship and the Syrian goddess (which would have been inappropriate for the ending considering her cult was parodied earlier in the narrative and because she was in Lucian's λουκιος η ονος), the Egyptian story of Seth/Osiris/Isis would have been far more familiar. 2) Isiac worship in the Hellenistic period onwards was popular, visible and strange; temples and inscriptions have been found all over the Graeco-Roman world and many of the rites involved were public, which would have allowed his audience, which would not always have been the elite and educated, to have knowledge of and understand the cult being described. The strangeness of the cult in terms of Egyptian style and origin, Winkler suggests, helps separate the earlier Lucius from the later Lucius after his conversion and revelation. 3) Isis is often featured in tales of saving as the aretalogies and others sources especially Artemidorus indicate: "Serapis and Isis and Anoubis and Harpocrates – these gods...signify disturbances and dangers and threats and crises from which they save people contrary to every expectation and hope. For these gods are universally considered to be the saviours of those who have gone through everything and reached the ultimate danger; people who are in such a fix are suddenly saved by these gods" (*Oneirokritika* 2.39). Apuleius' transformation of the original tale, originally called μεταμορθοσιες by 'Lucius of Patrae' and λουκιος η ονος by Lucian, although officially called *Metamorphoses*, was also called *Asinus Aureus*; the Latin word *aureus* – golden – connoted an element of blessed luckiness, perhaps a reference to Book 11 where Lucius finally loses the unluckiness of the previous ten books and achieves bliss and peacefulness in the form of religious conversion.

However, it seems unlikely that Apuleius would have had *no* sources to use or influence his narrative in Book 11 considering the degree of borrowing done in the rest of the book. But, if Book 11 really is a relatively factual autobiographical account would this still apply? It is a question which is difficult to determine without more information about Apuleius' life and even then there would be doubts about details. If we take the view that Apuleius was not initiated into the cult himself then he will most probably have used various sources, like that for the rest of the novel. As it has already been suggested above, it is possible that, for Book 11, Apuleius may have used, with or without an autobiographical knowledge of the procession and the internal workings of the cult, other sources on the cult of Isis and Osiris such as Plutarch's *Isis and Osiris* and perhaps those which are no longer available to us. Then again, this could also represent common knowledge, or at least common knowledge to the educated, as none of the secrets or revelations of initiation or ritual are described, or if so only in very vague terms. Despite the presence of that ever-present caution to the reader that such secrets could not be revealed, there is still the possibility that this only increases the believability of the tale to the reader and might not necessarily mean that Apuleius had been initiated into this particular cult. The words, "Accessi confinium mortis et calcato Proserpinae limine per omina vectus elementa remeavi" are reminiscent of those uttered in accounts describing the rites of initiation into the Eleusinian Mysteries. In light of the fact that Eleusinian Ceres and Proserpina (Demeter and Persephone) became identified with Isis, with their respective mythologies and rites merging within the Graeco-Roman world, it is not surprising that this phrase should appear. It reflects again that phenomenon of syncretism and assimilation that is evident within Platonism and which increases during the Hellenistic and Roman periods. With the knowledge of such connections and associations Apuleius would not necessarily have had to be initiated into this particular cult.

Apuleius' reliability concerning the cult of Isis and Osiris is difficult to determine. As we have no evidence to prove to the contrary, it appears that Apuleius was not himself initiated into the cult, and that his information derives from secondary reading and familiarity with mystery cults in general. Unfortunately this essay has not been able to cover some areas in as much detail, such as the purpose of Book 11, although it has touched on some plausible reasons for placing divine intervention at the end of the novel, and for that deity being Isis. Through cross-checking various details of the cult of Isis and Osiris with Plutarch (and if we were to have looked at the aretalogies we would have come to a similar conclusion) we can establish that many features of the procession and workings of the cult in the *Metamorphoses* seem to be accurate in so far as public knowledge can prove. Many of the elements are also apparent in other mystery cults, but these again are generally publicly known and not specific to one cult. We must therefore be careful in using Apuleius' *Metamorphoses* as a reliable source for the cult of Isis in the Graeco-Roman world as although some features seem to be genuine to the cult, others may be unspecific references to mystery cults which have little relevance to Isis.

Editors' Note: This essay was originally submitted by Nicholson for her Master's degree program at the University of London.

Notes

[1] Haight (1927: 24)
[2] See Ferguson 1961, esp. pp. 61-2
[3] Haight (1927: 24)
[4] Haight (1927: 26-28)
[5] Winkler (1985: 206)
[6] Smith (1977: 222)
[7] See Smith 1977, esp. pp. 201-2, 209
[8] Winkler (1985: 276-7)
[9] Scobie (1978:43)
[10] Mason (1978:7-12)
[11] Ferguson (1961:61)
[12] Mason (1978:12)
[13] Mason (1978:5)
[14] Walsh (1978:19)
[15] Bohm (1973:228)
[16] Scobie (1978:46-7)
[17] Mason (1978:11)

Bibliography

Apuleius, The Golden Ass; Being the Metamorphoses of Lucius Apuleius, trans by W. Adlington (1566) revised by S. Gaselee, The Loeb Classical Library
Apuleius, The Golden Ass, trans. by Robert Graves (1960) The Penguin Classics
Pausanias, Guide to Greece
Plutarch, Isis and Osiris – Online version of published trans. by Frank Cole Babbitt as printed in pp. 1-191 of Vol. V of the Loeb Classical Library edition of the Moralia, published in 1936 – http://penelope.uchicago.edu/Thayer/E/Roman/Texts/Plutarch/Moralia/Isis_and_Osiris*/home.html (07/04/09)
R.K. Bohm "The Isis Episode in Apuleius" in The Classical Journal, Vol. 68, No. 3 (Feb. - Mar., 1973), pp. 228-231
J. Ferguson, "Apuleius" in Greece & Rome, Second Series, vol. 8, no. 1 (Mar., 1961) pp. 61-74
J. Gwyn Griffiths "Isis in the Metamorphoses of Apuleius" in Aspects of Apuleius' Golden Ass, eds B.L. Hijmans Jr. & R. Th. Van der Paardt (1978) Groningen
E. Haight (1927) Apuleius and His Influence, George G. Harrap & Co. Ltd, London, Calcutta, Sydney

B.L. Hijmans Jr. & R. Th. Van der Paardt (eds.) (1978) *Aspects of Apuleius' Golden Ass*, Groningen

H.J. Mason (Toronto) "Fabula Graecania: Apuleius and his Greek Sources" in *Aspects of Apuleius' Golden Ass* eds. B.L. Hijmans Jr. & R. Th. Van der Paardt, (1978) Groningen

B.E. Perry "An Interpretation of Apuleius' *Metamorphosis*" in TAPA 57 (1926)

B.E. Perry (1920) *The "Metamorphoses "ascribed to Lucius of Patras* Lancaster

D.E. Smith "The Egyptian Cults at Corinth" in *The Harvard Theological Review*, vol. 70, no. 3/4 (Jul.-Oct., 1977) pp. 201-31

A. Scobie, "The Structure of Apuleius' Metamorphoses", in *Aspects of Apuleius' Golden Ass* eds B.L. Hijmans Jr. & R. Th. Van der Paardt, (1978) Groningen

P.G. Walsh, "Petronius and Apuleius", *Aspects of Apuleius' Golden Ass* eds. B.L. Hijmans Jr. & R. Th. Van der Paardt, (1978) Groningen

J.J. Winkler (1985) *Auctor & Actor; A Narratological Reading of Apuleius's Golden Ass*, University of California Press

Untitled

by Rebecca Buchanan

Wife of wives
Mother of mothers
Queen of queens
Never before was there one like You
Nor shall there be one ever after
    – mystery divine

(after the Sarum Breviary)

Inventio Osiridis

by Jeremy J. Baer

In the ancient Egyptian lunar calendar, the Discovery of Osiris occurred on the 17th of the month Hathyr, when the nights grew longer and the Nile receded. As nearly as can be determined the festival coincides with the Roman solar calendar on October 28th – November 3rd. The Roman adherents of the cult came to celebrate the festival after the emperor Caligula officially recognized Isiac worship and had a temple built to the cult on the Field of Mars, sometime during his reign between 37 and 41 CE.

In the earliest Egyptian myths, it seems Osiris, the embodiment of fecundity, drowned in the Nile on this date. Later myths have Osiris murdered at the hands of his scheming brother, Seth the god of chaos (whom Greeks equated with Typhon). Still later myths – the most complete version being preserved by the Greek writer, Plutarch, in his *On Isis and Osiris* – have Seth dismembering the corpse and scattering it across the lands. Isis and her friends among the gods search the lands to find the pieces and reassemble the body of Osiris. Isis, Great of Magic, resurrects Osiris, who later goes on to become the ruler of the underworld.

The Discovery of Osiris was like a passion play, commemorating the search for the murdered god and his magical resurrection. Statues of the goddess Isis were veiled in black, and it seems very probable that priestesses of the cult would have dressed so as well (it must be understood that in Ancient Egypt black was the color of the fertile Nile silt, and was thus a color of life not of death). Children wore a tress of long hair behind the right ear, identifying themselves with the iconic depictions of a young Horus. Both genders of all ages involved in the cult chanted laments and cries of grief. Some, in a ritual not unlike that of the Attis cults, beat their flesh with pine cones until bloodied.

A ritual idol of Osiris was dismembered and scattered along a predetermined route from the temple. The pieces were then gradually "rediscovered" and assembled. A priest of the cult wore a mask of Anubis, the jackal headed embalming god, whose sense of smell had helped Isis locate several of the pieces. On November 3rd the cult adherents joyously shouted "let us rejoice!" They proceeded happily in procession through town, shaking sistra.

Those living in the countryside surrounding the towns fashioned idols of Osiris out of damp earth and seeds, and consecrated the idols in hollowed pine trunks. Others decorated lamps or vases and offered them to the god.

Much like the Navigium Isidis, one did not have to be a duly initiated member to participate in this public festival. While mystae and clergy certainly formed the backbone of any observance, the wider public could and did participate in the processions. The festival championed the triumph of rebirth over death. On one level, it assured the prosperity of future harvests, as Osiris embodied the powers of fertile agriculture. On another level, those especially educated in Hellenistic philosophy (such as Plutarch) may have reinterpreted the myths of the cult through the prism of Platonic theology. The festival thus appealed to people with a variety of spiritual needs and backgrounds. It held practices and beliefs in common with other related cults, such as those of Attis and Demeter.

There is much about this cult that simply cannot be reconstructed by the solitary practitioner. Creating and then dismembering a cult idol of Osiris, only to reassemble it, is probably beyond most people's ken. Participating in a large procession is obviously impossible with the small numbers of modern adherents.

If one has a statue of Isis on one's domestic shrine, covering it in black would be entirely appropriate, and wearing black even more so. One could go to a park or one's backyard and fashion a makeshift Osiris idol out of damp earth and seeds, as was done in ancient times.

The festival falls conveniently enough during the modern Halloween, a time for remembering the dead (albeit secularly and with much humor and fun). Around the same time, Wiccans and Celtic pagans celebrate the festival of Samhain, a remembrance of the dead, and some Christians celebrate All Souls Day. It seems therefore fitting that modern Isiac cult adherents do likewise. Remember dearly departed loved ones during this occasion. Meditate on what they meant to you, and let it be not amiss to shed tears for them.

Then on November 3rd have a joyous occasion to celebrate the resurrection of the god Osiris. Light a candle or a lamp. Have a feast with living loved ones. Party! Know that death is but a doorway to another world. The memories of the dead live on in our hearts. The spirits of the dead pass on to the Underworld, and those who have contracted into cults of savior deities shall see their gods there to illumine the Stygian depths.

Bibliography

Pinch, Geraldine. *Egyptian Mythology: A Guide to Gods, Goddesses and Traditions of Ancient Egypt*. Oxford University Press. Oxford, England. 2002.

Turcan, Robert. *The Cults of the Roman Empire*. Translated by Antonia Nevill. Blackwell Publishing. Oxford, England. 1996.

Eternal Love

by Jocelyn Almond

Father

1 His face, his dear, beloved face,
    His golden, wise, eternal face;
    When I was held in his embrace,
    All I could see was his sweet face,
5 When he was all the world to me,
    When he was young and we were One,
    And love was all and we were free.

    How long? How many ages passed?
    Even for gods, youth passes fast –
10 When then I made that fatal slip,
    Slid, fell, splashed, plunged –
    I well-near died –
    I wallowed, flailed, breathed
    Into life, or death,
15 Where both ends meet.

Lost

    I drifted, lost,
    I wept, survived,
    And then in darkness floated on,
    Not dead, but scarce alive.

20 For life is hard, what is this life?
    And who are we who live it?
    What Love could ever mend that rift?
    What Love could e'er forgive it?
    Tears from a Mother's Eye we fall,
25 Sad, bitter, lost, forlorn,
    So far from that dear, sweet, sacred face
    Where once in Beauty we were born.

Mother

    Her fur, her breath,
    Soft, deep, close, warm;
30 Her mother-love, forgiving all –
    Purr! I shall not forget her call,
    When, weeping, she reached out for me!
    Oh, Mother, Lady, lion, cat,
    It does not matter –
35 She is All,
    As my dear mother was to me
    Before the darkness came again,
    And I was lost and she is free.

Salvation

    Osiris, once, he suffered and
40 He died, my love, he died,
    And tossed upon the ocean's surge,
    I cried for him, I cried.

Husband

    His face, his dear, beloved face,
    His wise, sweet, kind, his gentle face;
45 When I am held in his embrace,
    All I can see is his dear face.
    When in this mortal life we be,
    We are not young, we are not free,
    But he is all the world –
50 My love, my dearest husband is to me.

Notes

I wrote this poem at a time of personal crisis, and the feelings expressed were my sincere feelings at that time. However, my poem is meaningless unless the references in it are comprehensible to the reader. For those unfamiliar with ancient Egyptian myth, it may therefore make no sense. For this reason only, I provide the notes below. In no way do I intend these notes to explain, still less to 'explain away,' the emotional meaning of the poem. Both the poem and the notes are based on general knowledge about ancient Egypt which I have acquired over years of reading many books on the subject, so I am unable to provide specific references for the information provided. It can, however, be found repeatedly in many readily-available non-academic books about ancient Egypt.

Lines 1-2. In ancient Egypt, Horus, a form of the sun god, was perceived in one of his manifestations as the face of the sky, with the sun and the moon as his two eyes. A hieroglyph used to write his name is a human face. The sun god in general, under any of his various names is often spoken of as having the sun and moon as his eyes.

Line 3. The creator and sun god Atum came into being on a primeval mound emerging out of the primordial watery abyss, the Nun. Atum formed all that came into being out of his own being, starting with his two children: Shu, a boy, and Tefnut, a girl. He held them in a close embrace, which for the ancient Egyptians was expressed in the concept of Ka, a life-giving, perhaps breath-like or kissing energy, the word itself being written in the hieroglyph of a pair of extended arms.

Line 6. The triad of Atum, Shu and Tefnut may be regarded as a triple form of Deity which is essentially One, like the Christian Trinity.

Line 7. Love and free will are significant concepts in the relationship between God and human beings in many spiritual paths and religions. According to this way of thinking, love and free will are experienced by both God and humans.

Line 8. Myths take place in mythic time, but may be seen as symbolically applicable to any point in historical time, within ordinary human lives. It is important to recognise that they are not to be taken as literally true – a mistake often made by both religious fundamentalists and scientific-rationalist-atheists. Myths are poetic, symbolic, abstract and iconic, expressed through art, music, fiction, poetry, drama, dance, religion, and other variations of creative cultural phenomena. On a personal level, myths may often seem to 'break through' into the lives of human beings, which may be recognised consciously or sensed unconsciously. The Egyptian term for mythic time is Zep Tepi, the First Time.

Line 9. In myths, including Egyptian myths, the lives of the gods are often described in human terms, so that gods can be born, suffer, grow old and die. The gods' experience of this is assumed to be similar to human experience, even though a human might think of a god's life as lasting for aeons or for eternity. From the Christian point of view, of course, God incarnates in a human life. From the ancient Egyptian perspective, and from a general Pagan viewpoint, God manifests through all forms of life, and the essence of the Divine is within each human being, therefore within each human life.

Lines 10-13. In Egyptian myth, Shu and Tefnut slipped off the primeval mound and were swept away in the primordial watery abyss. This may be seen as a form of the myth of The Fall. The primordial perfection is lost through some slip, accident or fault, and humans are separated from Deity. In an individual human life, this is experienced through emerging from the waters of the mother's womb and growing up through a nurturing childhood to adult independence.

Lines 14-15. The symbol of the Ouroboros, the snake consuming its own tail, originated in ancient Egypt where the diurnal cycle was a snake called Sito. Life and death, experienced in all human lives, is part of a vast cycle of life, continuing on both physical and spiritual levels.

Lines 16-19. This theme of drifting in water is significant in Egyptian mythology and occurs again when the god Osiris drowns in the Nile. For the ancient Egyptians, the Nile was the fertilising life source of Egypt, but also hazardous because of its flooding and the bringing of plagues caused by environmental conditions around the river. The Nile was sacred to the Egyptians, as the Ganges is in India today. More generally, drifting aimlessly in water, or drowning, is a symbol of separation from God, a loss of consciousness, death, a return to the womb. Similar symbolism is readily found in myths of other cultures, where heroes fall into water and are drowned. The Judeo-Christian myth of Noah's Ark is a very different form of this water/fall/separation from God myth, but the meaning is essentially the same.

Line 21. In Egyptian mythology, the ultimate answer to the question, 'Who are we?' is, 'We are manifestations of God in his form as Khepera, the ever-becoming Creator, the scarab sun god.'

Lines 22-7. After Shu and Tefnut fell off the primeval mound, their grieving father, Atum, plucked out his own eye and sent it off in the form of a goddess into the watery abyss to find the missing children. The Eye Goddess is a very significant figure in Egyptian mythology – so significant that many other goddesses were frequently compared to this Eye or seen as forms of her. In her essential forms she is Hathor, the cow goddess of love and beauty, and Sekhmet, the lion goddess of destruction. This dual-aspect goddess can 'flip' abruptly from one aspect to the other, as the loving/punishing mother. Sekhmet, the bringer of plague, is also the goddess of healing. When the Eye Goddess brought Shu and Tefnut back to their father, she found that he had grown a new eye, and that she could never again return to her place on his face. She wept bitter tears of anger and grief, and as her tears fell to earth, they became human beings. This story relates to the fact that the Egyptian words for tears and humans are very similar. However, on a symbolic level, it obviously has a far greater significance to do with the human sense of loss, and the grief and anger that overwhelm so many people's lives. From the ancient Egyptian viewpoint, it could not be otherwise if we are the tears of God that fell from that great Goddess who is his Eye. To console her, Atum placed the Eye Goddess on his brow in the form of the serpent, the uraeus, his third eye, a symbol of wisdom, protection and power, the all-seeing Eye of God. Other well-known Egyptian goddesses portrayed in leonine or cat form are Tefnut, Mut and Bast.

Lines 22-3 and Lines 26-7. Love is the goddess Hathor. Generally speaking, in other religions, as well as this, the rift between humans and God is healed through love, which inevitably involves forgiveness, for all forms of emotional and spiritual separation rest on grievances, disputes, misunderstandings and, ultimately, wrong-doings. True love is unconditional, and no disputes, grievances or faults can stand as a barrier. The sacred face is the face of God, as explained in the Note above on Line 1. Beauty is of course Hathor again.

Lines 28-35. These lines refer to the Egyptian feline forms of the Goddess described in the Note above on Lines 22-7.

Lines 39-42. The god Osiris, the brother-husband of the goddess Isis, was attacked by his jealous brother Set and pushed into the Nile, where he drowned. In Egyptian myth, Isis and her twin sister Nephthys searched relentlessly for him, and eventually found his body in the marshes of the delta. In later Greco-Roman versions of the myth, Set deliberately trapped

Osiris in a chest or mummy case and cast it into the Nile, from where it drifted down to the sea and was carried across to another country. Isis, in a turmoil of grief, faithfully followed after her lost husband, taking to the surging ocean in a small boat. Both Osiris and Isis were both tossed on the ocean – continuing the themes of loss, grief, separation from God, and the turmoils and suffering of earthly life, in which, in some sense, we may all be seen as floundering or drowning. In the Greco-Roman culture, Isis came to be seen as the special protectress of sailors, and by extension the Saviour Goddess for anyone at all who might turn to her in distress.

Lines 43-50. The most common human experience of Divine love is through earthly love and through our relationships with those people who are most precious in our lives. This is recognised in religion and spirituality in other cultures, including Christianity today, but in ancient Egypt, this recognition was all part of the concept of God's manifesting throughout creation. In mythic thinking in general, the myth is meaningless to individuals unless they can find some echo of that myth within their own lives, when the myth becomes 'true,' not literally, but in a deep, heart-felt and life-renewing way.

First Sorrow of Creation

by Rebecca Buchanan

they stand around
in their white coats
and pastel scrubs
trying to look hopeful
failing
a chapel downstairs
nondenominational
just a few benches and stained glass
light a candle
light ten candles
a hundred
to creation's first widow
her tears flood the world
thunder her cries of pain
lightning her anger
grief to break the heart of the world
      – please not me too

Picking Up the Pieces

by Suzette Chan

Izzy still felt numb. Even after a weekend in the mountains, she still couldn't shake the lethargy that she'd fallen into since Roy died.

She dropped her bag in the foyer and looked at her living room as if it belonged to someone else. Feeling detached, her head filled with numbers: It's been eight years since she moved into this bungalow with Roy. Twenty-seven years since they met, nine since they married. Two years since Roy was promoted to a VP position he didn't want. Fifteen days since he died of a heart attack. Fourteen days since she went down to San Francisco, to wait for his body to be cut open, examined and sewn back together. Seven days since she gathered the body and brought it home. Five days since she buried it.

Taking care of Roy's body had been traumatic, but Izzy operated on automatic pilot. Most of the decisions she had to make were governed by medical and legal procedures, as well as Roy's will. Now came the hard part.

Roy had left to Izzy's discretion his collectibles and ephemera. Like Izzy, Roy had accumulated an enormous number of action figures, comics and movie tie-ins, from E. T. lunch pails to Lord of the Rings light-up goblets. Both had gradually stopped collecting. Roy was steered into senior management from actual engineering, while Izzy's easy job in a craft shop turned into busy management, and now challenging ownership.

She regretted being so distracted in the months since she took over the store. Roy was travelling a lot, especially to California, where his firm needed to lock down contracts jeopardized by the state budget crisis. Their last conversation was little more than a peck on the cheek at the airport.

Izzy moved slowly. Every moment she filled with little occupations was a moment she avoided Roy's things. She unpacked her hiking gear, sorted through the mail and newspapers, tended to the houseplants, then checked email. Tucked between the messages from Roy's friends and her shop contacts, one name caught her eye, but she dealt with it last. She hesitated over opening it, but curiosity won out over dread.

"Hi Izzy. It's Seth. Sorry I missed you at the funeral. It was nice. You might not know this, but I sent Roy a message a few weeks ago, before I heard what happened. It's about the chess set. The provincial museum is doing an exhibit about local collectors and asked about it. I gave it back to Roy when I moved to Lethbridge. Do you know if he kept it? Let me know."

Izzy never liked Roy's older brother. Roy was the more mature one, and could lead his brother to constructive activities, in spite of Seth's tendency to use disguise inaction as cynicism. Now Seth was playing out her nightmare scenario: someone she never accepted, asking for something she didn't feel she could give.

Still, his request prompted Izzy's curiosity. She made her way down to the basement and stepped into what was in theory the second guest room, but was in reality a private museum of artifacts from Izzy and Roy's past. She turned on the light. Dust motes swirled up from banged-up board games (his); milk crates of vinyl albums and cassette tapes (hers); action figures, blasphemously liberated from their original packaging (his); a fort of plastic containers filled with old craft projects and skeins of yarn that Izzy bought for projects that she would do "one day."

The chess set was Seth's idea, but Roy was the one who actually did something about it. Izzy met them in a first-year history of technology class. She thought the course would be useful whether she decided to go into the fine art stream or the industrial design stream. Roy, an engineer, took it as his arts elective. Seth was dragging out a three-year degree into four, expecting to crib from Roy, Izzy guessed. She had been surprised to discover that they were brothers. Seth was wiry, goat-like with his overbite and Beat poet beard. Roy was sweet, with an open face, shy smile and quiet, regal air.

Fascinated by the contrast, Izzy routinely eavesdropped on their conversations before class. One day, Seth mentioned that his local comic shop was sponsoring a window display contest. He said someone should do that Star Wars chess set he'd been thinking of since junior high. Roy became animated. "This is a great excuse to finally do it. It'll be easy." He proposed making a diorama, which Seth dismissed as being uncool. Roy suggested custom die-cast models (too expensive) or wood figurines (too time consuming).

Izzy recognized a cue. "You could use wax," she interrupted. "You can dye a batch black, and one white, and make the blocks big enough so that you don't have to carve small details."

The boys didn't say anything for a long time. Seth was giving her the evil eye for nudging his idle notion into reality. Roy, as he told Izzy years later, was just looking at her. Finally, Seth said, "You know a lot about this." They ditched their afternoon classes. Roy led the discussion to figure out which characters would be used for which chess pieces. Izzy knew enough to make the gender-bending suggestion that Darth Vader be the black queen, due to his position in the empire's hierarchy and his swishy ways with a cape. Seth left early for his weekly D & D game, so Roy started the character sketches. Izzy drew up a supply list (Roy was a whiz at figuring out volumes), and they both went out to get the materials.

Izzy and Roy spent almost every night of the next two weeks in the kitchen of her tiny apartment, which was really just an illegal suite in the converted attic of a house near campus. If it hadn't been November, the wax would have melted in their hands. They had hours of carving to do, but never felt rushed. Toward the end, Izzy wondered why chess couldn't have sixty-four pieces instead of just thirty-two. From old b-movies to new music, they never lacked for something to talk about.

"The ancient Egyptians used wax a lot," Izzy said. "They used it to make perfume cones for fashionable women – I guess it made them sexy enough to attract mates – and to make death masks."

"So wax was life and death for the Egyptians." Thus, Roy passed Izzy's test for tolerance of morbid humour.

As they were working, Izzy realized they were making a beautiful work of kitsch together. Roy was a quick learner, building on his experience carving model cars from balsa wood. But Izzy was fast and adept; she was already micro-famous for making cartoonish wax sculptures of the Ramones for friends. Looking back, Izzy realized that she'd made most of the Star Wars pieces.

She wasn't surprised that they won, but she couldn't believe that Seth never amended his original entry to include her and Roy as collaborators. Roy said he didn't mind because he considered Izzy to be the real prize, but Izzy considered it fraud. The chess set was an instantly iconic fixture (one of the older staff members used it to recreate famous chess matches, one move per day). Its association with Seth strengthened when he bought half-ownership of the shop. He had stopped going to university by then, and gained a reputation as a shrewd, if mean, businessman. Eventually, Seth made enough enemies to sell his stake and exile himself to the southern deserts of the province. About five years ago, just before he moved, Seth showed up at Izzy and Roy's house, drunk.

"I won't let them keep it – I won't," Seth slurred as he shoved a bunch of plastic grocery bags into Roy's hands. "It's yours." All three of them knew full well that the comic shop owned the set. None of them brought that up during the small talk they engaged in until Seth passed out on the couch. It was an annoying evening, but Izzy now had to admit that Seth's pathos-ridden act of thievery returned the set to Roy.

Plundering Roy's boxes like Indiana Jones, she exhausted his inventory in the main room and remembered the containers stacked in the closet. Roy had rearranged everything last summer, when a new engineer from the UK needed a place to stay until he found one of his own.

Near the bottom of the pile, she found a bag of the white pieces. There were Roy's x-wing fighter rooks, the white bishop Yoda, the black rook Jabba the Hutt and almost all the rebel soldier pawns. Izzy noticed a piece of paper at the bottom of the bag. "Rest belongs to Izzy." It was in Roy's handwriting. She zoned in on her half of the room. It didn't take long to unearth the remaining pieces.

She put the set together the way she and Roy did when they first assembled it. Stormtrooper pawns, Jedi horses, rebel command knights, the emperor and even Han Solo all placidly awaited to report for duty like shabti, the little slave figurines that were supposed to help the pharaoh carry out his responsibilities in the afterlife. Izzy chuckled at the thought of Osiris leading the rebel forces, with Roy in the elite command.

She would have to do a lot of work to breathe life into the pieces. The AT-AT walker rooks needed new legs, and warriors on either side needed nose jobs and finger reattachments. One piece was missing. She would have to carve a new one. It really was too much to expect that Seth would resist keeping Darth Vader.

Izzy drew up a new list of supplies, determined to complete what was now hers.

About a week later, she picked up the phone. "Seth? It's Izzy. I have something to give to you."

A Modern Festival for Serapis

by Jeremy J. Baer

Though it may be the relatively limited resources open to me, I have trouble finding references to ancient festivals for Serapis.

The Discovery of Osiris, which occurred in the Roman Empire from October 28th – November 3rd, seems to have been more a part of the cult of Isis than Serapis. Likewise, cult adherents of Serapis, particularly musicians, participated in another festival to Isis that happened on March 5th. The only festival exclusively for Serapis I have found is called the Serapia; it was celebrated on April 25th and may have been held to commemorate the giant temple dedicated to the god by the Roman emperor Caracalla. Details on this festival are lacking.

There is however no reason why a modern festival to Serapis could not be developed, so long as it seems like something the god would appreciate. To determine that, we would have to look to ancient sources, and fortunately there are enough sources to give us a taste of what the worship of the god was like.

Religious associations throughout the Hellenistic world were quite common, and often had a kind of central meal in honor of their presiding deity. This seems to have been true of Serapis as well; there are various invitations recorded to a celebratory feast in the god's honor. Clearly, food should be part of his worship.

Apuleius makes it clear that the cult of Serapis included sacred musicians who performed in the god's honor. These musicians were active not only in the temples of Serapis, but also in the joyous procession of Isis that transpired in March. Thus, festive music is at home in the god's worship.

Finally, there was a pronounced solar aspect in the worship of Serapis. In Egypt it was thought the sun god Ra nightly journeyed into the Underworld, where he mystically united with Osiris. Serapis too was often conflated with solar deities such as Helios and even Mithras. By the time of Caracalla the Romans knew him less as a god of the underworld and more as a god of the sun (a nice counterpoint to Isis, who was seen as a lunar deity in the Greco-Roman world).

Obviously then, it would not be amiss for a festival of Serapis to transpire at a time when one could appreciate the warmth of the sun. The ancient Serapia, which fell on April 25th, might not have had anything to do with the sun, but in the Northern Hemisphere the date is usually spring-like enough for most latitudes. Alternatively, a festival to Serapis might conceivably take place on the Summer Solstice, which is still celebrated with folk practices in many European countries, and which many modern Pagans have appropriated as a major holiday.

Finally we must remember what Serapis was. He was the principle god of Alexandria. He was a god of healing and dreams, a god of fertility and agriculture. He was the lord of the dead, savior of the living, and architect of human law and culture.

The following is a suggested festival to Serapis-Helios, Serapis in his solar aspect.

Time: the midsummer solstice, near sunset.
Place: outside if the weather is suitable, indoors if not.
Items Needed: an image of Serapis (can be printed off online), candles, incense, water, musical instruments, food and drink, a table and pedestal.

Arrange an altar to Serapis. The altar should be on a table or pedestal. It should contain an image of Serapis, at least one candle, an incense burner, and an empty bowl. It may also be decorated with flowers and food. Images of Isis and other Egyptian deities such as Anubis would not be out of place.

The participants should be dressed in colorful and festive attire. They should form a procession at some point away from the altar. If space is limited, they can circumambulate around the altar as required. The newer or lower ranking members of the group should be up front, with the presiding officers or priests in the back.

If any members are musicians, they should play a celebratory tune during the procession. If there are no musicians, then someone carrying a portable radio or CD player with a festive song should suffice.

Once at the altar, the music should cease. The lay members should stand respectfully silent. The presiding officer or priest should approach the altar with any attending officers or assistant clergy. The candle or candles should be lit.

At this point one must invoke Serapis with a prayer or hymn. There are numerous ancient hymns to Osiris available in translation that may suffice. Alternatively, one may construct one's own specifically to Serapis. It should invoke the major elements of the god. The following is only a suggestion:

"Serapis, great god of Alexandria. Lord of Eternity and Judge of the Dead. You taught men the useful art of agriculture, that they might feed themselves. You gave them laws and culture that they might no longer live in chaos. You taught them the sacred rites of religion that they might honor the gods. You send dreams of prophecy, and you cure the sick with miracles. The souls of the virtuous drink cool water at your feet in the Underworld, and in the sky you cast down warm rays over the world. Serapis, god of the sun, light our way!

May you delight in these offerings of fire and water. May you bless this group assembled to feast in your honor."

Pour the water reverently into the bowl, and light the incense.

At this point the feast should begin. Eat, drink and be merry, but remember to thank the god for the gifts of life.

The preceding was a bare bones suggestion for a celebratory rite. It is for individual and individual groups to foster their own relationship with this mighty deity, and construct rites that work best for them.

Bibliography

Turcan, Robert. *The Cults of the Roman Empire.* Translated by Antonia Nevill. Blackwell Publishing. Oxford, England. 1996.

Hymn to Serapis

by Sannion

Hail to thee, O great Serapis, lord of everlastingness
merciful god who hears all prayers and pours out his blessings
like the great river in flood season.
Thou art the bull-faced one in the land of shadows,
masterful and most potent, who makes the hearts of all spirits glad at his coming.
Thou art the glorious one, crowned with the rays of the sun,
exalted like no other god, whose fiery dance sets the stars in motion.
Thou art the snake-faced one,
who sleeps in the basket of grain and makes the barren earth fruitful once more.
Thou art the silent one, whose eyes shine from the darkness,
sending healing dreams to men while they sleep.
Every land knows thy name and men of every race solemnly celebrate thy mystic rites.
Hear my prayer, O Lord, and be kindly disposed towards me,
for thy name is sweet upon my lips,
and the thought of thee is never far from my mind.

NAVIGIUM ISIDIS

by Jeremy J. Baer

In Antiquity the Greco-Roman cult of Isis grew from the thousands year-old cult of the Kemetic goddess Aset. Through many centuries of evolution it received its definitive form under the Ptolemies, where it was linked with the cult of Serapis. Isis became the goddess of sailors, and sailors hailing from Ptolemy's capitol at Alexandria carried the cult all over the Hellenistic realms. As the Romans devoured the Hellenistic East, their lands in turn were consumed by the militants of the Isiac cult. By the time of Caligula, the cult of Isis which had been once repressed by the conservative Republican Senate seems to have infiltrated every imperial port, and had an especially heavy presence in Rome's port town of Ostia.

In the Roman solar calendar, March 5th and 6th was a time of celebration by the cult adherents. This was the Navigium Isidis, The Vessel of Isis. March 5th was the start of the sailing year in much of the Mediterranean, and Isis had become a divine patron of sailors, for myth told how she had searched the waters for remains of her murdered brother-husband Osiris. There was also a powerful metaphor at work: the sea was the waves of fate upon which humanity drifted, and Isis was the savior goddess whose intervention could steer humanity on the right course.

In his *Golden Ass*, Apuleius gives us an interesting look at this colorful festival. There was a kind of carnival costumed procession of people, many of whom were not necessarily initiates in the cult but simple participants in the joyous activities. The men arrived first. Some dressed as a certain profession, some as animals, still others as mythological figures. A few cross-dressed as women, perhaps imitating a practice of the Dionysian cults. Then came the women. They were clothed in white, and had flowers in their hair. They flung flower petals to the streets as they passed by.

The truly faithful of the cult followed behind. Many carried lamps - lamps having a connotation of protective magic in Ancient Egypt. Others carried torches and candles. Singers and musicians dedicated to the god Serapis proceeded next, who with flute and pipe played cultic melodies. Next came new initiates to the cult. The women were veiled, the men shaven headed, all were clad in linen and shaking sistra.

The priests and ministers of the cult were next in procession. They carried holy water to preside over the ceremonies, as well as various items of cultic significance. Some of the priests were dressed as gods connected with the Isiac cult, such as Anubis. Finally, the high priest of the cult brought up the rear.

A newly fashioned boat decked with Egyptian symbols was waiting for the procession in port. There the high priest prayed over the boat and ritually consecrated it with a torch, an egg, and some sulphur. The vessel was filled with spice and other offerings. The ropes were cut, and off the boat drifted into the high seas.

Back at the temples, the high priest and his ministers said prayers for the health of the emperor, the Senatorial and Equestrian orders, and the Roman people (rather generous of a cult once persecuted by the Romans). In Greek the priests blessed sailors and announced the start of the sailing season. The crowd then adorned a silver statue of Isis with flowers and greenery, and kissed her feet.

The cult may have varied from port to port, but in general it was cause for spring time merriment.

A Modern Navigium Isidis

Modern recreations present the adherent with difficulty. The numbers of followers are few and scattered. Even if they could congregate in one place, there would be obvious financial difficulty in buying a boat and filling it with exotic spices (not to mention that setting an empty boat adrift with goods might violate local maritime laws).

Then there are those like myself who do not even reside in a port town. I live in the hills of a landlocked state, hundreds of miles from the sea. Robert Turcan can find little evidence for the cult of Isis in rural areas of the Roman Empire where sailors did not tread, but nonetheless that is modern reality for some of us.

We can only do the best with what we have, and try to recreate the spirit of the occasion if not the actual events. As I see it, there are three forces at work here:

1) reverence to Isis, especially in her aspect as a patron of sailors
2) a general sense of spring time merry making, almost carnival in scope
3) prayers for the broader social order

As to the first, reverence for Isis by the solitary modern can be done with sincerity if not always pomp. Lighting a candle or lamp to Isis and keeping it burning for as long as practical that day seems appropriate. Also appropriate is burning some exotic incense or spice to the goddess in lieu of actually filling a boat. If one lives near a body of water (be it an ocean, a lake, or even a decent sized stream), casting a votive object into the water might prove satisfying to the goddess. The one problem here is that local micro-climates vary – March 5 may be the start of Spring in the Mediterranean, but in some locales it may be the dead of winter, complete with frozen bodies of water! Finally, prayers of one's choosing should be made to the goddess. While most of us aren't sailors, we can pray to Isis in her higher aspect as Mistress of Heaven, deliverer from fate.

The second element of merry making should provide no problem. Who doesn't want to have some fun? Of course, everyone's definition of fun is different. I do not see myself cross-dressing as some ancient males did, but perhaps a night out in town with some friends would not be amiss. Let adherents decide as individuals or as individual groups how best to swing into the mood of things.

Finally, the prayers of the high priest demonstrated a concern for broader social reality, and as concerned citizens we should be no different. Prayers can be made for the heath and guidance of one's modern head of state and other leading statesmen – unless it offends one's political sensibilities. But even if individual politicians can offend, certainly a prayer for the general welfare of one's society can be embraced by someone of any politics. Living in ecologically sensitive times as we do, and given that Isis was linked with fertility and abundance, praying for the health of the planet and its ecosystem might be in order for those so inclined. If nothing else, pray for one's loved ones and their safety and happiness.

As every port probably celebrated the Navigium a little differently, we can afford a variety of modern recreations of this ancient festival. What matters most is that whatever we chose to do, we remain true to our goddess and ourselves. By doing so we can happily and reverently resurrect an ancient faith into contemporary reality.

Bibliography

Turcan, Robert. *The Cults of the Roman Empire*. Translated by Antonia Nevill. Blackwell Publishing. Oxford, England. 1996.

Isis Poetic

by Russell Goodman

Looking out past me,
past the realistic scene before me,
past the veil of reality,
into some unknown space.

Isis, hiding behind there,
secrets of the tapestry of life,
woven carefully with fine threads.

A single knot unravels,
a thin line my life unspun
set back into place,
under your watchful eye.

Here I am.

Trying to see beyond where I am,
projecting forward into time,
desiring a place not there yet,
willing a moment to arrive unripened.

Watch over our lives with compassion,
reach out your gentle hand of nurture,
hold our rocking souls in your embrace.

Saturate my moments with a rich life,
keep my soul nourished by the waters.

May I always know your home as mine,
may we receive your wisdom as enlightenment.

Cradle our consciousness to your heart,
provide us with your endless kindness,
blessed honey-sweet milk of love,

Mother-Above-All, Deathless Isis.

A Mother's Love

by Grace

The sharp stones still burn from the heat of the day as I settle down upon the ledge. My eyes scan the lands before me, the dunes of nearly endless sand still and peaceful in the glow of twilight. This is my favorite time of day, for it is where I am: not a part of day or a part of night. My home lies in the space between the golden light of life and the serene stillness of death, and I am one of the few who finds easy joy in slipping between both. As I am seated upon the highest point of the Western mountains, with Ra sliding into the Dark Beneath behind me, and the winding down of frantic mortal life before me, I have time to pause and reflect.

There are so many things my mind flickers over, the thoughts and prayers of both the Easterners and Westerners for guidance, protection, and mere blessings ever present. My sharp ears perk, as I sit in contemplation, when I pick up the distressed cries of a child. The tears tug at my heart and draw me from my place upon the mountain until I am pacing the streets of a busy city, looking for the source. The child, when I find him, is huddled against the wall of a building, tears streaking down his dirty face as he looks around in fear and cries for the mother he cannot find. The sky is darkening; it really is far too unsafe for a babe so young to be lost. It reminds me of darker, lonelier times and I move forward without thought, gently touching the dark hair. The child knows I am there and turns, pressing against my legs. His tears quiet as he finds comfort in my presence. It draws a smile from me and I stroke his hair with affection. No one will bother him, not while I stand guard over him.

"Your face... there is so much love there," a voice says from the center of the street.

My eyes lift. The mortals go about their lives, perhaps unaware of me in the shadows standing guard and She who stands amongst them in the street. Still, they stay away from my corner, and the crossroads in which She stands are left alone and untouched in unconscious reverence for Her grace. Even as far as I am from Her, I feel Her love for both me and the boy like the gentle kiss of the dawning sun.

"I feel for him," I respond to Her. "Those who are lost are mine to protect. I remember the pain they feel, but you know this, of course. You were there."

"And I was the one who showed you the way home," Isis says. She smiles again, and then a woman is moving through the crowds toward me and the boy, calling his name. The child turns from me as his mother runs up, pulling him into her arms. On her lips are praises to myself and to the Great Mother. I watch them and give them my blessings as she gathers up her son and moves on toward the safety of home. With a small chuckle, I move through the thinning crowd toward the glowing goddess who watches me.

"Have you come to guide a frantic mother to her lost child?" I ask Her, standing like a shadow by Her glorious side.

"Yes, but not only this. I'm an efficient multi-tasker," She replies with a playful wink. "Walk with me?"

"Always," I reply, taking Her hand.

We walk side by side through the city, allowing the prayers of the people to flow around us in a pleasant hum as they let the evening take them. Soon enough, we step from city streets into sand, and continue our silent walk out into the moon-kissed dunes that glow like silver.

"You have been distant of late," She says once we are alone.

"Have I?" I ask calmly. Despite the serenity of my tone, there is a fine edge of worry in my belly. I know I will always have Her love, but I worry for Her feelings. Does She feel neglected? I hope not.

She laughs, a throbbing, musical sound. "I see past your masks, my fond companion," She says. "I assure you I do not feel abandoned by you. I merely worry that there is something that gnaws at your mind and disturbs your thoughts."

I shake my head, watching as a scorpion scuttles across the sands. "Nothing special," I reply. "The world is changing. People are becoming something new and different. I wonder sometimes if their progression will ever be something we cannot control."

"Do you want to control them?" She asks curiously.

"Perhaps control was not the word I desired," I say. "My concern lies more in the fact that there are so many of them, and more to come as time passes. As the years pass, who we are and what they need of us changes. I wonder sometimes how they will change in future years, and how we will have to change with them."

"Are you afraid of these changes?"

I smile slightly, shaking my head. "No. No matter how much they change, when they are lost, I will be there to guide them. I just wonder about it sometimes. Ma'at has told me that such wonders are similar to trying to predict the direction of water flow. She says progression happens for a reason, so why concern myself over the results of such progression?"

Isis grins at me, again impish and playful. "Ma'at is very logical. Wonder is the playground of the innocent, and those who do not step into innocence once in a while soon find their existence cumbersome."

"Do you ever wonder about it?" I ask Her, curious to Her answer. Isis is grace and glory, love in its greatest form, and she can be as playful as Bast, but I wonder sometimes if She worries. I have seen Her in sorrow, but never worry.

Her beautiful eyes, dark as the night itself, look over the merciless lands of the Red God as She considers my question. "There comes a time in every mother's life," She replies, "where she wonders if she made a mistake. When the house is empty and the hearth cold and her children are out in the world to make use of the life she has given them, there is a shadow in her soul that wonders if they will forget her love for them and feel alone as she does then. That is the greatest fear of a mother's heart: not that she is alone, but that her children feel they are." She stops and turns Her radiance on me. "They are all my children, and I do not wonder what they will become, for Ma'at is great and all will eventually succumb to Her will. I wonder instead if, in the dying light of day, when all feels like it is coming to an end, will they fear that they are alone?"

Her words are powerful, and I understand what She is saying to me. "In the dying light of day," I say softly, "when all feels like it is coming to an end, they will open their hearts to You, my Queen, and they will feel their Mother's love fill their hearts, and they will know peace."

She smiles brilliantly at me and reaches forward, stroking her hand over my cheek and down one ear lovingly. "You're such a good boy, Anubis," She says delightfully, and turns to continue across the sands. I am left, slightly surprised at both the tender words and their amusing context. I laugh, and then catch up to Her as She makes Her way down to the kingdom of Her Husband.

THE ISIDIS NAVIGIUM:
GRECO ROMAN RITUAL OF ANTIQUITY IN A MODERN CONTEXT; PEOPLE ARE RETURNING TO THE ANCIENT WAYS*

by Karen Tate

It is my honor and privilege to present to the American Academy of Religion's Western Region, the impact Isis, She of Ten Thousand Names, can have on contemporary minds and hearts. She has inspired my two published books – *Sacred Places of Goddess: 108 Destinations*, which has been endorsed by the Joseph Campbell Foundation, and my second book, *Walking An Ancient Path; Rebirthing Goddess on Planet Earth*. And today I share with you the history of the Isidis Navigium, on the tenth anniversary of the Iseum of Isis Navigium and The Isis Ancient Culture Society, reviving this ancient ritual of Isis in contemporary culture each year for the last decade. We believe that when this Festival of Isis began to be celebrated on the beaches of Los Angeles in 1998, the founders and volunteers made history. It was probably the first time this festival was recreated in such grandeur to celebrate the worship of Isis, She of Ten Thousand Names, in modern times.

These artifacts and reliefs depict the annual festival of the launching of the ships, also called the Isidis Navigium or Ploephesia, usually held the first weekend in March by devotees of Isis in ancient Greece, Rome, Turkey and Egypt. You may recall in *The Golden Ass*, also known as *The Metamorphoses*, one of the great works of literature, the character Apuleius received salvation and hope from Isis during the Navigium as he was transformed from an ass, back into a man.

Our modern ritual is held just before the Neo-Pagan Spring Equinox celebrations, thus likewise for contemporary devotees it is a time when the light and spring dew is upon us bringing hope and promise for the coming year. Today and in ancient times, the Isis celebration, which included dancing, feasting and processions, focused on seeking the Goddess' blessing for ships, sailors and travelers, as well as for successful journeys. Practitioners of Egyptian mysteries, who were well versed in recognizing cosmic meaning in mundane symbols also assumed multiple layers of meaning for ritual action and would have understood that the sea voyages being blessed during this ritual of Egyptian and Roman antiquity were synonymous with the individual's voyage through life.

When re-creating this ancient-modern ritual today, we focused closely on this concept in adapting ancient practices to modern sensibilities. We also borrowed heavily from the material culture and symbolism of this period in history and retained as many of the actual elements of the original ritual as possible. But before comparing the second century rituals with those of the twentieth century, let us examine just why Isis deserved such devotion then and now.

According to the 2nd century CE writer, Aelius Aristides, Isis may herself be Holy Wisdom, the Creatrix of the material world, when he refers to Wisdom as, "the mediatrix between Serapis and men." In the Nag Hammadi scriptures Isis is Sophia, and we hear her beseeching her children not to forget her in the Gnostic texts called "Thunder, Perfect Mind." Isis, or Auset, a descendant of the Creator Gods of Egypt has always been looked upon as a beneficent mother and savior goddess. It was she who bestowed sovereignty upon the pharaohs giving the god-kings the right to rule their kingdoms.

Her devotion transcended class and culture. Her worship spread from the shores of Egypt, throughout the Mediterranean, into Ireland, England, Gaul, Anatolia, the Middle East and along the Silk Road, into Russia. She was a healer, a wife and lover, a mother, and not just to her son Horus, but to her devoted. She resurrected the dead and provided her milk of abundance.

One of her most important attributes was her accessibility. By her myths, not only was she powerful, savvy and a loving protectress, but equally important, the people felt she could understand their pain. The people knew her as a Goddess who had experienced the sorrow of loss, betrayal, and strife. They believed she could understand and alleviate their sorrow and if they performed the right rituals and curried her favor, they too might have some control over the forces of chaos that threatened their lives. She could provide light, truth, salvation and security.

According to R. E. Witt, author of *Isis in the Ancient World*, "If western civilization could have somehow developed on a matriarchal basis, Isis might have been too stubborn a mistress to dethrone." She became an enormous universal power in the post-Alexandrian world, a foe to Jesus and his Apostles as they preached Christianity because she was all things to men.

Dare I say an entire conference might be devoted to her and her worship across time, continents and cultures, similar to the vast 1997 exhibit compiled at the Palazzo Reale in conjunction with the Department of Culture of Milan entitled *Iside, The Myth, The Mystery, The Magic*. This *Iside* exhibit was comprised of thousands of artifacts from across the globe representative of her earliest devotion forward to 17th century opera playbills and 19th century magic shows of Robert Houdin honoring Isis, the Mistress of Magic, further showing how Isis has lived on in popular culture.

Contemporary Isian practitioners of the Isidis Navigium, equally enamored with Isis, invoked her at each corner, above and below with the words, "Isis is All Things and All Things are Isis." To them, she is considered the Oldest of the Old, her aspects and epithets dating back to Inanna and Ishtar, and her essence a primary ingredient in the primordial stew of pre-history. No matter their ancestry, Isis calls to women and men today for all the same reasons she was beloved in ancient times. She hears, understands and provides. Isis transcends time and culture. All Goddesses are embodied in Isis, as her own aretalogy professes. The All-Powerful, All-Knowing Isis could provide her devotees with a fuller, more abundant and satisfying life. She is the Great Mother who suckles all of humanity at her breast. And the Isidis Navigium, seen to have so much over-lap with Neo-Pagan Spring Equinox, was the perfect ritual or common ground, to bring together practitioners of all traditions under one umbrella to worship their Mother Goddess.

But let us delay no longer. I invite you to close your eyes for the telling of the ritual itself. Close your eyes if you will. Allow yourself to be transported back. Let us "Make Way for the Procession," as was shouted in ancient and recent times, to announce the beginning of the sacred spectacle.

At the head of the Greco Roman procession were magistrates, gladiators, philosophers, men wearing dresses, wigs and gilt sandals. Exotic animals such as a she-bear, monkeys and donkeys walked alongside their handlers. Next came women in shining white dresses, garlanded with spring blossoms, who tossed flowers along the route. They carried polished mirrors and combs which they applied to the hair of their divine Queen. Others perfumed the path with scented oils. Throngs of men and women carried all manner of illumination - torches, lamps, and wax tapers. There were singers and musicians playing flutes. Then in line came the initiates dressed in their white linen robes. The women were adorned in gauze veils while the men sported shaved or tonsured heads. The tinkling of their sistra, the sacred rattles of Isis, could be heard. Next came the priests holding representations of the deities Isis and Sarapis, and miniature altars. Another lifted up emblems of Justice, still another held the golden pitcher from which droplets of milk trickled onto the path. The last priest carried the vannus mystica, a branched winnowing fan of gold. Deities walked in the procession. Spectators could see

Anubis, with half his face black and half gold and Isis in her bovine aspect resembling Hathor or Io.

During some Navigiums, people [paused at] stations along the way, reminiscent of Stations of the Cross where hymns were sung to the Goddess. Lucius Apuleius made his way forward to nibble upon roses so that he might be transformed once again into a man. Transfiguration over, we focus on the Ship of Isis near the seashore. The white sails are emblazoned with prayers to Isis for successful conduct of the season's navigation. The High Priest held a lighted torch, an egg and some sulphur with which he symbolically cleansed the vessel before uttering more prayers to dedicate the ship laden with offerings to Isis. Upon the waves libations were made and milk was poured. Soon, cables cast off, the ship slipped down into the water and glided out to sea with no crew to guide her as she disappeared toward the horizon. State prayers were said and concluded with the formula dismissal, "The ship has been let go." Glad tidings had all around, the people now returned to their homes but not before gathering up garland and greenery left behind from the ritual and kissing the feet of the silver statue of Isis which had been set up upon the temple steps.

Isis, as a maritime deity, was depicted on coins in various forms – with sistrum and sacred vessel in her hand, aboard a boat holding its sails, and in the palanquin which parades her image. As late as the latter half of the fourth century Rome's mints provided various depictions of Isis on coins as protectress of harbors, patroness of navigation, inventor of the sails - all declaring open war on Christianity. A vota publica coin can still be seen depicting Constantine on one side with Isis looking forward from her ship on the other. The people were hardly giving up on the Goddess who literally and spiritually provided them their daily bread.

Flash forward to the twentieth century Navigium. It took three months of intense preparation to plan the Ploephesia and re-create clothing, decorations and accoutrement reflective of the material culture of the Egyptian and Greco-Roman Isis ritual, bringing alive this time and place so many of us found so provocative and full of power, mystery and magic. Labors of love and devotion, ritual garb and sacred tools such as sistra and menat collars were developed, both items from antiquity which enable the clergy who wears them to embody the Goddess, bestow blessings and ward off evil. Craftspersons devised ways to make copper ankhs and was scepters. From four-inch tall line drawings in the books of E.A. Wallis Budge, images of deities were transferred onto large surfaces by artists, painters and carpenters to create life-size mobile temple walls. Then finally on the first weekend in March, under the rays of a powerful noontime sun, an auspicious time for Egyptian magical work, the ritual would finally be unveiled to the public on Pt. Dume State Beach in Malibu, California. What follows is a composite re-telling of several rituals held on the Pacific Coast shores over ten years, combining not just ancient and modern ritual practices, but revitalizing that connection between devotees of the Great Mother Goddess, then and now, using the red cord of Isis as a lynch-pin.

A herald shouted, "Let the procession begin!" Facilitators and spectators dressed in their most elaborate and festive ritual attire began chanting and attendees followed suit. "People are returning to the ancient ways." Clergy who embodied the Egyptian deities with whom they felt the most reverence and connection came first – representatives of Isis, Anubis and Bast, followed by priests and priestesses dressed in white carrying sistra. People wearing masks, drummers, participants carrying golden fans, mirrors, candles, depictions of Hathor as the golden cow, golden pitchers of milk for the blessing of the ships and statues of Isis and Anubis. Along the path was a doubloon tosser who threw into the crowd plastic gold and silver coins from the New Orleans' Mardi Gras carnival krewes of Isis, Cleopatra and Thoth, connecting modern festivals with those of the ancient Egyptians. Participants scurried to pick up the doubloons hailing down upon them, excited to have these mementos to take home in remembrance of this sacred and glorious day! And yes, there were the altars and animals – snakes, dogs, and birds. Facilitators felt Goddess herself blessed the rite by sending her creatures of the sea to attend. No Navigium held on the beach was ever held without the presence of either a dolphin, sea lion or pod of whales in attendance. And participants felt inspired to set up their own impromptu altars of devotion along the ritual path.

Serpentining along the beach, chanting and drumming, the group stopped at several stations, where the clergy of these Temples of various deities imparted either spiritual guidance or sacred amulets upon those in the procession. After honoring Isis with songs of praise, the procession moved on, with the ultimate destination, her temple, then the launching of the Isis boats. At the Isis Temple the doors were symbolically opened and therein were meditations and drama, with prayers from yesteryear and today read from scrolls. Offerings of songs and dance, along with flowers, food and drink were made to She of Ten Thousand Names. With rites within the cella complete, bearers of the golden and veiled palanquin of Isis lifted up her statue and carried her to the beach to oversee the launching of her ship and the climax of the ritual. At the water's edge, after libations with milk, beer and honey, Isis bestowed her blessings on those gathered for their abundance in the coming year, while her boat was launched.

As one might imagine this element of the Navigium posed quite a challenge, for certainly we had no actual wooden ship laden with offerings that might be launched on the shores of Malibu beach. But the challenge was met and overcome with creativity and flair. In fact it became an integral and much anticipated part of the ritual over the years. The solution to this dilemma came to the founder of the ritual in the same way as much of the inspiration for this entire rite – in a dream. To launch the boat of Isis, contemporary clergy handed each participant an ecologically friendly boat made of colored ice, which they were to launch into the Pacific Ocean imbued with their breath of intention for the coming year. Next, now having cast their "vessel of desire" upon the waves, the group, still chanting and drumming proceeded to a life-size image of Isis mounted on the beach to make their final offerings of incense and rose petals, in thanks to their Mother Goddess for hearing their prayer. The ritual was concluded with the song, "We are an old people. We are a new people. We are the same people, stronger than before."

As can be seen from the aforementioned account, the contemporary Isidis Navigium retained many of the qualities of its ancient predecessor, including the flexibility to change its pattern as circumstances sometimes dictated. Away from the beach, or for indoor Navigium rituals, a water channel depicting the Nile River with temples along its banks was created. Attendees launched not boats of ice, but palm-size red-colored ice in the shape of hearts – "their heart's desire" upon the moving life-giving waters. And at the Japanese Gardens, many of the ritual elements remained the same. There were dancers and processions complemented with banner carriers. Within the cella the rite reflected performances and ritual theatre with a pronouncement from Isis herself. The launching of the boats was overseen by Isis and Anubis, and first to cast her boat upon the waters was our contemporary Cleopatra who issued forth her prayers for the people of her kingdom.

Scholar R. E. Witt cites Herodotus who states the first people to institute festivals, processions and religious presentations were the Egyptians, from whom the Greeks received their knowledge. Ancient writers detail the Isidis Navigium already being held during the reign of Tutankhamen during the 18th Dynasty in Egypt, in the Greco Roman world by the 1st century BC, continuing on until possibly as late as the 5th century CE. There is evidence the Navigium was celebrated in Paris, in Turkey along the shores of the Black Sea, and in Germany during the

Middle Ages. Today there are vestiges of the ritual being performed during Christian rituals such as the Blessing of the Fleet and the Feast of St. Agatha in Sicily. Other close associations are the Festival of Lights, or the Epiphany of the Christians and Coptics. And Muslims, on the second day of the Eid el Adha feast, embark on small boats and take to the waters, hearkening back to the Isidis Navigium. We cannot forget, cultural celebrations such as Carnivale and Mardi Gras which owe much to the sacred spectacles that was the Isidis Navigium honoring Isis. And finally, Isis passes her baton to Mary the Mother of Jesus, who becomes Stella Maris, the new "watcher of the waters" as people attempt to navigate the treacherous waters of their life's journey.

Yes, people today see that the dominant patriarchal cultures and religions serve the few and not the many. Like their ancestors, they are seeking alternative ways to restore order from chaos. With the contemporary Isidis Navigium, new people look back and cherry-pick old ways, to have a meaningful spiritual experience and as activists, make a political statement, right here on the Pacific coast of California. The people are hardly giving up on the Goddess who literally and spiritually provides them their daily bread.

Editors' Note: Excerpted with permission from Walking an Ancient Path: Rebirthing Goddess on Planet Earth *(O Books, 2008). This paper was read at WESCOR American Academy of Religion Conference in March 2008.*

Isis, Nuit, Sol and the Ox

by Payam Nabarz

(A poem about river Isis in Oxford, inspired by the floods last year)

She has burst her banks,
She is very wet today;
Isis flows everywhere.
Isis is reaching for Nuit;
water levels rise higher.
Dawn arrives before the Sun's chariot,
Nuit is moved by her daughter's overnight labour.
She reaches down, clouds descend
haze engulfs the land of the Ox.

Mist and river meet, sisterly gossip follows.
Swans and ducks swim where a week ago
the footballers played.
Ducks in the rugby field cheer
the swans in the football pitch paddling
between the goal posts.
A feathered goal keeper
in the game of Isis v Ox.

There will be no Oxen fording today.
Bridges surrounded by water,
wooden islands with no visible paths
of entry or escape,
Footpaths, tow paths, deer tracks
all are submerged,
a highway for the fishes.

Only a single path remains,
one made by Man
from stone, rock and sweat.
The path is just visible above the water line,
like a water snake swimming in the Isis.

Walking on this narrow path,
or is it walking on water?
Through the mists of Oxon.
Heading towards the dawn,
which appears at the end of the golden path.
Nuit leaves her daughter, mists disappear,
as the sun begins its daily journey across the sky;

but Isis keeps on rising up heavenward,
this time reaching for her lover; Sol.
Sol-Osiris too is reaching for her
with his penetrating rays.
His reflection is engulfed by her,
a fiery globe floating in the river of space,
together bringing nourishment to the land of Ox.
It's going to be a beautiful day
on the Port Meadow sea front.

Note: as I finished writing this prose and headed back from Port Meadow, Oxford, along the towpath, I ended up accidentally ankle deep in the river on one of the flooded paths. Moral of the story is: you can't write about a flood and not get wet!

Isis Worship for Hellenic Polytheists

by Sannion

Aset (or Isis to give the more familiar Greco-Roman form of her name) is one of the most popular "gateway gods" in the Kemetic pantheon. One is perhaps not too surprised by this, for she was also one of the most important goddesses in ancient Egypt, and one of the most popular outside of Egypt as well. Her worship spread like wildfire through Greece and Italy during the Hellenistic era (it is truly startling to see how often Pausanias mentions a temple or festival of the goddess during his travels through mainland Greece). Under the Roman Empire her cult was carried to lands as distant as Spain, Germany, and the British Isles in the West and Turkey, Afghanistan and Russia in the East. (One aretalogy even claims that Isis is the goddess of the Ganges River in India, but I do not recall any archaeological evidence in support of this claim. However, I wouldn't be the least bit surprised to discover that the wandering goddess had made it that far by the end of antiquity.) So clearly Isis was an ecumenical goddess, as the praise poems written in her honor constantly remind us.

In this essay, I shall focus on how a contemporary practitioner of Hellenic polytheism might worship the goddess today, without necessarily adopting Kemetic reconstructionism in full.

The first thing that I would suggest, however, is familiarizing yourself with those traditions, even if you do not intend to incorporate them into your practice. Kemetic worship is similar in many regards to traditional Hellenic worship. Offerings are given, hymns recited, incense is burned, food and drink is shared with the gods, and before the worship begins purification is to be performed. In all this they are strikingly similar.

But there are also differences between them, usually involving a degree of emphasis, the order that things are done, and the amount of repetition involved. In Egyptian practice each step of the service is accompanied by specific ritual phrases that need to be repeated a number of times to increase their potency. These phrases often allude to mythological events or personalities that may or may not be directly connected to the deity who is being honored. In this way a network of associations is established, and the act of worship takes on profound – even cosmological – significance.

Another important distinction to consider is how the offerings are to be treated once they are given. In Hellenismos the libation is poured out, either upon the god's altar or into a trench dug into the earth. The portion of the god's meal is either burnt on the altar or left out for them. After it is given it is not to be touched again, except when we respectfully dispose of it if we are making our offerings in our own home and do not have access to fire or a pit. In the temples of Egypt things were done differently. The offering was presented to the god. It was invited to partake of the spiritual substance of the meal and then the priest consumed the physical substance of the offering himself, with no part of it being wasted, as such things were considered an affront in a land of scarcity where the desert always threatens to destroy and consume life and its precious resources.

You may have noted an important point in the above paragraph: I said in the temples. The Egyptians had an elaborate daily ritual that they performed for the gods in their temples. While temples belonged to the gods in Greece as well, they were not necessarily thought of as the house of the god in the same way that the Egyptians did. For the Egyptians, the god actually resided in his or her temple. The cult statue was not meant merely to represent the deity – it was the physical body in which the spirit of the god resided. Each morning the priests would rouse the god from its slumber, wash and clothe it, feed and entertain it throughout the day, before finally putting it to sleep at night. These rituals were thought necessary to increase the potency of the god and make it well-disposed towards mankind.

The temple was the house of the god, but it was also in some sense a battery that stored the spiritual energy of the god and channeled it out into the surrounding countryside to ensure the health, prosperity, and protection of the people that lived nearby. As a result, the average person never set foot inside the temple. It was too holy, being the residence of the deity, and it was too dangerous, being the repository of the god's power. Only specially trained priests were ever permitted inside and even then only the most senior priests were granted entrance into the remotest parts of the temple, where the cult image was stored. The closest that the average person ever got to seeing the god was during festival days when the deity's image was carried out in procession.

Now, it is false to assume that the common Egyptians never had anything to do with their gods as a result of this. They were permitted into the outer courts of the temple, and some temples had chambers reserved for pilgrims or people seeking healing miracles, oracles, or dream incubation. The common people also worshipped the gods on their own, keeping small, cheaply produced terracotta or wood statues in small niches carved into the walls of their homes where they performed their own regular – even daily – rites in honor of the deity.

However, we don't know a whole lot about what they actually did in that domestic worship. They didn't bother to write down most of it, or if they did it hasn't survived through the centuries. You can get an idea of what that was like by reading my article on Greco-Egyptian domestic worship (http://www.neosalexandria.org/domestic_worship.htm). But one thing that we can say with certainty is that it wasn't the same as the temple cultus. It couldn't be, for the commoner had only a representation of the god whereas the priests cared for the actual body of the deity, whose spirit had been installed in the statue through specific rites. As such, different things needed to be done on a daily basis.

Now, since much better information has come down to us about the temple cultus – including complete rituals – many modern Kemetic practitioners have turned to this information in reconstructing ancient Egyptian religion. They perform the elaborate ceremonies and observe all of the religious prohibitions attached to them. They have brought the spirit of the god into its statue and they clothe and feed it and keep it locked away in a naos-shrine or covered with a cloth when they are not actively engaged in worship. This is a fine and very effective way to honor the deity – however it is not the only method open to us. Nor is it necessarily the best one if you are not intending to act the part of a priest. After all, as a Hellenic polytheist interested in the goddess Isis, you are much more in the position of the common Egyptian than his priestly brother, and therefore it is probably to these traditions that you should look when determining the form of worship that you intend to use when honoring the deity, not the temple rites.

Thus in making your offerings to the god you have several options open to you. You may do it like the Egyptian priest in the temple, presenting it to the god so that it may consume the spiritual substance, then eat the remains yourself. This can be a powerful thing, sharing a meal with them and enjoying their company as you do so. But if the "No! What is given to the gods belong to them! Touching it afterwards is bad and destroys the mojo!" approach of Hellenismos is too hard-wired into your brain, you may also leave it for them, since it appears that this is what many regular Egyptians did when they visited the temple. (There were even offering tables and niches to house statues outside the temple, intended for use by the commoners. Although this appears to be a late development, since we generally find them around the time of the New Kingdom, when things became more democratized and a more personally-focused piety became evident in the prayers and inscriptions of the period, that still makes it part of the traditional religion, with a long history. After all the New Kingdom is roughly 1550–1070 BCE and thus still pretty damn old!) And some of us who identify as Greco-Egyptian polytheists have developed a nice compromise. We will share a portion of the offering with the god, eating some and leaving the rest.

There are, however, no definite answers here, and through trial and error you will have to determine the methods that are most effective. However, keep in mind that worship isn't just about what we like, what makes us feel good. Yes, that is an important element. If you never get anything out of it, if you're only ever just going through the motions – something is wrong, and you may need to look elsewhere to fix it. But religion is about building up a reciprocal relationship, about cultivating the good favor of the gods. You need to be respectful and pay attention to what they want and need, just like with any type of relationship. If your human partner wanted you to do the dishes and you always left them in the sink or if they had an allergic reaction to your perfume and you wore it anyway – how well do you think your relationship would be going then? When you are worshiping a god you are supposed to be making them feel good. Giving them things, saying nice things about them, spending time focused on them and in their presence.

So, as you do this pay attention. Try different things and see if they work. Do you get a feeling of intensified connection or does it feel flat and meaningless to you? Do certain ritual actions work better than others, certain types of music, certain scents, certain offerings? Do you get a feeling of "no – not this" or does the god make their opinion known through other ways: an offering bowl cracking, incense refusing to light, noxious clouds of charcoal smoke filling the room, you start to feel queasy and ill for no good reason every time you start to do ____, etc. These can all be signs that something needs to change and you should pay attention to them. And if you aren't particularly sensitive or have trouble picking up divine clues from gods you haven't worked with extensively in the past, you can always resort to divination. There's nothing wrong with asking "How did the ritual go – would you like me to do something different?" After all, we're doing this for the gods – so why not ask the gods directly how they feel about it? That way we're not wasting their time – or our own.

One thing in particular that Isis is concerned with – and many of the other Egyptian gods as well – is purity. In Egypt the lowest level of priests were called *wabu* "the pure ones" – and the level of purity and discipline demanded of them only increased as they rose higher in the ranks. They had to be pure in body and soul. This meant abstaining from sex and certain foods (like pork, fish, and beans), adhering to a stringent ethical system, avoiding whole classes of people (such as swineherds) and so forth. They bathed multiple times a day and even shaved off all of the hair on their body – and yes, I do mean all of it – in order to maintain physical cleanliness. The demands of priestly purity were so great that they felt a normal person could only observe them for a short period of time. Therefore priests belonged to a *phyle* or tribe, and each tribe served in the temple for a period of three to four months in continuous rotation. When a priest's *phyle* was not on duty he returned to his normal life and family, often with a completely unrelated occupation. (Some off-duty priests, however, rented out their services as religious experts, becoming magicians or itinerant folk-healers/shamans. And a few groups or exceptional individuals served full-time in the temples, particularly when the priesthood was a hereditary position.)

This aspect of the religion was not left behind in Egypt when Isis was carried to foreign lands. If anything it intensified so that Isiacs gained a reputation for being especially devoted, austere, and concerned with purity. The poet Propertius found this aspect of Isis-worship especially annoying when his girlfriend took it up. He complained about her frequent baths in the frigid waters of the Tiber and how she was always doing this or that ritual, and worst of all, her refusal to sleep with him at various times of the month because of her devotion to that Egyptian goddess.

Considering all of that, I think it is important to observe great concern regarding matters of purity when worshipping Isis. Before Kemetics approach their naos-shrine they always bathe, and often sprinkle themselves and the sacred area with a mixture of water and natron for added effect. Natron is a naturally occurring mixture of sodium carbonate, sodium bicarbonate, salt, and sodium sulfate found in certain parts of Egypt. However it can be manufactured by mixing salt and baking soda together and baking it until it hardens. This is then broken up and stored until needed for ritual purposes, when small granules of the natron are dissolved in water. (Many prefer to use pure spring water for this. I have also provided only the most basic description of the process of making natron: if you're interested in using the substance you can find numerous recipes for it online.) The water is then daubed on the eyes, ears, face, hands, and the rest of the body (with some washing their mouths with it as well) to ensure that the whole body is clean. Certain ritual phrases are often recited at each instance. Now, you may choose to do this as well, or substitute your own Hellenic *khernips* or burn bay leaves or smudge with sage, or you may instead just choose to bathe thoroughly beforehand. Whatever method you employ, make sure that you are clean – and more importantly that you feel pure afterwards.

Then you should dress in new, clean clothing. Ideally these should not be your regular street clothes (certainly not what you were wearing before you bathed!) though it is not necessary to dress up in an elaborate Egyptian costume, complete with robe, sash, a big old ankh hanging from your neck, and a striped *nemes* head-dress. (Seriously: don't wear the *nemes*. It's just...wrong.) Some people have special sets of clothing that they wear only for ritual use – a simple robe or *gellabiya* or loose fitting trousers and shirt. Some wear normal modern attire, but just make sure that they are nice, neat, and clean.

It's really up to you and what you're most comfortable with; however, there are two things to consider. One, Egyptians were forbidden to wear wool or other animal products into the temple (except for certain ranks of priests who wore animal skins over their priestly robes as a sign of their high office) and instead wore simple linen garments. Secondly, color is very important. You should never wear red when worshiping Isis or her husband. Red is the color of Seth, and considering their history with him, it's not the sort of thing you want to bring into their sacred space. There are even admonitions against using things like lamps or bowls that are red in the Greek magical papyri, so consider that color off limits in your Isiac devotions unless she specifically tells you otherwise. If possible you should wear white clothing, for white symbolized purity and was the color that most Egyptian priests wore. Black is also a good Isis color, for black signified the rich, fertile earth of Egypt (which was originally called Kemet, "the Black Land") and gold is also a good color, for gold suggests the sun and the gods were frequently described as having golden skin.

Even before you get to the point of bathing, dressing and setting up the altar, you should be focused on internal purity: quieting your mind, leaving behind anger, frustration, and other negative emotions, and cultivating a joyous, reverent, and peaceful manner. Since Isis is so concerned with purity, you should try your best to lead a pure lifestyle leading up to your ritual. To get a better understanding of what this means you may want to read up on Egyptian religion and the priestly purity codes. You should generally abstain from sex, eating meat, ingesting harmful substances, and engaging in activities that you know to be ethically dubious leading up to your ritual.

One issue that might prove problematic for Hellenic polytheists is menstruation. While the ancient Greeks do not seem to have regarded menstruation as a thing of miasma or ritual pollution (Robert Parker's

Miasma: Pollution and Purification in Early Greek Religion has a good discussion of this), the ancient Egyptians did. As a result, many modern Kemetic women avoid approaching their naos and performing *senut* or their daily ritual while on their period. Whether you choose to do likewise is, of course, up to you, but I would advise feeling Isis out on the matter (perhaps with the aid of divination) before proceeding.

One of the differences between Kemeticism and Hellenismos is how sacred space is established. Within Hellenismos this is often not a very involved procedure. The shrine and altar are already considered holy because of their proximity to the deity. Often nothing more than sprinkling *khernips*, scattering barley, and burning incense or bay leaves is considered necessary. Kemetics, on the other hand, often perform elaborate preliminary rituals before they even approach the shrine. These involve circumnavigating the space multiple times, sprinkling with natron-water, fumigating with incense, untying cords, and so forth. The place needs to be charged with energy and returned to a state of primal purity, like the mound of creation that arose at *Zep Tepi*, the First Time.

If you are not following a strict reconstruction of the temple rites, you may feel that such elaborate procedures are unnecessary. The average Egyptian in their home probably didn't do this, after all. Therefore you may choose to do things in a more informal Hellenic style – or you could opt to include some elements from the Egyptian repertoire, producing a hybrid or Greco-Egyptian style. This is usually the method that I employ. While I am not as given to the ornate gestures and verbose repetition that my Kemetic brothers and sisters are, I often feel that something more is expected when I'm honoring Egyptian deities. And those methods can be very effective and beautiful, especially when you pause to consider the deeper meaning that lies behind the ritual actions and phrases. A whole cosmology is embedded in those things, and that can profoundly affect the outcome of your ritual when you make an effort to be mindful of it.

One of the most important aspects of Kemetic ritual which I do not recommend that Hellenics leave out, even if they choose not to incorporate the rest, is *hennu*. In Greek this act was called *proskynesis* which meant inclining towards, bowing, or kissing the earth. This is a powerful act, full of deep symbolic value. It is a humble acknowledgment of the awesome power of the deity, a reminder of our place in the world and its social hierarchy, that we are mortal and they are a god. It is not a servile act, a groveling at the feet of the master you fear, though some no doubt have interpreted it as such. It is rather a sign of admiration, of awe, and of love. When the Egyptian went down on his knees, bowing his head, he also pounded his chest with his closed fist, then extended the hand out to the god openly.

This dramatizes the experience of reverence. The kneeling brings us to the level of the earth, firm of foundation, just as the gods are the source of all life, all stability, all permanence in the universe. The bowed head acknowledges that we are in the presence of something greater than ourselves, and we pound our chest to show the effect that this has upon us, how it strikes us to our core and stirs the deepest emotions within us. We hit our hearts, for that is where the epiphany occurs, in the seat of our emotions. We touch our heart, as the gods touch us, and then we draw the hand from our heart back to the god, showing that our love is focused outwards, towards them.

Although the full *hennu* involved complete bowing, there was also the half *hennu*, more in keeping with the Greek *proskynesis*. This involved a nod of the head, a kissing of the hand, and waving the hand back towards the image of the god. Either way you choose to do it, I think this element should be incorporated. For in addition to all of the above symbolism, it shows something else, that we worship our gods through our bodies, with all that we have and all that we are. It is too easy for worship to become a mechanical thing, a series of memorized lines, of automatic acts. You scatter the barley, light the candles, pour the wine, and say a couple of pretty verses and you're done. Worship should be more than that, involving us on all levels. Not just something in our minds – but in our hearts, in our souls, and in our bodies as well. This gesture ensures this by requiring us to be conscious and thoughtful and active participants, as opposed to just passive spectators in our own worship. Plus it seems an especially appropriate action for Isis who is a very proud and regal deity, as she will no doubt remind you numerous times throughout the years.

So, what sort of things are fitting offerings for Isis? Well, many of the same things that we give to the Greek gods, actually. There are the standard food and drink offerings, and incense and candles and such, and she likes votive gifts as well. Actually, she likes them quite a lot. You see, Isis is a capital-L Lady. She is a high society goddess, the very personification of royalty. (Quite literally, as the name Aset means "the Throne".) She likes rare and expensive things, fine things and pretty things. We're talking gold and silver, shiny jewels, fine silks and delicate fabrics, and the very best perfumes. Nothing gaudy or overdone – she has very elegant, refined tastes and detests showiness. Of course, being who she is she will no doubt graciously accept whatever you offer her – for there is definitely a kind, nurturing maternal aspect to her – but she will also really let you know when you get her something that she likes.

Here are a couple good sites to give you an idea of what sorts of things people normally offer to Isis:

http://neosalexandria.org/isis.htm
http://www.llewellyn.com/bookstore/article.php?id=861
http://www.wepwawet.org/wiki/index.php?title=Isis

Something that Isis really likes is music. She was often represented holding a sistrum and her temples always had trained musicians and dancers, both for the entertainment of the goddess and her devotees. She seems to like a wide variety of musical styles, but a lot of people seem to come back to Middle Eastern or belly-dancing music for her.

Experiment with different things and see which produce the best results for you. You may also want to get – or better yet make – your own musical instruments and play them for her. Rattles, drums, and flutes are all traditional and easy to make, and more importantly easy to play, too! This can add a whole new level to your devotional practice. As can dancing, which is an especially Isiac form of worship, since she is a strongly sensual, alluring goddess who mastered the arts of deception and seduction. (She used these to trick Re into revealing his True Name, the source of his power, and also managed to outwit the god Seth on several occasions, including one that involved sexual games. And let us not forget that she revived her dead husband so that she could have sex with him to produce a legitimate heir. Although she may be concerned with purity, she is anything but a prude!)

Oh, you may be saying, *that is a very nice idea, but I have no musical ability and bad body image issues, so I couldn't possibly do those things.* Fine. Stop reading this article and go find yourself another goddess to worship, because in the long run you are not going to get along well with Isis.

And no, I'm not saying that you have to be a dancer or musician to honor her. Far from it! She may never even ask such things from you. But I'll tell you right now that there will be something that she does eventually ask of you, some way that she is going to challenge you, push you out of your comfort zone, and you had better be willing to bend – because she won't. Isis may wear a delicate and pretty silken glove – but the fist that goes in it is iron-hard and you do not want to get on her bad side. The more involved you get with her the more demands she is likely to make on you. And that, my friend, is why I have kept a respectful distance from her. She is a wonderful goddess and I have certainly warmed up to her over the last couple years, but there is no way I am getting any closer than this, because she isn't a goddess who does things by half measures, and she doesn't put up with a lot of whining and excuses.

Isis is into a lot of traditionally "girly things" and many times the closer people get to her, the more they find themselves attracted to such things as well. It's often not even on a conscious level and the person may not realize that it's happening until it's already too late. They start to dress nicer, begin wearing more jewelry and perfume, start noticing their appearance more and taking better care of their grooming and adopt healthier eating habits and an exercise routine, start eating things like fine chocolates, expensive wines, and taking long, sensual baths with scented oils and salts and, well, you get the picture. It's really rather amusing to watch all of this happen when the person had zero interest in such things before their involvement with Isis.

It makes perfect sense, I suppose. She is a seductive and strongly feminine goddess who is very good at persuading and influencing people, with or without their knowledge. At an early period she began acquiring a lot of the traits normally associated with Hathor, the goddess of love, seduction, and joyous celebration. The Greeks frequently equated Isis with their own Aphrodite, making her the patron of courtesans and dancing girls. She was also said to be incarnate in the person of Kleopatra, the last of the Ptolemaic monarchs, and we see there the wedding of a strong, powerful, fiercely independent femininity with a sensual, pleasure-loving personality that knew how to use deception, seduction, charm and the flesh to get what she wanted. Kleopatra, of all people, deserved to be called the New Isis.

In keeping with all this you should remember that Isis is very fond of flowers, the rose in particular. One of her most important festivals in Greco-Roman Egypt was the Rhodophoria, during which her statues were garlanded with wreaths of roses. Roses also adorned the ship on which Kleopatra, acting as Isis, met Marcus Antonius, acting as Dionysos – and it was also roses at an Isis festival that transformed Lucius from his asinine form back into human guise. In addition to roses you may give Isis lotus flowers, which are important symbols of rebirth and renewal in Egyptian religion, as well as lilies which were the flower of Hera, the marriage goddess in Greece, since Isis is so strongly identified with her role as the dutiful spouse. Pretty much any flowers will do, though – the bigger and lovelier and more expensive, the better. But you might want to avoid the melilote or sweet clover. It was a garland of these that brought to light the affair between Osiris and Nephthys, and while they have all no doubt kissed and made up, I imagine that might still be a sore spot, and not something you really want to rub in her face, you know?

(Especially as the end result of that affair was the murder of Osiris by Nephthys' husband Seth.)

Now, since I am writing this article with a Hellenic polytheist audience in mind I'm going to go ahead and do something radical and leave out all of the traditional Egyptian festivals for Isis. You can find plenty of information about those online or in books about Isis' ancient worship, and I'm sure that they will be covered much better than I could here. For instance, here is a really good site on her traditional Egyptian festivals: http://www.philae.nu/akhet/AsetFestivals.html. There are dozens, if not hundreds of other sites out there, some of which provide complete ritual scripts and further ideas on how to celebrate them. Repeat after me: Google is your friend.

And, hopefully that should give you a feel for how the ancient Greeks and Romans worshipped Isis. If you wanted to add another element of authenticity to your worship you can read some of the ancients' hymns and poems during your rituals. The amount of devotional literature that has come down to us for the goddess is quite striking. Here are a few volumes that you should consider getting:

Hymns, Prayers and Songs: An Anthology of Ancient Egyptian Lyric Poetry by John L. Foster
Ancient Egyptian Literature: Volumes I, II, and III by Miriam Lichtheim
Hellenistic Religions: The Age of Syncretism by Frederick C. Grant
Hymns to Isis in Her Temple at Philae by Louis V. Zabkar
The Four Greek Hymns of Isidorus and the Cult of Isis by Vera F. Vanderlip
The Metamorphoses/Golden Ass by Apuleius (various translations are available)

Additionally, there are poems about Isis by Ovid, Tibullus, Propertius, and others that are very lovely, and usually included in any decent collection of their works.

So, there you go! Hopefully that's enough to begin your journey with Isis: and what an interesting journey it's going to be.

Approaching the Altar of Isis

by Amanda Sioux Blake

I approach your altar with trepidation
A bouquet of roses clutched tightly in my hands
A mixture of awe and fear stirs in my breast
Along with an odd sense of guilt.
Isis of the ten thousand names,
You are the all-welcoming
The all-knowing
And the all-nourishing.
I have always been intrigued by you,
Always been captivated in a small way
But I have always been a daughter of Greece
And although eternally respectful,
I paid no homage to foreign Gods.
I named you the Hera of the Egyptians
Or perhaps Golden Aphrodite, or earthy Demeter
And I went on my way,
Ignoring your gentle nudgings.
But the truth is that you are none of these Goddesses, worthy as they are.
Your Divinity shines through my preconceptions –
I cannot diminish you to a mere mask for one of my ancestral Gods.
I recognize you now, as a powerful Goddess in your own right
And you who enfold all of humanity in your wings
Make no demands for me to renounce my Gods
Who for so long I have poured out sweet wine to
And sung hymns in their honor.
I need not jealously guard the walls of my mind
To keep out "foreign" influences.
Your ancient worship spread far from your ancestral land of Aigyptos
Into all of the known world.
Your Mysteries reached great Roma Herself.
The Nile flows into the Tiber
As far as the Germanic Rhine.
Perhaps it flows into the Mississippi
And the Great Lakes as well.

I have never seen the banks of the Nile
And I will forever remain a daughter of Greece,
A devotee of Athena Owl-Eyed.
I will continue to pay homage to those who dwell on Olympos
But, Isis – or Aset as you were once called –
I will resist you no longer.
I now open myself to you,
Lead me where you will.

My Travels with Serapis (and Antinous)

by P. Sufenas Virius Lupus

While I have not been able to travel as extensively as I'd like, I have been fortunate enough to have visited a number of ancient sites and excellent museums over the last twelve years or so that have significant Graeco-Roman-Egyptian content. I was particularly lucky to have done this on several occasions during my stints in higher education at Wadham College, Oxford University, and at University College Cork in Ireland, and on a few trips to academic conferences elsewhere in Europe. I was also able to make a concerted "pilgrimage" in July of 2003 to Newcastle-upon-Tyne, an important site for Romano-British archaeology (which is, amongst other things, the beginning/eastern end of Hadrian's Wall and the site of his city foundation, Pons Aelius). These various pilgrimages have been motivated by my involvement with the modern cultus for the god Antinous, the deified lover of the Emperor Hadrian, whose original cultus was Greek, Roman, and Egyptian in its roots, and highly syncretistic.

Unfortunately, on many occasions, I have set out to find a particular Antinous statue in a museum, and have been stymied in my efforts to see it for various reasons. But, it was not until mid-2008 that I finally realized something: though I had often not seen Antinous, the deity I did see on many occasions was Serapis. Serapis, too, was a syncretistic deity, originally Egyptian, then Graeco-Egyptian, and eventually his cult was taken up in the Roman world as well. Syncretism, as an historical phenomenon as well as a useful methodology for modern polytheistic practice,[1] has always had an appeal for me, and of the various deities to emerge in the Hellenistic, Roman Imperial, and Late Antique periods, Serapis and Antinous are among the most prominent and the most successful. After realizing this, I began pursuing a relationship of devotion with Serapis, and have had some intriguing results from it, that have lead me to have an expanded sense of what might be involved in many divine relationships, and how the supposed "lack of mythology" that Serapis and other syncretistic deities are said to have can be filled in other ways.

The present discussion, therefore, will outline my travels (with Antinous) to Serapis; the historical relationship between the cult of

Serapis and the cult of Antinous through the person of the latter's founder, the Emperor Hadrian; some reflections on the identity of Antinous and Serapis as "gods of syncretism" and the theological implications of this; and, finally, the way in which I have re-envisioned the relationship between these two deities into a theological schema that has proven both interesting and productive for engaging in devotion to them.

Itinerarium Serapis Antinoique

In many respects, my travels with Serapis began even before I was in active cultus to (much less knowledge of) Antinous. In my year at Oxford, I made a trip with a friend up to the city of York in March of 1997, which was a wonderful place to experience. The walled city has many upstanding medieval remains, including the impressive York Minster cathedral, which has survived several fires and is the largest cathedral in Britain, and contains the largest expanse of medieval stained glass anywhere. The interior of the cathedral is so expansive that there can be several, separate church services occurring in different side chapels and areas while tourists mill around otherwise, without any difficulty. There are also several areas of the cathedral which cost a small entrance fee to explore, including the upper levels and steeple, the crypt (which contains a "treasury" of sorts of medieval liturgical gear), and an intriguing area called "the foundations," which I ended up exploring on my own.

Beneath the foundations of the previous cathedral of York, and the current one, was the ruins of a Roman fort, which by amazing feats of engineering, can still be explored. At one particularly unassuming portion, there is a covered well, but the plaque next to the well reveals something rather impressive: very near to that site, the Emperor Constantine the Great was declared Augustus on July 25, 306 CE, and of course we know how history took its turns after that event. At that particular time and place, I was having my own struggles with an appealing but ultimately unconvincing Christianity and a vapid-in-execution but compelling-in-content paganism, and standing amidst those Roman ruins beneath a Christian cathedral seemed an apt place to sum up that conflict. Constantine the Great died on May 22, 337; on that very same day, 1639 years later, I was born. His death on the date of my birth had a significance for me, then as now, which was also not lost upon me, given my current religious affiliation, and the direction that I decided to take spiritually, once and for all, during those last months in Oxford.

The city of York, which used to be called Eboracum, had one of the only temples to Serapis in Britain, which was founded there in the early third century, by a legate of the Legion VI Victrix, Claudius Hieronymianus.[2] On a "ghost walk" of the city one evening, we were taken to what we were told was the second most haunted location in all of Britain (after the Tower of London), which was the site of the Roman fort at Eboracum, just behind York Minster. A ghostly Roman Legion had been reported at the site on a number of occasions. Could Serapis' devotees have been speaking to me as early as that? It's anyone's guess, of course, but nonetheless the experience was a striking one for a variety of reasons.

At the British Museum in London during the years between 2003 and 2005, I saw many Serapis artifacts. The first time I went to the museum looking for the Townley Antinous,[3] that bust was unfortunately being packed up for shipping to another museum for an exhibition, and was thus not on display. This particular occasion was in late August of 2003, on the date of the 21st, which in the modern Ekklesía Antínoou is the first day of the two-day festival of the Lion Hunt and the Miracle of the Red Lotus, which is the subject of a great deal of the surviving poetry and at least one sculpture from the Antinoan cultus.[4] The lion hunt was nearly fatal for Antinous, who was too eager in his attack on the lion and not cautious enough, but Hadrian allowed him to test his mettle in this manner, intervening before the lion could do more than wound Antinous' pride. The significance of the holiday for modern devotees, partially, is of the effects of failure, and how disaster can be averted through the help and support of friends and lovers. My total failure to see Antinous for myself on this day seemed driven home even further by the exit from which I chose to leave the museum in dejection—an exit flanked by two huge lion statues!

Some time later, I went looking for the Walbrook Mithraeum in London, and before getting thoroughly lost and discouraged in my attempts to locate it before being successful, I first visited the Museum of London near St. Paul's, which I was under the impression contained the Mithraeum itself. One of the objects on display there was the head of Serapis which was found in the ruins of the Mithraeum.[5] After a circuitous walk, a confusing set of tube transfers and misdirections, and nearly giving up all hope in desperation, I finally found where the remains of the Walbrook Mithraeum had been placed, in the front courtyard of a large multi-storey office building, railed off to keep unwanted passers-by from enjoying their lunches on its bench-like foundations. I stood admiring it for a while, and then finally made a move, crossed over the low railings, and walked slowly up the central aisle and left a small food offering where the relief of Mithras that I saw the remains of earlier at the museum would have once been installed.

When I went to Bonn, Germany in July-August of 2007 for an academic conference, I noted before going that there were Serapis temples in that region of Germania (particularly in Colonia, the Roman settlement on the site of present day Köln/Cologne, just across the river from Bonn).[6] I made a specific intention to see an exhibit on "Egypt's Sunken Treasures"[7] with one of my co-religionists, and during this exhibit I saw a particularly interesting Serapis head, of which I ended up purchasing a postcard, and have since been using it as my only image of the deity for devotional purposes. One of the other exciting aspects of this exhibit was the only known colossal statue of Hapi, the androgynous god of the Nile, known to exist. One of the original Egyptian syncretisms that created Serapis was Osir-Hapi.[8] My friend and I performed a short Antinoan devotion before the colossal statue, since Hapi is mentioned on Antinous' Obelisk as well.[9]

What perhaps drew all of this together most definitively for me was what occurred in March of 2008, when myself and several others went to visit the Roman Art from the Louvre exhibit in Seattle, to specifically see an Antinous they had on tour. This particular Antinous bust was restored from some small fragments, and depicted an "Egyptianizing" form of the god, the fragments of which came from Hadrian's Villa.[10] Among the other pieces of statuary on display there was an especially fine head of Serapis that had an amazing sense of *gravitas*.[11] As I looked at his face, a strange idea struck me: this particular Serapis almost looks weighted down with his gigantic hairstyle as well as the grain measure (*modius*) on his head, so that his face appears almost nested within it...as if the accretions of so many layers of divinity and identity on him created their own presence represented by his thick cascading locks, so that the god was most certainly "there" amidst all of it, and yet struggling to hold it all together and actually raise his head under all of that authority. There is a Hebrew word, *kavod*, which usually gets translated as "glory," but it can also mean "weight"; some people and things certainly do have a heavy presence, a majestic quality, while also being very overpowering in that way.

The reason that this experience in Seattle was so important was because it followed a number of other significant events. In mid-2007, the Ekklesía Antínoou was formed after a break from the earlier group I had helped to found, due to irreconcilable theological and ecclesiological differences with one of the original founders and his deputies. Since that time, I had traveled to Germany and initiated my co-religionist there into the Antinoan Mysteries while at the academic conference, and had also initiated six other people into these mysteries in Seattle in early February, and also at PantheaCon in San Jose later that month. And suddenly, out of the blue, I found out that an original Antinous statue — something of which the actual in-person viewing had eluded me for five years — would not only be coming to the U.S., but would be coming to the very city where I was living. But, not surprisingly, Serapis also got in on the action. The epiphany, as it were, of Antinous in my life at last being accompanied by Serapis seemed to be the culmination of a particular theological trend that I had been pursuing for years, and of which I finally began to realize the significance.

Sadly, however, on that occasion one essential part of this developing theology was missing: though many artifacts on display from the Louvre came from Hadrian's Villa, there had been a reconstructed painting of what Hadrian's Villa may have looked like prominently on the wall near where the Antinous bust was displayed, and there was a whole room next to this dedicated to statues of Emperors, there was no depiction of Hadrian to be found anywhere. This was all the stranger, since after Octavian/Augustus, there are more surviving statues of Hadrian than there are of anyone else from the ancient world. Hadrian and Serapis definitely had a connection, though, and it is to this matter that I will now turn in the present discussion.

Hadrian and Serapis

Hadrian seemed to have a great interest in the cult of Serapis, and was quite connected to it in many ways. When Hadrian was being installed as Emperor, there were several "miracles" (*mirabilis*, which essentially means "thing to be marveled at") that occurred in Egypt: the appearance of the phoenix for the first time in ages, and the re-appearance of the Apis-bull.[12] By this period (i.e., 117 CE), the Apis-bull and Serapis would have been nearly inextricably linked in the minds of most people, so this would have been a good sign for Hadrian, and indeed we find in Alexandria several statues of the Apis-bull that were either made by the Emperor at some point in his regin, or made for or on behalf of him and these events.[13] On January 24, 126 CE, a temple sanctuary was dedicated on the occasion of Hadrian's birthday to Serapis in Thebae/Luxor,[14] and the following year, on the same date, another Serapis temple was dedicated in Ostia.[15] These were gifts, no doubt, intended to please and flatter the Emperor and to gain imperial favor, and which we must therefore take seriously as things that Hadrian would have appreciated and enjoyed.[16] On Hadrian's visit to Egypt in 129-131, he honored Serapis along with Jupiter/Zeus as principal gods of the Empire, and he established a chapel in the Alexandrian Serapeum to himself, as depicted on coin issues.[17]

In the area of Jerusalem that was developed into Aelia Capitolina under Hadrian's direct planning, there is evidence of a cult of Serapis-Asklepios;[18] and in the aftermath of the Jewish War, there is a small sculpture which might in fact be an allegory of Hadrian putting down the Second Jewish War/Bar Kochba Rebellion in 135, in which the imperial armored figure has Serapis and Harpocrates pictured in circular medallions on his breastplate.[19]

At Hadrian's Villa, the famous Canopus room, which was outfitted with a huge rectangular pool, crocodiles, and a great deal of statuary, had, at one end, what was long considered a Serapeum[20] (though some disagree with this now, and think it a mere *triclinium*, i.e., a fancy dining room).[21] There was a famous Serapeum at Canopus in Egypt as well,[22] and the overall design of the Emperor's villa was thought to have reflected his various journeys throughout the Empire.[23] Several Serapis and Isis artifacts have been recovered from the site of Hadrian's Villa generally,[24] and several Antinous images also seem to have been found in the vicinity of the Canopus room of the villa specifically.[25]

Serapis and Isis had mysteries celebrated in their honor, much in the same way that Osiris seems to have done (though perhaps with some input of an Eleusinian-like element, since Isis was syncretized to Demeter/Ceres as well in the Greek and Roman spheres), and we know that not only was Hadrian interested in, took part in, and founded or endowed many mystery traditions in different cities,[26] but that Antinous participated in the Eleusinian Mysteries with him on one occasion,[27] and eventually had mysteries celebrated in his honor that were thought of as similar to the Osirian mysteries (as we hear on the Obelisk).[28] In this latter regard, as well as many others, it appears that Serapis and Antinous are not only connected, but in fact the cult of the younger deity might have been modeled deliberately upon that of the older.

Serapis and Antinous: Gods of Syncretism

Serapis was a deity that many (even among academics) still believe that Ptolemy "invented" in order to fuse together the Greek and Egyptian populations in the Nilotic region.²⁹ Needless to say, this is, at very least, a vast overstatement. There was a general Egyptian tendency to have their own gods syncretize with one another in new and interesting ways from a fairly early period, and this happened in the case of the "proto-Serapis" as well. The god Osiris, who we all know as the just ruler of the underworld and husband of Isis, was combined with either Hapy/Hapi (the androgynous god of the Nile) or the Apis-bull, the animal representative of divine kingship on earth, to become Osr-Hapi or Osorapis.³⁰ It was only when the Ptolemies took this cult up and began to portray this deity with Greek rather than Egyptian attributes that things really began to change. Originally, two cults of Serapis emerged in the early Ptolemaic period: the Memphis cult (which was the seat of the old Osorapis cult), which emphasized the deity's role as god of the dead, and the Alexandria cult, which emphasized a "kingly" and regal aspect of the deity.³¹ However, very early on, it began to emerge that this deity, in either place, was a deity very directly involved in the lives of his followers, who made things easier for them and blessed them on an everyday and practical level, and the cult was taken up with verve as a result, and spread over the next two centuries quite far. There was an intermediate period in which cult activity seems to have died down (from the late second to the late first centuries BCE), but then in the Roman period, the cult began spreading again. Isis' cult was established outside of Egypt well before the time of Alexander (even in Athens), but once Serapis' cult emerged, the two often spread together, for obvious reasons.

What is most interesting is that Serapis picked up the qualities of many different deities along the way in this process. He was initially linked to Osiris, of course, and it was a commonplace for many Greeks to assume a basic identity between Osiris and Dionysos, so certain ways in which Dionysos was active and present in everyday life went along with the Serapis package.³² However, as Osiris was also the god of the underworld, Serapis took on these characteristics in the form of a connection to Pluto/Hades, but in a much more "friendly" and approachable form than Pluto/Hades ever had for the Greeks previously³³ (his name was often not even mentioned for fear of him). The Apis-bull cult was also linked with Serapis,³⁴ but also a Greek legendary royal figure called Apis was connected to him.³⁵ As time went on, Serapis also gained the attributes of Zeus and Zeus-Ammon (a syncretized/Hellenized Egyptian deity), Helios, Asklepios (especially as an oracular and healing deity), Aion, Pan,³⁶ Poseidon, Herakles, and Agathos-Daimon.³⁷ He was further connected to a number of deities — most commonly Isis, Anubis or Hermanubis, and Harpocrates, but also to plain, good old-fashioned Osiris, as well as Dionysos, Zeus, and others from whom he inherited attributes,[38] and in the later centuries of the Roman Empire, he came into the orbit of Mithras and his mysteries as well.[39] There is even an audacious but plausible suggestion that the Ptolemaic syncretistic strategy with Serapis was intended to unite the Greeks, Egyptians, and the Jews of Alexandria by combining into one deity their major gods Zeus, Osiris, and YHWH/Iao.[40]

If the cultus of Antinous can be said to have had a methodology in its spread and acceptance in a great variety of geographical locations (especially in the Greek East of the Empire), then syncretism of the type witnessed by the cultus of Serapis is the most likely and accurate candidate. In the city of Antinoöpolis itself, Antinous was revered as Antinosiris or Osirantinous,[41] and a *phylum* of Antinoöpolis bears this name as well.[42] Because of his drowning in the Nile, Antinous' syncretization to Osiris initially follows Egyptian custom.[43] At Hadrian's Villa, and in a few other locations, Antinous was portrayed in Egyptian garb,[44] probably with the Osiris identification foremost in the minds of those who created these statues. The Obelisk of Antinous, now known to have stood originally amidst the Antinoeion at Hadrian's Villa,[45] also refers to Antinous under this name.[46] While it is obvious that Serapis was likewise connected to Osiris through syncretism (and likewise, Antinous was linked to Dionysos, on which more presently), and thus the two deities share this linking deity in common, the other deities to whom Antinous is most often connected are markedly different than those for which known syncretisms with Serapis are attested.

The most common syncretism in literature and inscriptions for Antinous is that with the god Hermes. He is called the "Neos Hermes" in some inscriptions,[47] the "son of the Argus-slayer" (*Argeiphontiadas*) in a poetic fragment,[48] the "Hero Before-the-Gates" (Heros Propylaios),[49] "the God Hermes under Hadrian" in an acrostich appearing in the poem *Periegete* of Dionysius of Alexandria,[50] and possibly the son of Hermes in the fragments of a papyrus hymn from Oxyrynchus dated to the beginning of Diocletian's principate.[51] Pausanias reports that the most common visual depictions of Antinous in Greece had him resembling Dionysos,[52] and in inscriptions he is given the Dionysian epithets Epiphanes[53] and Choreios.[54] Other syncretisms of Antinous include Adonis,[55] Belenus,[56] Eros,[57] Silvanus,[58] and a variety of other deities or local heroes on coins.[59]

Apart from the Osiris connection, their far-flung cultus, and their promiscuous syncretisms, Antinous and Serapis also share a phenomenon in common: the existence of oracles and healing miracles attested through dreams and incubation. Serapis' temple in Canopus was famed for this,[60] and likewise the very origins of his cultus are connected to dreams.[61] The Obelisk of Antinous records that healing dreams were a major part of his cultus.[62] Incubation is a part of many other cults which were popular in the Hellenistic and Roman periods, including the highly syncretistic cults of Asklepios[63] and of the Romano-British Nodons.[64]

A number of aspects about the similarities between these two cults are noteworthy. Hadrian's evident interest in the cult of Serapis in the pre-Antinoan period, and his numerous connections to it, suggest that it is possible that he took the theological model of Serapis and employed it in new and interesting ways to propagate the cult of Antinous. But instead of creating a supreme syncretistic god to integrate many populations and appeal to a wide variety of cultural viewpoints, it seems that the younger god was instead meant to be subordinate, and yet powerful — no less so than the powerful sons of Zeus, Hermes and Dionysos. Antinous was a "junior" deity in the overall Graeco-Roman-Egyptian pantheon, in every respect, and yet no less important nor less appealing for that. With the theme of rebirth and renewal that Hadrian attempted to emphasize during his principate, a more youthful and less authoritative deity would have been more appropriate to propagate than an elder deity at the head of several respective cultures' pantheons.

I do not take syncretism as a phenomenon — especially in late antiquity — as a symptom of decadent and sloppy religion in which even the senseless pagans were slouching slowly toward a unified and sensible (often solar) monotheism. One hears this type of statement often in academic circles. Instead, I see syncretism as a fascinating and vital, natural tendency in multicultural and polytheistic societies that reflects, if nothing else, something which Christians have only scratched the surface of considering in the last century or so, which they have termed "process theology." In essence, this is the idea that (put into polytheistic terms) the gods change as much as humans do, and no deity is "set in stone" forever, or in only one manner. One simply need look at the history of various polytheistic religions worldwide to see that this is the case, and I would go as far as saying it is the default state of polytheism and most healthy and sensible religious outlooks. Hinduism, Buddhism, and Shinto are all highly syncretistic, and in the early centuries of Christianity, syncretism as a methodology for assimilating pagan figures and practices into Christian saints and liturgical holidays was the rule rather than the exception. As one among many examples, especially appropriate to the present context, consider the figure of St. Christopher, who was adapted from the Graeco-Egyptian cynocephalic deity Hermanubis.[65]

Especially in times of great upheaval and cultural change, syncretism becomes necessary to prevent a cultural encounter from becoming a cultural clash. The Hellenistic world of Alexander and the early Ptolemies, and the expanded and consolidating Empire of Hadrian, were both periods in which this type of religious activity amongst a polytheistic culture would have been highly desirable, and the figures of Serapis and Antinous were ideal divine figures through which to accomplish this goal. The overarching figures could be respected and worshipped across great geographic and ethnic boundaries in a universalizing manner, and yet localization and individual communal interpretations of the deities' epiphanies could also be observed and developed.

But this is not to say that the humanistic dimension of syncretism is the only important or valid understanding of the phenomenon. The deities themselves may have changed and developed, adapted their appearances and adopted new attributes, in the face of these sweeping and transforming cultural and religious realities. Those who believe that they have the divine world and its many deities fully figured out in a systematic and infallible manner are, at best, sadly mistaken, and at worst asking for trouble from a deity that may decide to show them how mistaken they are. This idea of deities who change as a result of their interactions with others, just as humans change, is not so much an effect of an over-anthropomorphic or humanistic understanding of the gods, but instead a recognition at a theological level of the evolving nature of the universe and everything in it.

As there are many people in the modern world who fear or even subtly advocate (and create by their assertions) a "culture war" between Christianity and Islam, or between various brands and interpretations of Christianity (usually more influenced by liberal versus conservative politics), are quite illustrative of the way in which creedal monotheism and its monistic and exclusivist tendencies are not well suited to such a diverse and rapidly changing world as the one we live in at present. Perhaps not surprisingly, then, the deities Antinous and Serapis are reasserting themselves rather strongly in certain circles, and offer their potential devotees a variety of options in engaging with this wondrous but often mystifying socio-cultural landscape of the early twenty-first century.

The Divine Triad

As noted above, there are many connections between the historical cults of Antinous and Serapis, which are both attributable to Hadrian's direct influence, as well as arising from independent causes. Serapis and Isis had at least one major temple in the holy city of Antinoöpolis.[66] It has also been suggested that the limited cult relics of Antinoan devotion in the city of Rome itself were likely from the Iseum Campense on the Campus Martius, where Isis and Serapis were worshipped.[67] And, of course, Isis and Serapis were also worshipped and commemorated along with Antinous at Hadrian's Villa outside of Rome. While Antinous and Serapis are never linked specifically in any of these known instances, their ultimately similar backgrounds and their related provenances on these occasions is at least suggestive, and could be productively developed in a modern Graeco-Roman-Egyptian polytheistic practice in a variety of ways.

In the modern Ekklesía Antínoou,[68] the figure of Antinous is understood in a number of different ways, but one common manner is in three particular aspects: Antinous the Lover, Antinous the Navigator, and Antinous the Liberator, each of whom has a season during which he is primarily acknowledged, and holidays marking the transformation from one to the other. Likewise, other divine triads have been developed or suggested, including the triad of Julia Balbilla, Diva Sabina and Diva Matidia as Poetry, Fidelity and Philosophy,[69] the three Divine Emperors (Trajan, Hadrian, and Antoninus Pius), Hadrian and his adopted successors (Aelius Caesar and Antoninus Pius), and the three *kouroi* of Lucius Marius Vitalis, Antinous, and Polydeukion.[70]

While the Ekklesía Antínoou has a large and noticeable emphasis on Antinous, there has been a growing interest within Antinoan practice to include divine figures who are of a "more mature" character than Antinous. The great majority of the group is made up of males over the age of 30, and despite the appeal of youth and the idea that there is wisdom to be found in youth, younger men have always been in the minority in the group. For this purpose, taking Divus Hadrianus very seriously — indeed as an essential and necessary companion figure to Antinous in almost all things (for there would have been no cult of Antinous without Hadrian) — has been a more and more common and widespread interpretation and practice in the group. Hadrian very aptly fills the somewhat "middle-aged" category for divine figures quite well, and is much easier to relate to and identify with for many members of the group. But, there has also been an interest in a further divine category which until 2008 had remained lacking in the group's outlook. There has been a need to have an older-aged deity for the third part of the triad, and Serapis fills that role admirably.

Previous to this understanding, there was a purposeful, post-Wiccan avoidance of any theological formulation which would in any manner mirror the "triple goddess" idea of Maiden, Mother, and Crone[71] as the archetype for all goddesses, and some sort of triple god likewise mirroring the expected heteronormative life cycle for males. As the Ekklesía Antínoou is first and foremost a queer cultus, it seeks to question and critique these heteronormative theological and psychological assumptions wherever they are found, and as a result, these types of schemata have not been attractive to many in the modern cultus. However, when it is realized that the reproductive and heteronormative imperatives can be jettisoned easily, the life cycle of youth (Antinous), maturity (Hadrian) and elderhood (Serapis), perhaps exhibited by the lack of facial hair on Antinous, the trim Greek beard of Hadrian, and the overabundant beard and hair of Serapis, can work in a queer theological schema quite easily.

While Antinous was primarily connected to ever-youthful deities like Hermes, Dionysos,[72] and Eros, he does have the Osiris connection as well, which further links him to Serapis. Hadrian was syncretized, even to an extent before his death, to Zeus, which also links him to Serapis. And thus, while the connections between them are not necessarily linear, and are not based on direct descent, Serapis is in some sense the "spiritual father" of Hadrian and the "spiritual grandfather" of Antinous. The *erastes/eromenos* relationship can still remain between Hadrian and Antinous in this schema, just as the erotic relationship between Julia Balbilla and Diva Sabina can exist in the triad mentioned earlier. This type of queer triad, in which the assumptions of relationship between various figures at different stages of life can be problematized, questioned, nuanced, and even enhanced, is a fertile ground for speculation and individual interpretation.

In the yearly calendar of the Ekklesía Antínoou, each of these three divine figures is celebrated on certain days, and some occasions allow the different members of the triad to share holidays. Serapis is given his Serapeia festival on April 25th,[73] which falls midway between two other (mostly modern) holidays – the Megala Antinoeia on April 21st, and the Venatio Apri on May 1. Hadrian's death is commemorated on July 10, but his birth (which was the usual date for celebrating a deified Emperor in the ancient Roman imperial cult) on January 24th[74] is also marked, and since two Serapis temples were dedicated on that day, it would also make an excellent time to have a further festival for Serapis. Additionally, the Sacred Nights of Antinous are celebrated from October 24th to November 1st, with the most important festival being October 30th – the day of the foundation of the cultus and of the city of Antinoöpolis – but the first day of the festival is the feast of Osiris, and this could also be given as a date to honor Serapis.

I believe that the connections — theological, cultic, and historical — between Antinous and Serapis (and Hadrian!) have been aptly demonstrated in this examination, and the way in which these connections became known to me through my own devotional wanderings, both scholarly and in terms of travel, have enriched my practice, and influenced the workings of the religious communities with which I am affiliated. While not everyone who is interested in or worships Serapis need have any interest in or devotion to Antinous, and vice versa, their common roots within a Hellenistic and Graeco-Roman-Egyptian syncretistic religious context can provide ample opportunities and productive avenues for exploring the splendor and the near infinite variation and adaptability available through syncretistic forms of polytheistic practice and theology. Only time will tell how Serapis, Antinous, and the development of the polytheistic divine process in general will further make itself known to those people willing to pursue such an understanding.

Notes

[1] I would note that I see a major distinction between syncretism—the connection between deities from different pantheons or even within the same pantheon, to the point that a new deity or a varied interpretation of the deities involved emerges — and what has been called "soft polytheism," the idea that the deities in question are simply one being with different names or forms according to the cultures which recognized them. The latter is very close to the Jungian idea of archetypes, and as an intellectual possibility is intriguing, and even productive; but on some level, this interpretive tendency can run the gamut of assertions ranging from arguments of the ultimate identity of two different deities (e.g., Mars and Ares being functionally equivalent in many people's minds), to monistic ideas that in effect make all deities simply aspects of a unified divine energy. For myself, I recognize that different deities have distinct and identifiable personalities that can be easily distinguished, and thus I would classify myself as following a syncretistic rather than a soft polytheistic theological model in almost every case.

[2] See Guy de la Bédoyère, *Gods with Thunderbolts: Religion in Roman Britain* (Stroud: Tempus Publishing Ltd., 2002), pp. 173-174.

[3] See Thorsten Opper, *Hadrian: Empire and Conflict* (Cambridge: Harvard University Press, 2008), pp. 182-183.

[4] Opper, pp. 171-173.

⁵ Peter Marsden, *Roman London* (London: Thames and Hudson, 1980), pp. 137-147, with Serapis photos on 138, 145.

⁶ See the relevant section in G. J. F. Kater-Sibbes, *Preliminary Catalogue of Sarapis Monuments* (Leiden: E. J. Brill, 1973).

⁷ See Franck Goddio, Manfred Clauss, and Christoph Gerigk, *Egypt's Sunken Treasures* (Munich and New York: Prestel, 2006).

⁸ In an early modern Antinoan liturgy I wrote for the first Foundation Day on October 30, 2002 (the official re-foundation date of the modern cult of Antinous), I included a litany of various deities, and though I was painfully underinformed about many aspects of the historical cult of Antinous at that stage, nonetheless, by sheer happenstance, Hapi and Serapis appeared in the same line of the litany.

⁹ See my translation of the Obelisk in *The Phillupic Hymns* (Eugene: Bibliotheca Alexandrina/CreateSpace, 2008), p. 20.

¹⁰ Cécile Giroire and Daniel Roger, *Roman Art from the Louvre* (New York and Manchester, VT: American Federation of Arts and Hudson Hills Press, 2007), p. 86.

¹¹ Giroire and Roger, p. 240.

¹² Anthony R. Birley (trans.), *Lives of the Later Caesars: The first part of the Augustan History, with newly compiled Lives of Nerva and Trajan* (London: Penguin, 1976), pp. 69-70; Birley, *Hadrian the Restless Emperor* (London and New York: Routledge, 2001), pp. 142, 245. Also note the Tebtynis Papyrus prose miscellany, which includes what may be some of the earliest writings on Antinous, that also details the Phoenix and its appearance; *Phillupic Hymns*, pp. 54-55 and 260.

¹³ See, for example, the one pictured in Jean-Yves Empereur, *Alexandria: Jewel of Egypt*, trans. Jane Brenton (New York: Harry N. Abrams, Inc., 2002), p. 24.

¹⁴ Kater-Sibbes, pp. 22-23 §122.

¹⁵ Kater-Sibbes, p. 101 §543.

¹⁶ Why get someone something that isn't on their "wish-list" if one is out to impress them and are trying to get them to like oneself? Additionally, temples are very hard to take back, even if one does save the receipts, and exchanging them or getting store credit is practically impossible!

¹⁷ Royston Lambert, *Beloved and God: The Story of Hadrian and Antinous* (New York: Viking, 1984), p. 117; Birley, *Hadrian*, p. 238.

¹⁸ Kater-Sibbes, p. 81 §462. Coin issues also indicate that Serapis was worshipped there: Birley, *Hadrian*, pp. 276.

¹⁹ Kater-Sibbes, p. 17 §87; Birley, *Hadrian*, pp. 276-277.

²⁰ Mary Taliaferro Boatwright, *Hadrian and the City of Rome* (Princeton: Princeton University Press, 1987), pp. 142-150.

[21] Opper, p. 160.
[22] William L. MacDonald and John A. Pinto, *Hadrian's Villa and Its Legacy* (New Haven and London: Yale University Press, 1995), p. 109.
[23] Birley, *Hadrian*, pp. 242-243.
[24] MacDonald and Pinto, p. 133.
[25] MacDonald and Pinto, pp. 149-150.
[26] Mary Taliaferro Boatwright, *Hadrian and the Cities of the Roman Empire* (Princeton: Princeton University Press, 2000), pp. 100-101.
[27] MacDonald and Pinto, p. 132.
[28] *Phillupic Hymns*, p. 20.
[29] John Ferguson, *The Religions of the Roman Empire* (Ithaca: Cornell University Press, 1970), p. 36.
[30] John E. Stambaugh, *Sarapis Under the Early Ptolemies* (Leiden: E. J. Brill, 1972), pp. 61. Ferguson, *ibid.*, notes this pre-existence of Osorapis, despite insisting on Ptolemy's invention of the deity.
[31] Stambaugh, pp. 18-25.
[32] Stambaugh, pp. 36-59.
[33] Stambaugh, pp. 27-35.
[34] Stambaugh, pp. 60-67.
[35] Stambaugh, pp. 68-74.
[36] Stambaugh, pp. 75-87.
[37] See Kater-Sibbes' indices.
[38] *Ibid.*
[39] See the earlier references above on note 5, as well as Ferguson, pp. 36-37, and Manfred Clauss, *The Roman Cult of Mithras: The God and His Mysteries*, trans. Richard Gordon (Edinburgh: Edinburgh University Press, 2000), pp. 158, 161, 165.
[40] Stambaugh, pp. 95-96.
[41] Hugo Meyer, *Antinoos: Die archäologischen Denkmäler unter Einbeziehung des numismatischen und epigraphischen Materials sowie der literarischen Nachrichten, Ein Beitrag zur Kunst- und Kulturgeschichte der hadrianish-frühantoninischen Zeit* (Munich: Wilhelm Fink Verlag, 1991), p.
[42] Boatwright, *Hadrian and the Cities*, p. 194 note 124.
[43] Jack Lindsay, *Men and Gods on the Roman Nile* (New York: Barnes & Noble, Inc., 1968), pp. 304-305.
[44] Giroire and Roger, p. 86; Opper, pp. 174-178.
[45] Zaccaria Mari and Sergio Sgalambro, "The Antinoeion of Hadrian's Villa: Interpretation and Architectural Reconstruction," *American Journal of Archaeology* 111 (2007), pp. 83-104; Opper, p. 178.
[46] *Phillupic Hymns*, pp. 19-22.

[47] Hugo Meyer, *Antinoos: Die archäologischen Denkmäler unter Einbeziehung des numismatischen und epigraphischen Materials sowie der literarischen Nachrichten, Ein Beitrag zur Kunst- und Kulturgeschichte der hadrianish-frühantoninischen Zeit* (Munich: Wilhelm Fink Verlag, 1991), pp. 169-170.
[48] Meyer, p. 164.
[49] Meyer, pp. 170-171
[50] *Phillupic Hymns*, pp. 135, 263-264.
[51] J. R. Rea (ed./trans.), *The Oxyrynchus Papyri*, Vol. 63 (London: Egypt Exploration Society, 1996), p. 10.
[52] Lambert, p. 166.
[53] Meyer, pp. 167-168.
[54] Meyer, p. 165.
[55] Meyer, pp. 163-164; *Phillupic Hymns* pp. 227, 269-270.
[56] Meyer, pp. 164-165.
[57] Meyer, p. 168.
[58] Boatwright, *Hadrian and the City*, pp. 255-256; Peter F. Dorcey, *The Cult of Silvanus: A Study in Roman Folk Religion* (Leiden: E. J. Brill, 1992), pp. 100-102, 112.
[59] For further possibilities, see Lambert; Caroline Vout, *Power and Eroticism in Imperial Rome* (Cambridge: Cambridge University Press, 2007).
[60] Birley, p. 242.
[61] Frederick Grant, *Hellenistic Religions: The Age of Syncretism*, The Library of Liberal Arts #134 (Indianapolis and New York: The Bobbs-Merril Co., Inc., 1953), pp. 144-145.
[62] *Phillupic Hymns*, p. 21.
[63] Grant, pp. 53-59.
[64] de la Bédoyère, pp. 198-200. My own experiences of and visions of Antinous have often been through dreams.
[65] See David Gordon White, *Myths of the Dog-Man* (Chicago: University of Chicago Press, 1991), pp. 22-46.
[66] Lambert, p. 202.
[67] Boatwright, *Hadrian and the City*, p. 255.
[68] The Ekklesía Antínoou is a queer, Graeco-Roman-Egyptian, syncretist, reconstructionist, polytheist organization dedicated to Antinous, as well as to Divus Hadrianus, Diva Sabina, and a number of other deities, divinized mortals, and figures of note.
[69] Forthcoming work by Erynn Rowan Laurie on this topic is eagerly awaited!
[70] Ekklesía Antínoou and Neos Alexandria member and contributor Kallimachus has introduced the intriguing idea that Kleovis and Viton, the two earliest *kouroi* (youthful heroes who died before their time) known to

Greek tradition, might have had an influence on the cultus of Antinous and how it was interpreted in a Hellenic context, which is both likely and attractive. Details on Lucius Marius Vitalis can be found in Lambert, pp. 101-102, and his reception into the Ekklesía Antínoou's wider mythology in *Phillupic Hymns*, pp. 250-251, 271-272. Polydeukion was a *trophimos* (foster-son) of the wealthy Athenian sophist and benefactor Herodes Attikos (and also an acquaintance of Hadrian and a devotee of Antinous), who died and was heroized by Herodes in a manner similar to Antinous, but in a far more localized and limited manner — see Opper, pp. 188-190, *Phillupic Hymns*, pp. 193-194, and Jennifer Tobin, *Herodes Attikos and the City of Athens: Patronage and Conflict under the Antonines* (Amsterdam: J. C. Gieben, 1997).

[71] This formulation rarely, if ever, actually played out in any attested historical cultus, and has much more to do with the influence of Robert Graves, than to anything found in ancient Greek, Celtic, or any other European polytheistic religion's remains.

[72] While bearded forms of Hermes and Dionysos are certainly well attested in the ancient world, the youthful exploits of these deities were often the most celebrated in myth.

[73] It is given as this date according to the mid-fourth century calendar of Filocalus; see Mary Beard, John North, and Simon Price (eds./trans.), *Religions of Rome, Volume 2: A Sourcebook* (Cambridge: Cambridge University Press, 1998), p. 68.

[74] Beard, North, and Price, p. 72.

To Apis

by Sannion

To Apis
O most holy Apis,
I sing your praises and ask you to come in peace,
for you are the source of all good things in life.
With your horns you drive off the foe,
keeping the two lands safe, and protecting those who love you.
You are solid, like truth, and your heaviness
speaks of the rich yields that we shall harvest with your blessing.
Your thunderous bellow stirs my soul and sends me into a frenzy of
    joyous ecstasy.
Your hooves are made of the stuff of stars and light my path
as I make my way through life.
Your gentle tongue wipes away my tears and soothes all my cares.
Come, O beautiful bull,
O mighty and majestic one,
that I might place a garland of sweet roses around your fragrant neck,
and rest in the presence of your godhood.

TRACING THE THREADS OF MY RELATIONSHIP WITH ISIS

by Amanda Sioux Blake

Until a few months ago, I considered myself to be strictly Hellenic. Oh, sure, the Egyptian Gods were interesting, and powerful in Their own right. I enjoyed a good research session as much as the next Reconstructionist, but I never thought my interest would develop into anything other than idle curiosity. Egyptian deities seemed so alien, so unapproachable – all those animal heads and the stiff, unnatural poses! How off-putting to my Greek senses! I had been a Pagan for nearly nine years, and Hellenic for eight of those years. The Gods of Greece, particularly Athena and Dionysos, were dear to my heart and had sustained my soul through many trials.

But in the last year or so, something has begun to change, and eventually it became clear that Someone was reaching out to me. Everywhere I went, Egypt seemed to be the topic of conversation. Pictures of mummies and Kleopatra graced the covers of magazines wherever I went. A stranger once stopped me on the street to comment on the weather, and her Isis pendant seemed to leap out at me. I began to dream about Isis, vague dreams of stumbling in darkness. All I could recall of them upon awaking was Her form illuminated in the darkness by the light of Her sun-disc headdress.

At first I ignored Her gentle nudgings. I dismissed the coincidences that seemed to follow me wherever I went, and sought to explain them away. I assumed that Egypt was in my consciousness because of the influence of an Isian friend. I had absorbed the propaganda of some Reconstructionists, the belief that worshiping deities of more than one pantheon or culture would automatically make me a fluffy bunny, a person with spiritual ADD, jumping from one shiny thing to the next with no real spiritual depth. What would my fellow Hellenics think? Surely I would be mocked and labeled a ramshackle eclectic. I stuck close to my religious home of Athens, to the gods who had first stirred my soul as a child.

This strange sequence of events finally came to a head the day after Christmas, 2008. I was visiting a friend, with whom I had made an agreement that we would not exchange presents, as neither of us could afford it. This friend was a fellow Pagan, and she was aware of my Greek inclinations, but not my recent experiences of being god-stalked by an Egyptian deity. Out of the blue, she suddenly reached into a drawer, withdrew a statuette and handed it to me, saying: "This is meant to be yours." It was a beautiful, bronzed representation of Isis, kneeling, Her face in profile, wings outstretched. I broke down. It was no longer deniable. There was something – or rather, Someone – to everything that had been happening to me recently.

That night, I spoke to Isis from the heart. I told Her that I finally acknowledged Her as a Goddess in Her own right. I told Her I was ready to begin a relationship with Her, but that I had made prior oaths to other gods and that She would have to wait a few months until they were fulfilled. I sensed She agreed, and indeed She withdrew while I carried out my other duties. She was still there, on the periphery, waiting for when I had the time to delve deeper into Her mysteries.

These past months since, I have been examining my preconceptions about this magnificent goddess, and doing what little research that time allows between the demands of daily life and my other projects. To my surprise, in my mental wanderings I have begun to see Her influence earlier in my life.

I remembered how, years ago, when it first became known that I was Pagan, my best friend's mother refused to let me see her daughter anymore. She was very Christian, of the charismatic sort, and both her daughter and I were fourteen. She feared that I would corrupt her daughter, when if anything it was the other way around. Unknown to her mother, my friend had been an Isian for years before I found Paganism.

Eventually we were allowed to see each other again, but only if I went to church with her and her mother. Missing my friend, I agreed. It was a megachurch with thousands of followers, all laser lights and fog machines and no spirituality. It was pure theatrics. My friend and I sang along with the Christian hymns, but we replaced the words "God" with "Goddess" and "Jesus" with "Isis." We sang our modified versions at the top of our lungs, sharing secret looks, with her mother standing right beside us. None of the faithful noticed. At one point I felt a powerful spirit rise up within me, and tears streamed down my face. No one knew I was experiencing a Pagan deity.

That was my first experience with Isis, although at that point I called Her simply The Goddess. I would continue to worship the Great Mother of Wicca and general Neopaganism for about a year before finding Hellenismos and the worship of the gods who had called to me while reading my big, leather-bound book of Greek myths under a blanket with a flashlight, so long ago.

It would be many years before I felt Her presence again. Since I broke down and accepted Her into my life, I have felt a change in myself, one that at times has struck terror in my heart. Since I began my studies on Isis, I have been much more drawn to children than ever before in my life. I found myself wondering what it would be like to raise a child, to teach him or her the ways of the gods, to feel the connection to them deeper than life itself. A few times I caught myself looking up information about adoption and fostering. As a career-driven woman who has for so long considered herself childless by choice, this about-face terrified me. It caused me to back off from Isis for a while.

I have a lot of issues when it comes to children and motherhood. My own mother was extremely abusive, and we have not talked in years. I have never known what real mother-love felt like, and I am somewhat doubtful if it is something I can ever give. It is not that I do not have a nurturing instinct; I do. I currently work with developmentally disabled adults after all, a very nurturing (and challenging!) position to be in. But having never had a healthy image of motherhood, I fear I would never be able to be a good mother.

Add to this the fact that in our culture women are not really given much choice in the matter. It is always assumed that a woman will have children. In many families, it is only a question of "when," never "if." The matter-of-fact statements of complete strangers – "You'll change your mind about having kids one day" – always pissed me off to no end. And so here Isis comes into my neat little world. Isis is many things, and one of Her many roles is that of Mother, to the child-king Horus, to the pharaoh, and to the world. The sudden thoughts of children surprised me, knocked me off balance. So I panicked. I ran as far from Her as possible.

But Isis was gentle, and patient with my neuroses. She waited, and did not push me past my limits. Eventually, I swallowed my fears and returned to my studies. Isis was ready with a gentle embrace. I realized that worshiping Her does not mean that I will automatically have children someday. I still have choice in the matter, and Isis would not want me to be a half-hearted parent. I am uncertain how I feel about children now, but I am still young. Isis is encouraging me to work on my issues and to own my feelings, all of them. I am still in a process of transformation into whatever I am becoming, so I cannot write certainties at this moment.

Recently, I held a ritual in my home on the Panegyris, a festival of thanksgiving to Isis as She was equated with Agathe Tykhe, the Hellenistic goddess of Good Fortune. It was the most important festival of Isis in the city of Medinet-Madi. This ritual was attended by several other local Pagans, although I was the only Reconstructionist. This was my first ritual honoring Isis since She entered my life this past year. The altar was set up in my living room, and I offered barley to the goddess. Her altar was laid with a silver cloth, Her image surrounded by flowers and semi-precious crystals.

We purified ourselves in consecrated water and the smoke of sage and rosemary. When the lights were turned off, the room was illuminated only by candlelight. In the quiet of anticipation I called the goddess, and She attended. The spirit of Isis was palpable in room, thick as incense. We meditated, and She met us in the fog of our subconscious. In the temple of my mind She clasped my hands in Hers, and told me She was proud of me and that we were only beginning. She kissed my forehead, and I was bathed in the sacred waters of the Nile River.

So here I am now. I don't know what my relationship with Isis is yet, or what it will develop into. I don't know if I will be called to worship other Egyptian deities. So far Isis has not led me to worship Her husband Osiris or Her son Horus, but I suspect that will come with a deepening of our relationship. Perhaps I will be drawn to explore the gods of Egypt as well as Greece. Or perhaps not. Perhaps Isis will be my sole connection to the desert sands of Egypt. I know that wherever my path may lead, I will not abandon the gods who have fed my soul and sustained me for these ten years. Greece is in my blood, too deep in my soul to ever be wrenched out, even if I wanted to. I will forever honor the Gods of my spiritual ancestors. I will forever pay tribute to my patroness, Athena: the warrior maiden, the scholar's goddess, owl-eyed daughter of Zeus, King of the Gods.

But the ancient city of Alexandria has developed new meaning for me. In the teeming bustle of the world's first truly cosmopolitan city, Greeks, Romans, Egyptians, Jews and people of many more cultures and ethnicities coexisted peacefully. The interaction of cultures and the exchange of religious ideas has always fascinated me on a scholarly level, devotee of Athena that I am. But now I see something else. Alexandria feels much more relevant to my spiritual practice now. I look to those brave Greeks who left their homeland and came to a new land, embracing the traditions of the people there, while staying true to the gods of their ancestors. I see myself reflected in them, men and women who passed from this world 2500 years ago. May I learn from them, and fearlessly embrace the wisdom and beauty of both cultures. May the gods of Greece and Egypt look on me favorably and bless my efforts to understand and to worship. In the names of all the Gods, I pray it will be so.

PRAYER TO ISIS I

by Theokleia

Great saviour Isis
You who cradle the lost
In your wings
Vulture-Mother
Clever, you know the Lord's name.
Great saviour Isis
Your mouth on my mouth
The breath of life
The opening of my lips
Great, glorious
Beautiful one.

Alone

by Jeremy J. Baer

A sleepwalk through the travesty of years
        buried beneath a broken age.
Discolored souls and idle pursuits to mock my forgotten face.
No sign to quell the thirsting wait of better days.
Where were You? If I had but eyes to see...
Too late it came, but suddenly I saw
The Immortal strand that imbues eternity.
The silver-fingered radiance that sears the heavens
        in answer to a whispered plea.
No more the long nights of hollow tasks
        toiled in sight of indifferent stars.
I gaze above and with practiced hands
        You cusp my heart to shelter's bliss.
I breathe in the Peace of the Gods.
I am here
        at home.
Bathed in a mistress' caress. O Isis.
Never again
        alone.

Seeking What Is Lost: An Isian Meditation

by Barbara Ardinger, Ph.D.

"You see me here...in answer to your prayer," said Isis to Lucius. "I am Nature, the universal Mother, mistress of all the elements, primordial child of time, sovereign of all things spiritual, queen of the dead, queen also of the immortals, the single manifestation of all gods and goddesses that are."[1]

Just as Lucius lost his human form and sought the help of the Great Goddess to be transformed again, so do we seek what is lost or what we imagine is missing from our lives. Whereas Lucius — and, 1800 years later, Wilfred and Molly Maxwell in Dion Fortune's novel, *The Sea Priestess* — met the goddess on the edge of the sea, however, we can meet her in the edges of our realities.

Before you begin this guided meditation, spend some time in quiet contemplation, perhaps with pen and paper to make notes. Ask yourself, What am I looking for? What have I lost? What do I want to find? Make a list if you want to. Perhaps you're seeking love, a lost friend or a missing animal companion, job security or a new job, confidence and optimism in these troubled times. What have you lost? Something small but precious? An opportunity? (Be aware, however, that if you're seeking your lost youth, you may not find it again in this life, though it is also true that our true age can be revealed in our actions.)

You can either record this meditation and play it back to yourself or do it in a group and ask one member to read it aloud. Pause at appropriate times, as when the judges and the goddess speak or for action to happen. At the end of the meditation, when you come back to your normal beta state (or something close to it), be sure to ground yourself. One good way to do this is to eat something made of root vegetables. (Potato chips work.)

If you would like to do so, cast a magical circle. Imagine the iconic throne of Isis at the cardinal points. You can use the standard Wiccan directions, but for this meditation, perhaps what the Farrars tell us about the elements in their meditation to Isis is more appropriate:

> Fire in the East (the rising Sun), Air in the West (the sky of the desert), Water in the South (whence the Nile

flows), and Earth in the North (to which the Nile brings fertility).[2]

Burn rose incense, for the rose is sacred to Isis and brings the powers of healing and protection as well as love. If you prefer, scatter rose petals in your circle. You may also use vervain, likewise sacred to Isis (and other deities). Vervain bears the powers of love, purification, money, and healing, among other things. Scatter the dried herb in your circle or set bundles of vervain in the directions. You can also burn an Isis incense that you've found in your favorite metaphysical store. (An Isian incense advertised on the Web says that its main ingredient is ambrosia.)

When you feel ready, sit comfortably, keeping your spine straight, and take a deep, easy breath. Feel your body begin to relax. Take another deep, easy breath, and feel your imagination quicken. Take a third deep, easy breath, and know that you are in a safe place and that if any outside noise disturbs you or there is an emergency, you can promptly return to normal consciousness and attend to your mundane business. But, just now...ahhh...just now, you are going to visit a marble temple surrounded by green fields beside the dark waters of the Nile.

In the eyes of your imagination, stand up and walk through the door of the room you're sitting in. Open the door. Like Dorothy landing in Oz, however, when you open your door you do not see the setting you're accustomed to. You are standing in your vision in the green and golden land of Egypt. Not too far away is a magnificent pillared temple, a reflecting pool beside it, date palms and sycamores growing around it. In the fields before you, perhaps you can see the Apis bull grazing. Perhaps, in the distance, you glimpse crews of men working on a tomb in a cliff. You can hear the faint voices of the distant workers chanting as they pile stone upon stone. Closer, you suddenly hear the rattling of the sistrum, its jangling sound clearing the air of troublesome influences and creating sacred space for you.

[Pause until this vision is clear and vivid in your mind.]

Before you lies the path to the temple. Step forward.

Because we know that the worship of Isis spread to the north shores of the Mediterranean Sea into Greece and Rome, and beyond, and that even the form of Her name that we use today is the Greek pronunciation of Auset, we begin our journey to her temple with a scene from Greek mythology.[3]

First you enter the anteroom of the temple. This is the dark, three-sided Chamber of the Judges. Minos, Aeacus, and Rhadamanthys are the three wise Lords of Endings and Beginnings. They represent justice, judgment, and balance. They tower above you, they stand as still as granite statues, they neither move nor smile. They are the Lords of the Dark Sun. You can see the dark sun reflected in the ebony columns of their chamber, shining on the walls, shining on the maze in the floor, jet inlaid in ebony.

Even though we know that Isis is a goddess of goodness and mercy, it takes courage to approach her. It also takes courage to encounter these three judges. Before you speak to them, think again about why you're here. What are you looking for? What is lost and must be found? Take stock of your life so far, recalling both successes and failures. These judges require gifts. When in your life have you been unjust? Give that injustice to Minos. What faulty judgments have you made? Give them to Aeacus. What part of your life is out of balance? Give the imbalance to Rhadamanthys.

[Pause to consider your life and give these parts away.]

Now the judges smile upon you.
"What are you seeking?" one asks.

What do you seek? Tell the judges. Ask for what you want.

[Pause as you tell them.]

Minos, Aeacus, and Rhadamanthys confer. They glance down at you several times, heads nodding, shaking, nodding again.

"What you seek is worthy," says one.
"Proceed into the temple," says the second.
"Go forward to meet the Great Goddess," says the third.

Give thanks to the three judges. They point to the doorway of the temple. Walk through it.

[Pause to give yourself time to enter the temple.]

You are now in the throne room of the great temple of Isis. It has a high ceiling supported by marble columns. It is filled with warm light and the sweet scent of incense. Before you see the goddess, you notice the sacred Abyssinian cats, with their ruddy, blue-gray fur, long tails, and intelligent faces. They are all around the throne room. Some are curled up and sleeping, others are grooming themselves, and some sit and gaze at you. If you listen carefully, you can hear them purring.

"My child."
She speaks.
"Come closer to me."

You are in the presence of Great Isis, who is also called Star of the Sea, the Power that Heals the World, She Who Initiates, Throne of the King, Mistress of the World.[4] She is the Goddess of Ten Thousand Names, Isis Panthea.

> "And so She came," Dion Fortune wrote:
> She is forever veiled, but there came to us the great exalted awe which some say is the gods and no other. This tingling fear took me by the heart and by the throat and by the eyes, gripping like a hand. And my hands began to burn and tingle with a pulsating force, and from behind my eyes it seemed to come out like a beam. And I broke out in that heavy sweat of the heat of the gods, which [the priestess] had told me always heralds their passing. ... Then slowly Great Isis turned, and drew Her veil closer about Her...[5]

Feel the awe, the awesome, awe-ful power, that Wilfred Maxwell felt in *The Sea Priestess*. Know now, understand, that you do not come on a frivolous errand. Know now, understand, that you are in the presence of the goddess who possesses the secret wisdom of Ra, the goddess whose magic is all powerful. Know now, understand, that she is both merciful and terrible.

It is proper to fear Isis, to be in awe of her. It is also proper to love and adore her.

> *[Pause until you feel the awe and the force of her power.]*

Today, Isis is approachable. She removes her veil. You see her more clearly now. She is sitting on her alabaster throne, wearing her crown of horns and the solar disk, her wide beaded necklace, her shimmering golden gown. Her wings are carved into the back of her throne. She is holding an ankh in her right hand.

She knows why you're here. "Speak, my child," she says in a gentle voice. "Approach me and tell me what you are looking for. Although thoughts are things," she says — and do you see her smile? — "you must say the words."

It's true. Mere silent wishing will not make it so. We must declare what we want. And then we must take action to find it. If we're looking for love, we must become more loving and more loveable. If we're looking for a friend we haven't seen in many years, it helps to do an Internet search. If we're looking for a wandering pet, it helps to post signs. If we're looking for job security, we may need to participate in office politics. If we're looking for a new job, we need to write a new resume or curriculum vitae. And if we're searching for optimism and confidence, then we must turn actively to the goddess, knowing that our chanting and prayers will focus our minds and prevent pessimistic thoughts from overwhelming us. What is the lesson here? Ask the goddess, then do your homework, too.

Tell Great Isis what you're seeking. Say the words out loud. Take your time and describe your desires in as much detail as you can. Even though you know that she may well lead you somewhere else, or give you something else (and probably better), be specific. (But don't be greedy.)

[Pause long enough to enumerate to Isis the things you seek.]

We've read about the search that Isis made for the body of her brother-husband, Osiris. We know how she searched throughout the world, how she even took a job as a nursemaid for a foreign queen before she found the body of Osiris. We know also that after Set cut the body of Osiris into pieces, Isis diligently searched again and found every piece but one. We know that she fashioned a new phallus out of gold, was inseminated, and bore the young god, Horus.

Are you willing to work as hard as Isis did to get what you're seeking?

With a gesture, Isis invites you to converse further with her. Speak honestly to the goddess about what you're seeking and tell her what you're willing to do to meet your goals and find what you want.

[Pause long enough for this conversation to reach its end.]

When you finish, stand quietly. You can hear the cats purring again. Accept this as a good sign. Accept the warm light in the temple as a good sign. Accept the scent of the burning incense as a good sign.

"My child," Isis says at last, "what you are seeking is worth seeking. You may find it. But you may also be surprised. You may find something better." She points her ankh at you. "I bless your search." She points the ankh a second time. "I bless your willingness to work to find what you want." She points the ankh at you a third time. "And I bless you for your strength and courage and determination."

The goddess nods, and now you know that your audience with her is concluded.

Thank her, bow if you want to, and turn and walk back out of the temple. Walk through the judges' anteroom and thank Aeacus, Minos, and Rhadamanthys, too. Follow the path back to your door.

Open your door. You are now back in your circle in your room. Use whatever technique you're accustomed to, to bring yourself back to normal, every-day consciousness. When you're ready, wiggle your toes and fingers, take a deep breath, and open your eyes. Be sure to ground yourself.

Know that if you think you've forgotten any detail of your conversation with Isis, what you need to know will come back to you, often in unexpected ways.

Notes

[1] Robert Graves, trans., *The Transformation of Lucius, Otherwise Known as The Golden Ass. From Apuleius* (New York: Farrar, Straus & Giroux, 1951), p. 264.

[2] Janet and Stewart Farrar, *The Witches' Goddess: The Feminine Principle of Divinity* (Custer, WA: Phoenix Publishing, Inc., 1987), p. 178.
[3] The anteroom and the three judges are adapted from a meditation in my book, *Goddess Meditations* (Llewellyn, 1999), p. 122. *Goddess Meditations* begins with a meditation to Isis, pages 3-6.
[4] Farrar, p. 176.
[5] Dion Fortune, *The Sea Priestess* (New York: Samuel Weiser, Inc., 1978; originally published in 1938), p. 304.

Ave Iside

by Rebecca Buchanan

Hail Holy Queen
    Mother of Mercy
    Mother of Peace
    Mother of Compassion

Lotus of the Sun
    To You we address our prayers
             our desires
             our mournful cries
Gracious
Loving
Sweet Goddess
    turn Your merciful gaze upon us

SLEEPING IN THE DESERT

by Normandi Ellis

I am waiting for night to overtake me
the way long purple shadows
beneath the wings of Isis
overtake the gleaming sands at dusk –
the way music that is only wind sings through you,
begins to use your throat.
I am waiting for beauty to crawl into my arms
like a long-eared desert hare
or like the peach-colored edges of an August sunset.
I imagine my own miraculous skin
changing colors like a salamander
– reds or blues
browns and greens –
or like a snake that sloughs itself off
all the way down to my eyelids
so that I might open them and gaze into distant vistas,
see far-off purple mountains,
see glowing orchards
pomegranates reddening in the dying sun.
May the old gray skins of my life
break apart and scatter
like clouds that open in the dark over this desert
revealing the milky skin of moonlight on the desert's face
and the enormity of stars
that we might otherwise miss
with our daylight eyes.

RITUAL TO ISIS

by Jeremy J. Baer

This ritual is designed to combine three broad strands: an opening invocation to the deities of the cult of Isis, based on Egyptian nomenclature; a hymn to Isis retelling the highlights of the death and resurrection of Osiris, composed in a manner similar to a Homeric hymn to a Hellenic god; and an invocation of Isis that is based on passages in the *The Golden Ass* where Lucius addresses Isis. Thus the ritual combines elements from the three great historical eras of Isiac worship: Egypt, Greece and Rome.

Items needed: statues or images of Isis, Osiris, Thoth, Anubis and Horus. Several candles or tea lights. A scented candle or incense and burner. A vessel for cold water.

Note: *Hennu* as discussed here means ritual prostration before the image of the gods as a sign of respect. In Egyptian style this would mean bowing to the gods and holding one's hand to one's heart, then displaying the open hand to the deities. In Greek style it means kissing the back of one's hand and then displaying the hand to the gods. Pick which version works for you.

Before the ritual, be sure to bathe. Conduct the ritual in clean clothes. Have the altar set up correctly before the ritual begins.

This ritual can be conducted at any time, but would work best during a full moon.

Opening Invocation

[light main candle]

[*hennu* to statue of Anubis]

"Lord of the Sacred Land, Prince of the Divine Court, Chief of the Holy Dwelling, Chief Over the Mysteries of Those in the Underworld, Guide of Souls Over the Long Road. I come to you, O Anubis, seeking purity and guidance. Accept this offering, Opener of the Ways!"

[light tea light or candle]

[*hennu* to statue of Thoth]

"He Who is like the Ibis, Scribe of Ma'at in the Company of the Gods, Lord of Divine Words, He Who Reckons the Heavens, the Pacifier of the Gods. I come to you, O Thoth, seeking wisdom and justice. Accept this offering, O God of Scribes."

[light tea light or candle]

[*hennu* to statue of Horus]

"The Avenger, Lord of the Two Lands, Son of Isis and Osiris, He Who Contends With Seth, He Who Sits Righteously on the Throne. I come to you. O Harpokrates, seeking strength and purpose. Accept this offering, O God of Royal Power!"

[*hennu* to statue of Osiris]

"Lord of All, Sovereign Over the Land of Silence, Lord of the Underworld, He Who Resides in the House of Conception, Lord of Ma'at. I come to you, O Osiris, seeking peace and plenty. Accept this offering, Greatest of the Great, Lord of Lords."

[light tea light or candle]

[*hennu* to statue of Isis]

"Queen of Heaven, Mother of the Gods, The One Who is All, Great Lady of Magic, Mistress of the House of Life. I come to you, O Isis, seeking protection and solace. Accept this offering, Lady of the Words of Power."

[light tea light or candle]

Hymn to the Gods

"Sing, Muses, of the terrible suffering of Isis. Sing of the death of Osiris and his resurrection to the world below. Sing of the love and magic of the great goddess who fills the world with light.

"14 years Osiris ruled as first king of Egypt. Agriculture and laws he gave to mankind. He taught men how to honor the gods.

"Then jealous Seth murdered him. The corpse of the mighty god was sealed in a coffin and floated to Byblos. And Isis wailed. She lost her brother-husband whom she had loved from the womb. Isis sailed the seas and retrieved the coffin; a great tree had grown around it.

"When the moon was full, Seth hunted. Coming upon the body of Osiris, he dismembered it. The pieces of Osiris were scattered afar.

"Isis led Thoth and Anubis in a great search. They restored Osiris. Through their magic the first mummy arose. Osiris lived again to rule Amenti, eternal judge of the dead! And the virtuous drink cool water at his throne. They never want for beer and bread.

"And Isis conceived her son Horus, a champion for her father. For 80 years Horus fought Seth for the throne. At last he was victorious.

"And so hail to you, Lady Isis, Queen of Heaven. Now I will remember you and another song too."

[light scented votive candle or incense]

Prayer to Isis*

"O holy, perennial savior of the human race, you are ever generous in your care for mortals, and you bestow a mother's sweet affection upon wretched people in misfortune. No day, no period of sleep, no trivial moment hastens by which is not endowed with your kind deeds. You do not refrain from protecting mortals on sea and land, or from extending your saving hand to disperse the storms of life. With that hand you even wind back the threads of the Fates, however irretrievably twisted. You appease the storms raised by Fortune, and restrain the harmful courses of the stars.

"The gods above cultivate you, the spirits below court you. You rotate the world, lend the sun its light, govern the universe, crush Tartarus beneath your heel. The stars are accountable to you, the seasons return at your behest, the deities rejoice before you, the elements serve you. At your nod breezes blow, clouds nurture the earth, seeds sprout, and buds swell. The birds coursing through the sky, the beats wandering on the mountains, the snakes lurking in the undergrowth, the monsters that swim in the deep all tremble at your majesty.

"But my talent is too puny to sing your praises, and my patrimony too meagre to offer you sacrificial victims; I have neither the richness of speech, nor a thousand mouths and as many tongues, nor an endless and uninhibited flow of words to express my feelings about your majesty. Therefore I shall be sure to perform the one thing that a pious but poor person can do: I shall preserve your divine countenance and your most holy godhead in the recess of my heart, and there I shall for ever guard it and gaze on it with the eyes of the mind."

[pour cool water into vessel]

[insert personal prayers to the goddess]

"May the blessings of the gods descend upon me. May the blessed gods watch over me while I follow Ma'at and hold dear the name of Isis."

[blow out main candle]

*Prayer to Isis taken from a passage in The Golden Ass by Apuleius

Hail Isis!

by Heather Cox

Behold the wondrous Isis!
Who unswervingly searched for her beloved Osiris after he had been slain.
Her tears upon finding his broken body could have overflowed the banks of the Nile,
while her smiling in rejoice of his return outshone the brightest stars in the night sky.
The vision of her loveliness is beyond compare –
lithe and graceful frame, bronze skin kissed by the sun, sparkling emerald eyes and wildflowers entangled in her braided hair.
She radiates power and carries herself with a regalness befitting only the Queen of Gods, and of man.
When fortunate enough to be in her presence one is filled with love and serenity;
yet she is also capable of defending those she favors with the ferocity of a mother lioness protecting her cubs.
Mankind is truly blessed by the gifts she has bestowed upon us – as countless as the grains of sand in the mighty desert.
May her wisdom and bounties continue to rain down on us as long as the sun blazes across the sky.
Hail she who is most vibrant! Hail Isis!

CRY TO ISIS

by Amanda Sioux Blake

The desert sands swirl about me
The realm of cruel Set envelops me
I am lost in the desert
No one hears my anguished cries
As the sands continue to blow
Stinging my squinted eyes
I cry out to You in desperation, O Isis
I cry out to You in anguish, O Isis
I have been betrayed by my friends, my confidants
As Your bother Set betrayed You.
O Isis, give me succor in my time of need!
Lead me to the oasis
For I cannot find it on my own.
I am parched, O Isis.
I am starved, O Isis.
I am lost, O Isis.
You appear to me
Long hair floating about Your shoulders
The staff of life in Your hands
Golden skin glowing, with the light of the Divine.
You are beautiful, unearthly so.
A kind smile plays on Your lips
You reach out for me
And I weep
Fearful that You are a mirage
Or an hallucination
Brought on by hunger and fatigue.
Your arms wrap around me,
Solid as the ground beneath us
Enfolding me in a Mother's embrace.
Holding me tightly,
You fly, taking me with You.
We leave the desert behind,
And drift among the stars,

In the bosom of Nyx Herself.
I cling to You,
Fearful of falling.
But You will not let me fall,
O Isis, my Mother, my Savior, my Rescuer.
You give me wings
So I may leave this world behind.
We dance together
Among the stars.

THE LADY OF TEARS

by Frater Eleuthereus

It was accursedly hot. The Sun rose upon the land. It looked almost as if Ra was glaring specifically at the robed lady. Ra's heat beat upon the land like bronze being smelted into spears of war. The paltry green in the desert oases was drying into tans and browns. Moisture and water were scarce, with soil parched like leather on a hide.

The Lady, a nearly all powerful goddess, was in hiding and had taken upon herself a human form and aspect (an avatar form). This limited her perceptions, her endurance and capabilities. Her avatar form also gave her a wider range of emotion and human sensibilities. She could not help but pause and feel regret as she traversed the land with her jet black hound, her son in spirit if not by full blood. Her Anupu, reduced from god to long-eared grinning jackal as they walked cautiously but firmly through once green fields, now desolate wastes, seeking her Treasure. Hers was a task she dare not entrust to any woman or man, neither acolyte nor champion, one of highest import.

Her garments were ripped, soiled and mottled from the elements. Still, she walked forward, continuing her sojourn. Her veil, a mottled gray once pure linen white, covered her bloodshot eyes but shielded her from the worst of the winds and sands in the wastes. Eyes which were red from dryness and grief, the salts of her tears caked upon her once lovely face.

She was undeniably beautiful. But this can be said of so many things or people. And to complicate matters, humans come in many forms and shapes. In the future, it would be their diversity that gave them their strength. What was beautiful to one might be only mildly pleasing to another. However, this lady radiated a beauty beyond her pink and copper skin. Her hair was the color of the night, not just black, but the starlight from which she was born. And if you looked closely, you could almost swear you saw it shimmer like an amber moon.

There was an aura about her, mild, cool, yet sparkling. In a land with people beaten by Darkness and Storm, she still walked with an air of refinement, not haughtiness or empty pride, but dignity. She might be broken, but she was unbowed. A moment's glance and one could tell she was royalty. The mud and dirt from her wanderings did nothing to extinguish or hide her elegance; rather they made her strong will and purity all the more hypnotic and fascinating.

Even in her self-restrained human form, she walked with poise and determination. She tried to exude a small sliver of light in the face of such suffering and fallowness in the Nile Delta. Even the areas which should have been the richest, by the Delta's salty sea and fresh river waters, once a deep flowing sapphire blue, were now trickles of their former glory, their normally darkened, nutrient-rich banks shriveled like dry fruit left out in Ra.

As she waded through the mingling of now noxious papyrus waters, she noted that they felt like scalded soup. The Sun reflected upon the water, back on her ivory skin. Solar power that would have caused a normal man to have second degree burns left Isis' skin copper interlaced with carnation, while her Anupu whose long ears were always perked and smiling, was completely unfazed and guided her forward.

The heat wave seemed as if it would never end. But from it, Isis learned a lot about her land. How odd that it took her becoming human to really understand the full putrefaction of Her Adversary.

Ask anyone of the desert, and they will tell you of its unique and harsh majesty of golden sands and colorful insects. You would hear with awe and reverence about a place vast and interspersed with rising vegetations of greens and reds a clear crisp scent and the smell of neroli or jasmine and other various herbs. But now the land reeked of burning compost and hints of sulfur on the breeze. You would also hear about another thing that Isis was discovering first hand, something that gave even her pause and care: the only thing worse than traveling during the heat of the desert's day was traveling during its nights.

The skies above Isis were clear, too clear during the days. Ra superheated the lands, thus making the surrounding air feel like a kiln's furnace. But at night time, the opposite occurred. The heat from the ground and the air radiated back into arid winds, without any moisture in the air, this yielded nightly and sudden temperature drops. And so, although the reflective light of the Moon was her guide, she chose to stay in encampments if possible during days, and traverse the waste in the mid-evening times; otherwise the temperatures were too frigid, even for Anupu in his current form.

The winds picked up and Isis continued to press on with her Anupu. She was always moving, attempting never to be in one area too long. And since everyone traveled at the same time, she had to be strategic to ensure she blended in to avoid guards and patrolmen. Her beauty and innate divinity at times made this challenging, so she kept her interactions with people to a minimum.

The distance between camps or villages was long and arduous. This constant transience left her little time or energy to think, only to be focused on the here and now. For a lady once a goddess, this limited definition of time was humbling. However, when she did have free time, it was focused on her Beloved and her Mission. Thoughts of him and union with him, drove her steps, her will, her every movement.

In this most recent settlement, where once roads were marble and tiled, now they were cracked and ill kept. She paced across dust laden streets and witnessed mite infested homes. Women and men and children ran to their errands. Securing their borders as the sands coalesced and stung eyes. Women and children tended to the donkeys, wrapping linens around their faces to ensure they would not be injured by the ongoing storms.

It was the same everywhere. Under her Adversary, the land refused to yield its fruits. Homes that were normally whitewashed and filled with lentils, meats and green leafy vegetables were now forced to make soups and stews from carrots and roots to stretch their resources as far as possible. The earthen streets of the settlement during the day were scorching to a human, but only a mild distraction to her on her bare feet. To such as her, it was nothing compared to the pain of her heart.

Perhaps the pain from the light of Ra above mimicked the pain in her heart as she walked below.

The people had so little, but still they did what they could to help her. Nomads and villagers, all offered her safety and sanctuary. She would only accept sparse fluids and rations since she knew that her people had barely anything to give. She thanked them each for their generosity and then continued onward. She had to maintain a low profile, ensuring that she could walk and avoid the patrols of her pursuers. The compassion she witnessed in the people as they struggled invigorated her. Even in the eye of a dark typhoon, there was light to be found. And so those times when she had to break and rest, entrusting her Anupu to guard her sparse slumbers, it was with hope dancing in her heart.

Isis helped as she could. She would give her water to little boys or girls but strangely, her water flasks burned skin, as if Ra personally had a grudge with her. How passive aggressive, she thought to herself bitterly. To make matters worse, there was no shade anywhere to allow them even to stay cool. Still dehydrated children found they were rejuvenated by her touch, and sometimes if a girl was watchful she might swear the mystery lady with the veil made flowers bloom as she walked or tell a parent that she saw water creep through cracks in the earth on the lady's path.

Isis wished she could do more, but she had to move on and left the encampment. Walking through a storm that had the village barricaded left her undaunted. And now, hills were coming next. With cane in hand she marched. By her side, prancing tongue panting in canine delight, was her Anupu. He barked and yipped and exhibited playfulness, an innocence that made her smile and lifted her spirits as it would many times on this quest.

The fugitive queen walked on, as if gliding on a current of unseen energy. Tireless, driven, in the early evening hour, she placed her hand over her eyes and left the encampment through wind and dust for the next oasis under a setting sun of purples and gold. Her heart tingled, she sensed that it was close, she knew it, and she felt it. Receiving a second burst of energy, the lady with over-fatigued muscles urged Anupu on and continued her pilgrimage through a now half-lit realm of sand and wind, until after what appeared like days, melding into weeks, the brown lands began to turn green.

Flora overran sand. Waters danced and cascaded before a magnificent tree. The waters were clear for once, not mottled with the taste of rotten egg... and they were finally... pure! She cupped her hands together and took a test taste of their nectar. A smile began to form on her lips, the water, such a blissful cooling fluid, its splendor rivaling the crystalline infinitude of Nun. Never would she take it for granted again. Tears trickled down her face, and flowers bloomed where they touched the verdant soils.

She was elated, for now she was sure she had found him.

An oak tree loomed before her, towering, impossibly tall. It jutted into the sky as if to challenge the clouds for mastery of the world's heights and air currents. But she was a creature of the Winds as well. Born from night and earth, a walking symbol of radiance, and now it was her turn to shine.

Words of Power were uttered. Holy words. Ineffable, unerring, vibrations of light, directed in a purity of love unseen before or since; this was not the love of happenstance or boys and girls. This was a love tempered by time and trials, one that might last beyond the grave. Her words paid homage to devotion, one that could never be broken, the power of true heart and love.

But even in the face of such love, the tree stood unmoved by the winds of her words or the power of her Will.

She spoke again and still nothing.

No. She did not come all this way, on the messages of birds and the hints of the green world, to be rebuked. She would not be denied in this, her urgent task. Never!

Arms raised themselves and revealed wings of jade and gold. Although still limited by her human form, she bore a crown disk that spilled sunlight upon the land. One of Her feathers blew off into the heightened wind and more light danced, touching the tree and caressing it, motivating it, awakening it. The tree saluted her, almost reluctantly recognizing its queen, and it leaned toward the gentle light. The tree was surprised to experience a light and coolness that was not scorching, but mild and comfortable within the confines of nature.

Isis called out again. The tree, hesitantly, released its fruitful treasure. But this vegetation did not have food, but rather her Other.

A coffin of gold lined with lead and scribed with onyx and ruby etchings fell from the tree's parted limbs. Reacting to protect the precious cargo, she quickly voiced another spell, and the fall of the coffin was stifled, not unlike a piece of linen or a feather in the breeze. And as the coffin came to earth, she cried in delight, a smile... she dared to smile holding the enchanted matrix.

"Asar Un-Nefer, Asar-Apis... Emerald of my heart, by blue and gold, and the white of salt I open thee coffin of dross. Thou art dispersed, your chains of bondage broken by word, will and," she paused, inhaling the sweetened air, "LOVE!"

One clang, and then another, and another grew in volume. Bolts burst, cracking at the sound of more pharyngeal vibrations of pure purpose, Holy Words. She used her godly strength to lift the metal casket top from its hinges. She grabbed the casket, heaving and grunting, muscles spasmed and stretched. Fibrous ligaments that she never knew she had begin to quiver. Why did it seem as if everything was exaggerated in this, her human form?

Finally, the casket opened and she dared another smile. Inside the sarcophagus was a male figure laying catatonic. He was youthful in appearance, square-jawed and toned. He was a lithe man with holly green skin his lips were the color of roses in summer and he smelled like the sweet air in the spring time. Bliss! Anupu barked in delight, his tail began wagging swiftly, making its own slight current. He knew his father when he saw him and licked him on the face with his tongue whimpering in happiness.

Upon a second glance at her Beloved, Isis' muscles tensed, she noted gravely there was a look of terror and dread upon his face.

"What are you seeing? How can I make it stop?" She asked her Beloved, kissing her love on his forehead. His pupils were dilated, they were not responding to the light of the now rising Sun on the horizon. She brushes her Osiris, her Serapis, her King, on his cheek... Yet, for all their efforts, the King remained comatose not responding to waving gestures or any stimuli. This concerned her but she was relieved for gazing upon him, his body glowed with the pulse of life. Laying prone, arms crossed in the casket her Beloved was immobilized. She picked him up slowly, and held him for a moment putting her fingers through his soft curly hair, and relished it.

And the etchings confirmed her suspicions. He was reduced to avatar form as well. The coffin that her Adversary had used was not just any box. It was specifically designed either restrain or tear out the alchemic divinity of a god; in effect leaving them bereft of the majority of their inherent miracles, their immortal vitality. It was why she had to traverse the land in this aspect and why the land was barren: it needed its green king.

But she was the Queen Physician and Alchemist. This could be reversed, this would be fixed. The two began to work in unison to reverse the spell. She wrapped Osiris in cloud-white linens, she anointed him with a special blend of oil and salts, an aromatic blend of neroli, amber and myrrh on various parts of his body.

Anupu's golden eyes shone and he opened his mouth. A mist of spiritual *ka* began to form. Isis, now with eyes closed deep in meditation, hummed and intoned, directing her Will and Anupu's spell-craft through her voice and body. Her jackal hound bowed on all fours, eyes shimmering a soft blue and with hints of gold, to assist his mistress.

The hands of Isis glowed softly and she began to sing a gentle lullaby a song of love, sorrow and life. "Wake love, into my arms you fly. From word to heart and back to ka the light of life returns to heart. Bodies of heaven and space, join your power to this song and rise love forever stirred."

The stars in the sky started to flicker, and even the planets shimmered, moved to action by their Rightful Queen, restoring her mate.

And then the world went red with blood and a bludgeoned impact to her skull.

A crash, and Isis winced, stunned by an injury that radiated through her spine. A frightful yip was all she heard as a mysterious hand grabbed her jackal's tail, flinging him. Anupu was knocked unconscious with a concussive blast, sending him hundreds of feet. He was deathly still; a foot twitched, his ribs elevating minimally.

Isis turned around, barely avoiding the back end of a lance made from golden Sun. That smell of sulfur and electricity was unmistakable. No shadow was that strong, no living being that swift or sure.

Only one could it be, Her Adversary.

Curse her foolish naiveté. Her task was too simple. Even on the run, she was never overrun. She tried to dodge for she knew that Lance's power. It had the power to sever Chaos from Order, Darkness from Light. It would kill her in this form.

But death wasn't on Seth's agenda for her today. An impossibly strong and brash red-haired humanoid in red and gold armor, accented with royal blues and the black of soot on the legs placed his foot upon her. His voice was the rumble of thunder on the wind. Clouds that whitened at her arrival now began to converge into a mottled mountain range of inky black, and the water began to turn a rotten apple green.

"So you are a woman after all..." he said, pushing his foot harder into her chest, grinning like a crocodile ready to swallow a bird.

Shifting her body weight, seeing that he left himself open, she swiftly struck Seth with her heel to his groin. He grimaced, yelling in temporary pain, releasing his grip. This gave her time to get back on her feet and to fly. But that kick should have immobilized him and all he did was shudder a moment, blinking and was fine. He stopped chasing her and ran to the coffin.

No, anything but that!

She witnessed in her opponent her own fire, her own will but magnified. Looking upon Seth he was force incarnate. The heat of his fire was the unbridled Solar winds. His options for destruction were limited only by his rage or creativity. He could hurl meteors upon her, his fists could crack the planet with ease. He was a force of nature and unpredictable.

And now Seth was at speed.

How was it he was able to keep his divinity when she and her Beloved were mortal on this plane? Or were things not as they appeared? While over thinking her plight, Seth swung his lance in an arc. Isis twisted in the sky, but still received a glancing blow from the weapon, which was enough to cause her to shriek, falling from the sky to earth leaving a streak of uprooted vegetation as she scraped across the ground.

Nearly triumphant, Seth walked toward his brother and then aimed his Lance upon the newly awakened Green God. The lance he normally used to destroy the Un-named one carved into his brother Osiris with appalling ease. Osiris, was aghast, looking saddened and confused. As his heart was gorged, Osiris grasped onto the spear, in vain trying to pull it out of his entrails, his head arched contorting itself. Realizing the wound was mortal, he looked up at his Isis somber and mild. Getting back on her feet, her infusion of bravery melted away as she stared into those earthen brown eyes of her Beloved's losing their *ka*.

This was *not* how it was supposed to end.

The oak-skinned lord bled green sap. His life force spilling onto the land and Isis' clothing... making flowers, vines, grapes, all matters of vegetation form. As the world began to dim, he saw something. The sun began to eclipse on the land, blanketing it in a primal darkness.

He knew that darkness... this was a dark that sucked the heat from fire, gorged on mishap, accident and murder. And now it was feasting upon Ra. And it was then Asar saw out of the corner of his blood-tinged vision a Serpentine Presence. Born of Nothing, filled with anger, seething and sulking, snickering and reveling in the stink of Its own filth and havoc. His arms stretched out, attempting to point to what he saw, urging the assassin to pause, but it was for naught.

"I forgive you," he whispered, his life fading.

"You forgive me?! You adulterous pig!" Seth's eyes turned embers of iron red, his voice became cacophonous, he ripped off Osiris' hand in rage, "I gave you my heart and loyalty, and you repaid me by sleeping with my wife." Seth arced his lance, slicing the rest of the arm to the shoulder. Osiris quivered in his brother's grip.

"You stack every indulgence and pleasure upon yourself. Dalliance with goddess after goddess and since she would forgive you anything, so should I?" Asar's eyes widened with the knowledge that he would be dead soon. There was no reasoning with this anger.

"And then tricking Isis into raising that, that mutant? How dare you make this about you?"

Arms outstretched and grasped Seth in an upward arc. She called on the winds to enhance her speed. Though mortal, Isis soars higher and higher toward the atmosphere's upper layers, friction burning her face. Her Adversary glares. "How can you forgive him? Time, after time?"

However, the higher Isis flew, she realized her limitations. Air was scarce the higher she went; her body and fluids started to freeze in a dark ice. Her arms spasmed and tightened, she grunted in pain, noting her fingers were slipping and she was too high. She let Seth go and began to plummet back to earth like a comet, faster and faster. Now the speed caused friction that burned her skin, turning it a cooked red. Seth unfazed threw her off him and she plummeted faster; if she hit the earth at this speed she would die.

She uttered the spell used on the falling coffin, again and again, something, anything, to dampen the fall. She called to all her hidden power, even to the power stolen from Ra, power that seemed to betray her before. *Don't let this be the end.*

And it was not. A light refracted upon her frame of jetting red, elegant purple, and fire gold. She was stopped inches above the ground, hovering above the soil. But Seth was back upon her, a blur of crimson slapping her and in its wake a boom of thunder. She struggled against his force vainly, "not today, birdling." Seth punched Isis in the gut, ribs broke and she doubled over in a slump of blood and bone. And now he grinned, standing over her, the strength of his frame negating her wings or any hope of mechanical or magical advantage.

Seth went back to his brother. His laugh is fell. A strike, a slice, a rip a tear, Seth appeared mad. Too injured and weak to break Seth's grasp, Isis watched, crying begging him to stop. Impotent for the moment, forced to watch as each piece of the body was tossed half a world away by hands more powerful than anything.

"There." As if a comet jetted from the bowels of land to sky, an arm careened at an upward arc hundreds of miles per hour. Isis blanched in disgust, a lump of heartbreak accumulating in her throat suppressing hiccups of grief which she dared not express in front of Him.

"There." Another limb flew, breaking trees, hill, and mountain as it impacted on the other side of the world in a crater of blood and grief.

Seth chuckled, throwing another piece of His brother, "There... and there is your love, your dear, tender love." Somewhat recovered, Isis managed to twist out of Seth's grasp while he was focused on his bloody act.

She vowed not to give Him the satisfaction of submission. He would be upon her in a moment. She called on the towering trees to become missiles, and they lifted themselves from rich top soil and darted at Seth. He brushed them away as if they were hay straw flung at the winds. Next, she summoned vines to act as ropes to spindle his legs in cords. Those ropes would normally restrain a mountain, but to Seth they were as yarn on a loom. He freed himself in but a moment, but that fraction of time saved her life.

And then Seth began to feel the pain of fang and claw upon his shoulder. This time he was the one who bled and yelped. Anupu had regained consciousness and was upon Seth. Teeth glowing with magick, his jaw became an iron grip holding on to his pray. Irritated, face contorted in pain, Seth grabbed the jackal under its nose and rubbed hard.

A reaction Anupu did not anticipate began. Anupu's long jaw unlocked. Anupu flailed with his back paws to scratch Seth, but he was unfazed. Grabbing Anubis by his neck and scruff, Seth began bashing him into the ground like a child with a toy having a tantrum. Not once, not twice, at least six times. The poor jackal's body left a crater, and Seth threw him in the hole, tossing him aside to bleed in his own filth.

At least he was alive, Isis noted with relief.

Regretting the necessity of it, Isis hid herself within an invisibility spell. Blending in with her surroundings in a distortion of light, she was safe, but there was a catch to this spell. She would have to move soon, to run, and thus become a target; or she could try to strike the mad god and thus become visible, giving up her temporary advantage. Even flight would disperse the spell.

She meditated, using a skill of mind to blot out Seth's ranting and raving. Seth shrieked to the Stars and the Winds of his own anger, blustering for her to show herself. She glared at her brother within her magickal Veil. Concentrating, she called upon her wings, her body to become enchanted copper. Her nails became claws. Light and durable, but magickally enhanced. Finally she revealed herself and stole up behind Him, boxing his ears, then scratching his back, leaving gashes, swiftly tearing into his armored shoulders, her aim was true and she stabbed into him. Making the most of her temporary advantage she grabbed him with her arms, slashing with her enchanted claws down his legs, severing the muscles of his upper legs, through his sartorius muscles, into his femoral arteries cutting beyond, into bone.

The power of her fury even in this human form was such that Seth did more than bleed, His sinew and godly fluids splotched the land and waters, contaminating what they touched. Had he not been fully divine, he would have had but minutes to live. Unfortunately this was not the case. Even wounds this grievous would do little more than slow him down. Seth flopped and quaked, losing His balance, falling to the ground.

"There! There! There!" Clang upon clang, radiating in pulses, and she struck again... again, if she stopped, in this rage, he'd kill her. "Where has your sense gone?! What has gotten into you?! I remember when your word meant something, when you were a hero, kind and brave!" She met her brother defiantly, standing on top of him while he nursed his ear drums and she continued.

"You were brothers. He loved you, almost more than anything, always forgiving your outbursts. And you cannot forgive him for one error of loneliness and a drunken stupor? Instead you repay him with *murder*?!"

Her eyes burned white hot like a nova of a star. "You've doomed us all." At this final statement, faint on the wind a serpentine chuckle was hissed, so silently Isis had to stop her attack to focus and hear it. What was that, and why did it sound so chillingly familiar? Apophis, the Feared Destroyer!

"Brother, look! Stop this, we must save Ra!" The Lord of Deserts had healed with the speed of a god. Taking advantage of her distraction, he slapped her across the face again, holding her so she could not fly away, kicked into her chest with his knee causing even Aset's enchanted copper to shatter like potters clay. Her face swelled like a damaged pomegranate, and was on the ground, wings and bone broken sliding on her visceral life essence.

A fist charged by the accumulated thunder and rages of wrongs both real and imagined struck the oak tree that held Osiris. The punch vibrated with a spheroid concussion, splintering the oak, sending it flying into millions of pieces. He then turned His attentions back to her, His sister.

"Give my whore of a wife my regards." A final punch to her face. It was too much and she fell. Her injuries were too many. Her vision clouded, turning black and feeble.

Pain. Red. Swelling.

Drought, shadow, failure.

When Isis came to, the oak tree was in shards, the coffin twisted and mauled, and green-brown sap-blood stained her dress and the ground of the oasis.

Seth was gone, and with him the hurricane of his self-propelling Chaos. Shock and pain filled her nerves and the fibers of her flesh. There was also the agony of fractures and internal bleeding. Much too much for her body to comprehend right now. She could barely move, and why would it matter?

It was all for naught, for Her Osiris was gone, again. She had failed.

A hole of darkness bleeds from the sky where Ra should have been. Black, blacker than a void with its own eerie eyes and wispy mouth with ephemeral fangs began to consume the sun and stars pervading upon the land. Another lady stared into that darkness, gulping and sighing. The Land was in its dying fits, Apophis was ascending.

A woman emerged from the shadows gliding toward Aset, torch held in the air by magic alone dimly lighting her way. Her eyes were a deep blue, her skin tanned and taut. Someone watching would perhaps consider them twins, but for the difference in their hair. Where Isis' hair was a soft pleasing shimmer of amber on black, hers was the dark between stars.

She was the greatest Nurse the land had known or would know. And she too knew Words that could make Gods yield, could set bones, and stave infections. But even with all that power, and having mended the wounds of her jackal son the best she could, Nephtys, Empress of the Red Land, looked into her sister's bruised and swollen eyes and was chilled.

It was because of her this happened. Had she been brave, like her sister, Isis would not be near death's door. All these wounds, this carnage, this anger a string of errors bound in moments. A fleeting loneliness, the warmth of his embrace, to feel green and alive rather than this barrenness. And for her failing, this, her sister broken and crumpled and their other brother dead, scattered everywhere.

She gingerly lifted her precious Isis. The white lady whimpered into the woman's black and red robe. Isis began a coughing fit, and spasmed while Nebhet-te wiped off blood redder than her robes from her sister. She began voicing spells welling from her heart; Isis' bones set themselves and her bruises healed. Purple and blue turn brown and gold, and the body healed itself. Though Nebhet-te could heal the body, she had no word or potion, no song or ritual to mend Isis' broken spirit.

There were no more azure waters, for the oasis that was of green pasture was now a husk. Even Ra was in its dying fits. It was the land's darkest night.

The Sister offered Isis new linen and a shoulder. Where one was broken the other was supple and strong. Enough was enough. Nephtys willed her emotions into check. Now was not the time for such things. Now was the time to be the anchor for her sister.

Her sister Nephtys carried her to a secluded area. "Let it out. You are safe for now. I loved him, too. You can be a widow, just like anyone else. Come into the darkness for a moment let it absorb your pain." Deep in those obsidian eyes there was a compassion born of the pains and sorrows and helping others during their nights.

Isis shrieked as if a wounded animal and finally the drought broke.

Everywhere across the land, clouds of gray poured their sorrow in lances of diamond water. The land devoured the moisture at first. But then hour after hour, Isis' cries were without end. No matter where one was, you could hear and see the hounds join in, standing in puddles, or on top hills, howling their grief. The birds fell from the sky. Lions refused to hunt, and elephants blew their snouts somberly, for their Isis has lost her One and Only.

The masses felt it too. They knew that Osiris was dead. Whether far away in city or village they all wept with her. Felines yowled, sister held brother as they wept into their pillows, husbands cried alongside wives for the Rightful King was dead.

The land could not bear these tears. The Nile river convulsed, spilling upon the desert. Though its nutrient rich earths and water brought life for all else... its dissolution was flooding, destroying, giving form to the pain of an exiled queen and a helpless populace.

She didn't care, *let them die*, for what worth were their lives if they were all to waste away in this putrid mockery of sustenance?

No. A sisterly hand grabbed Isis flinging her out of the dark and vanished. "Be the hero I cannot be right now. I shall see you soon, wellspring of my heart."

Hours later, a pregnant silence.

Isis, bald, her locks shaved in mourning and armored in her grief and purity, holding Anupu with her godly strength, took to the skies. Though it might take a year or generations, they would scour land and sea, the pits of volcanoes, for every piece of her Beloved. Seth be damned, they would be together once again with he who was lover, father, redeemer, her Beloved Serapis.

And rising in the sky stood the boat of Ra in his fight against a Serpent of Old. He shined a slight halo of orange and gold Isis' way. She smiled, a tear of joy like a pearl falling from her face.

And this time the light of Ra held her, guiding her like a friend, filling her with hope.

ISIS

by Logan Gore

How does one truly capture the essence of Isis? Can it be done through essay, studies, or ritual? In my personal experience, it is all of the above plus one extremely important detail: devotional work. Devoting oneself and opening up one's mind to Isis creates a never-ending supply of unconditional love, protection, and friendship.

I first encountered the never ending love of Isis through the interpretation of popular Egyptian mythology. It is here that we find Isis in her natural environment. The archetype of devoted wife and mother is epitomized at its peak with Isis. One only has to look at how she handled herself with the death of Osiris, or how she showed unconditional love to Horus to see this.

Meditation on the love and motherhood that Isis shows is a great first step for the potential Kemetic devotee. When I first began my workings with Isis, I took great care in paying attention to how the myths made me feel. When I thought I had captured the essence of her love I began devotional work, magick and ritual. In this heightened state on consciousness I opened myself up to her messages.

Wife and mother are not the only roles that Isis plays. She is also the epitome of the strong, independent woman. Consider the way she ruled Egypt while Osiris was away, or how she obtained the Sun God's secret name. My personal favorite example is in the passion in which she made love to the resurrected Osiris to conceive her son. In this myth we see a woman with extreme sexual power, for Osiris had no phallus when Horus was conceived.

Here, we can meditate again on the different faces of Isis. By tapping into her sexual side we can obtain a tremendous amount of knowledge on how love and passion should be handled. For those of us who are in the process of gaining our personal independence, she is the perfect role model. Here, we see the perfect balance of personal and financial independence, and sexual and personal freedom.

The protection that Isis offers is unlike any other we may encounter. At first, it is almost intimidating. Let's look again at myth. During the contending of Horus and Set, Isis went to great lengths to protect her son from the same fate as his father. And, considering that we are all spiritual children of the union of Isis and Osiris, she will protect us to this same extent.

It is here that some of us find trouble in furthering our devotional work. If Isis gives us this much, what can we possibly give her in return? The answer is simple. We offer her the same intangibles that she offers us. We can easily offer her our love and devotion. We can protect her name from slander, and we can use her stories to better our own life. Isis demands no sacrifice or blood spilled in her name. Only perfect love and trust. This is surely sufficient enough.

Friendship is the best gift that Isis has to offer. After we invite her into our lives, she is always there to experience everything that our path has to offer. And if we quiet ourselves often enough, she has an infinite amount of wisdom and guidance to share with us. As we walk our path, we know that we are never alone. As if Isis was not enough, she brings with her all of her friends and family! She will introduce you to Osiris, Horus, Thoth, Ra, Nuit, Bast and many more!

In conclusion, we all have so much to learn from Isis. Her beauty is as strong as her will, and her lessons are priceless. Devotion, meditation, and interpretation of myth are three key ingredients to forming a never-ending bond with Isis. And maybe once you have cemented your relationship with her, you can make many myths of your own.

Prayer to Isis II

by Theokleia

Omnipresent Mother, I am always in the shadow of your wings.
With each inhalation:
may I learn the path you have chosen for me.
With each exhalation:
may I walk upon it in honour.
In each moment:
may you find me worthy of your love
Vulture-Mother, I keep your shrine in the deep pools of my heart.

The Message of Osiris

by Sannion

Do not turn your face from Osiris;
look instead at what he shows you,
carefully, closely, inspecting the vision in all its particulars.
Once supple skin turned into hard brown leather by the centuries,
stretched taut over protruding cheekbones,
empty sockets staring blindly up to the heavens,
razor-thin lips set in an eternal grimace, silently howling through eternity,
wisps of fine hair hanging loosely from the back of the head,
bony fingers still clutching amulets to its sunken chest,
blackened, bug-eaten bandages crumbling into dust all around the frail
    figure.
Resist the temptation - do not look away, do not flee from the horror,
desperate to drive it from your memory.
Stop your skin from crawling,
refuse to let your mind play tricks on you,
convincing you that this is some thing,
some monster,
that it was never human,
that it was not once like you.
Let your eyes linger –
search for the traces of mortality still present in the mummy.
See the beauty that hides in the midst of the horror.
Imagine what he was like in life:
what pleasure he got from eating bread and drinking beer,
what games he played,
how he laughed,
what joy he took in kissing his wife and bouncing his baby son on his
    knee.
This thing was human once –
all that you experience in life, he did too.
And one day you shall stand where he stands,
a corpse returning to the elements.
We cannot flee death.
It overtakes us all

– even the gods, in their time, must endure finality's kiss.
This is a bond which all life shares,
which makes us all brothers and sisters in mortality.
That is the message Osiris has for you.
He was the first to die,
the first to make that long journey West.
But it is only a matter of time until you set out on that road yourself.
Do not squander your days.
Do not idly waste them, thinking that you can escape your fate.
Cherish each day that comes to you,
fill your life with abundant experiences,
taking pleasure in all you do
and see
and feel.
Stockpile your memories –
for they are the only riches we carry with us into the next world.

How Aset Learned Ra's Name

*based on a Ramesside papyrus
reinterpreted by Rev. Tamara Siuda*

I sing of the Self-Created:
God Who made Sky, Earth and Water.
Breath of life and fire of men and gods,
cattle and snakes, birds and fish.
King of Men and Gods both,
Lord to the Limit, having no years;
Whose Name is hidden from all.

I sing of Aset, clever Lady:
more cunning than a million men,
more thorough than a million gods,
more observant than a million spirits.

She knew the secrets of heaven and earth,
Like Ra, Who created both and all therein.
Except one thing:
She wanted to know Ra's Secret Name,
the Name that founded creation,
and all the things She knew.
This one thing She did not know,
and wanted it more than anything else:
to be equal to Her Father.

Every day Ra went to his Millions Boat
and sat at the head of the crew,
in his Throne of Two Horizons.
He was old; age had loosened His lips.
Moisture fell there, unknown, from His mouth
to drip down on the ground by the Boat.

Aset found the moist place on the earth
and set it to work in Her hands.
She made it into a snake

unlike snakes of Ra's creation.
With a stroke, it was straight like a dart,
and did not move.
She put it where Ra liked to walk,
at the crossroads,
and left it to wait.

Great Ra went outside with His following,
to stroll His creation, as He does every day.
The snake-dart struck – and hit.
Fire, Ra's blood, burned the grass of the road
and He fell.
His screams shook Heaven's foundation.

"What is it?" said the Great Nine.
"What?" shouted His bodyguards.
But Ra could not answer.
The poison, like the Nile flood, was cresting.
His lips trembled and His limbs shook.

Ra tried to be calm. He told them:
"Come, My children, of my body myself,
Let me say what has happened!
A painful, strange thing has struck.
My heart does not know it,
My eyes do not see it
and My hand did not make it.
This thing is not of My creation.
I have never felt anything like it.

"I am a king, the son of a king:
the divine seed being as a god.
I am a great one, the son of a great one:
Whose Name came straight from His Father.
I have many Names and forms,
and My forms are every god.
I am Tem and Heru Who Praises.

"My father and mother told Me My true Name,
and I hid it, from you, in My body,
lest someone steal creation from Me.

I came out to see these creations;
I walked the Two Lands, which I made.
A thing bit me, this unknown thing.
It is not of fire or water.
My heart burns, my body shakes;
my limbs, they grow cold.

"Bring My children, all the gods, to Me:
The ones Who know words of power,
Whose knowledge is higher than Heaven."
The Children of Ra came in tears.
None of them could undo it.

At last Aset came, with her powerful words,
The words that could drive away sickness,
and the words that raise the dead.
"What is it, My Father?" She asked. "What,
a snake? Has a snake shot its ill into You?
Has one of Your Children raised His head,
to defy His Creator?
I will destroy it with my perfect words,
make it retreat from Your shining rays."

Ra said "I was walking the road of the Two Lands,
as I like to do, to see all my Creation.
I was struck by this snake which I have never seen.
It is not fire or water. I sweat, shake,
My eyes are unsteady and I cannot see.
It is moist on my face like the flood."

"Tell Me Your Name, Divine Father," Aset said.
"Tell Me now. For he who is called
by his true Name must live."

"I am He who made Heaven and Earth," Ra replied,
"Who knotted the mountains, made all to exist.
I made water for Great Flood, the Divine Cow.
I made the bull for the cow, that pleasure might be.
I made heaven and the Two Horizons' mysteries,
and placed the souls of gods therein.
When I open My eyes it is light;

when I close them, darkness comes.
By My order the Nile flows.
My Name is unknown.
I made hours and days,
made the festivals separate, and bring the river.
I make the fire of life which makes men to become.
I am Khepera in the dawn,
Ra at the noon
and Temu in evening."

The poison stayed put.
Ra did not recover.

"Your titles are there," Aset said,
"not your Name.
Tell it to Me and the poison will go,
For he who is called by his true Name must live."

And the poison burned brighter,
more than Ra's own fire.

"Give me Your ear, Daughter Aset," Ra sighed,
"that My Name might be told from My body to Yours.
The Father of Gods hid it in Me
so My place in the Boat would be made.
When it goes from My heart into You,
You can only tell Heru, Your son,
if You bind Him with oaths with My image as witness."

The Great God told His Name to Aset, Great of Magic,
and She shared in His power.

"Flow forth, poison!" Aset cried.
"Creator of pain, at my word you will come forth from Ra!
I act and you go down into the earth, as
the Great God has told Me His very Name!
Ra lives and the poison is dead!"

And Ra lived and the poison died
by the words of Aset the Great,
Mistress of the Gods,
Who alone knows Ra's True Name.

OUR CONTRIBUTORS

[Editors' Note: we did not receive biographies for Seti Apollonius and Heather Cox before this volume went to press. We regret the omission.]

Jocelyn Almond is an Archpriestess-Hierophant in the Fellowship of Isis. She has a B.A. Degree in Studies in the Humanities and a Ph.D. in Philosophy. She is the co-author of *Egyptian Paganism for Beginners: Bringing the Gods and Goddesses of Ancient Egypt into Daily Life* and *An Egyptian Book of Shadows.*

Barbara Ardinger, Ph.D. (www.barbaraardinger.com), is the author of *Pagan Every Day: Finding the Extraordinary in Our Ordinary Lives* (Red Wheel/Weiser, 2006), a unique daybook of daily meditations, stories, and activities. Her earlier books include *Goddess Meditations, Finding New Goddesses* (a parody of goddess encyclopedias), and *Quicksilver Moon*, a novel. Her day job is freelance editing for people who have good ideas but don't want to embarrass themselves in print. To date, she has edited close to two hundred books, both fiction and nonfiction, on a wide range of topics. Barbara lives in southern California.

Jeremy Baer has been an avid admirer of ancient history and classical civilizations since grade school, and his parallel interest in cultural polytheism led him naturally to the study of Greco-Roman and Egyptian religions. Jeremy loves nature, the arts, and a good beer. He helps moderate the United Nations of Rome Victorious (www.unrv.com), a classical history discussion site.

Anne Baring (www.annebaring.com) is a retired Jungian analyst – author and co-author of seven books including *The Myth of the Goddess: Evolution of an Image; Soul Power: An Agenda for a Conscious Humanity,* and *The Dream of the Cosmos.* Her work is devoted to the recognition that we live in an ensouled world and to the restoration of the lost sense of communion between us and the invisible dimension of the universe that is the source or ground of all that we call 'life.'

Christa A. Bergerson is a guardian of Nature who finds pleasure traversing the wilds of Illinois, but would prefer to explore a warmer climate. She is also a spiritualist, a polytheist (there are too many wondrous deities to adore) and a Luddite. Her poetry has appeared or is forthcoming in *Doorways*, *Illumen*, *The Beltane Papers*, *Lalitamba*, *Faerie Nation Magazine*, *Sinister Tales*, and *Lady Churchill's Rosebud Wristlet*, among other publications. In 2008, her poem "Sekhmet Upon the Horizon" garnered third place in the B.S.F.S. Poetry Contest.

Birdsong is a teacher, artist, and writer living in rural Maine. Her great love is making books and teaching book art to others. She has chosen to use the anonymous name "Birdsong" for her poetry because the words often surprise her in their sudden appearance, as if they came from some place deeper or larger than herself – a place without a name but which we all have access to if we will only listen.

Amanda Sioux Blake has been Pagan for nearly ten years, since age thirteen, but remembers being called by Athena at age seven. She lives in South Bend, Indiana, where she splits her time between writing, school, volunteering, work, and caring for the many animals that find their way to her home. She is the author of *Ink In My Veins: A Collection of Contemporary Pagan Poetry* and the forthcoming titles *Journey to Olympos: A Modern Spiritual Odyssey* and *Songs of Praise: Hymns to the Gods of Greece*.

Rebecca Buchanan has a Master's Degree in Women's Studies in Religion, and is an editor with the webzine *Sequential Tart*. She has published a number of short stories and poems (thank you, Muses), including "Aoroi," "Black Leopard," "Gavrel," and "The Gray Lady of Gettysburg." No, she doesn't have a blog.

Jules Cashford read philosophy at St. Andrews, did post-graduate research in literature at Cambridge and earned a Ph.D. on Tragedy in the novels of Joseph Conrad. A Supervisor in Tragedy at Trinity College, she also studied Psychology of Consciousness with Max Cade and lectured on Mythology at Birkbeck College of Extra-Mural Studies, University of London. A member of the International Association of Analytical Psychology, she is the co-author (with Anne Baring) of *The Myth of the Goddess: Evolution of an Image*. She is also the author of *The Moon: Myth and Image*; the children's books *The Myth of Isis and Osiris* and *Theseus and the Minotaur*; and has published a translation of *The Homeric Hymns*.

Suzette Chan lives in Edmonton, Alberta. She writes for the comics and pop culture webzine, *Sequential Tart*.

Frater Eleuthereus has been pagan and has worked in the helping professions for over eleven years. He contributed several pieces to *Unbound: A Devotional Anthology for Artemis*. He is also working on his first book, which will focus on rituals and modern era material for the lunar goddess, Diana.

Normandi Ellis (www.normandiellis.com) is the author of three books on ancient Egypt, including *Awakening Osiris*, *Dreams of Isis* and *Feasts of Light: Celebrations for the Seasons of Life*. She leads workshops in writing as a spiritual practice and also leads trips to Egypt with Shamanic Journeys.

Russell Goodman is a college student, studying Dance Performance with a minor in Writing. He has a passion for role-playing games and hopes to be published one day. Independently, he studies astrology and mysticism.

Logan Gore has been a practitioner of Egyptian Paganism for three years, and a Priest of Isis for two. He has been featured in numerous magazines for his writings on the furthering of the Kemetic religion, and is currently working on his first book for the entire Pagan community. He lives in Columbus, Georgia and can be reached at lagore2009@yahoo.com.

Grace is a devotee of Anubis. She has been studying shamanism for two years, and has belonged to her Master even longer.

P. Sufenas Virius Lupus is the Doctor, mystagogue, and functioning priest of the Ekklesía Antínoou – a queer, Graeco-Roman-Egyptian syncretist reconstructionist polytheist group dedicated to the god Antinous, the deified lover of the Roman Emperor Hadrian – as well as a contributing member of Neos Alexandria. He previously published the book *The Phillupic Hymns* (Bibliotheca Alexandrina), and has contributed to several of the other current and forthcoming anthologies. When not involved in the things mentioned above, Phillupus is occupied with the overwhelming concerns of the everyday world, which are nowhere near as interesting or as important.

D. Jasmine Merced has studied classical history, language and art in both Greece and Rome, and is currently a graduate student at the University of Arkansas. Her specific research interest is classical religion, its architecture, and its effects on politics and society at large.

Payam Nabarz (www.myspace.com/nabarz) is author of *The Mysteries of Mithras: The Pagan Belief That Shaped the Christian World* (Inner Traditions,

2005), *The Persian Mar Nameh: The Zoroastrian Book of the Snake Omens & Calendar* (Twin Serpents, 2006), and *Divine Comedy of Neophyte Corax and Goddess Morrigan* (Web of Wyrd, 2008). He is also the editor of *Mithras Reader: An Academic and Religious Journal of Greek, Roman and Persian Studies Volume 1 and Volume 2*. His forthcoming book *Stellar Magic: A Beginner's Guide to Rites of the Moon, Planets, Stars and Constellations* is due out in 2009.

Brandon Newberg is an English teacher in Hokkaido, Japan. His interests include ancient religions and philosophies, ethics, and humanitarian concerns. Find him at the Polytheist Charity group (http://groups.google.com/group/polytheistcharity), or at his blog, Lilies and Cedars and Corn (http://brandondedicant.livejournal.com/).

Emma Nicholson is a postgraduate student at the University of London studying ancient history. She specializes in Greek religion, particularly in 'mystery' cults, and is currently working on her thesis about the cults of Isis and Serapis in Greece. Her passion for the ancient world started at a young age, and she wishes to convey and impart her joy of it by writing and teaching.

Sannion is a Greco-Egyptian polytheist who has been actively honoring the gods since around 1993. He has lived all over the country and currently resides in the state of Oregon. He divides his time between an insanely intense religious practice, writing, research, helping to organize the activities of Neos Alexandria, and directing the Bibliotheca Alexandrina. There isn't much time for anything else.

Tamara L. Siuda is the founder and current Nisut (spiritual leader) of the Kemetic Orthodox Faith, a modern practice of the ancient Egyptian religion. She established the religion in its present form and founded its first modern temple, the Kemetic Orthodox House of Netjer, in Chicago, Illinois in February, 1989. She is also a professional Egyptologist with a Master's degree in Egyptology from the University of Chicago (2000) and a second Master's degree in Coptic (later Egyptian) Studies from Macquarie University Sydney (2007). Rev. Siuda is currently engaged in doctoral research on the surviving traditions of ancient Egypt via a joint project between Macquarie and the Universität Göttingen in Germany.

Karen Tate (www.karentate.com) is an independent scholar, speaker, workshop presenter, sacred tour leader, minister, author and radio show host. As a Priestess of Isis, Karen also holds a Mistress of Goddess Spirituality degree from Reformed Congregations of the Goddess International (RCGI), she's an Adepta within the Fellowship of Isis, and has founded both the Iseum of Isis Navigatum and the Isis Ancient Cultures Society. Her travels around the globe visiting sacred sites of the Divine Feminine culminated in her first book, *Sacred Places of Goddess: 108 Destinations*, which has garnered many prestigious endorsements. Her second book, *Walking An Ancient Path: Rebirthing Goddess on Planet Earth*, was a finalist in the USA National Best Books of 2008 Awards in the spirituality category. Karen hosts two radio shows, *Voices of the Sacred Feminine* and *Earth's Sacred Places*. She still leads sacred tours to Goddess sites around the globe.

Theokleia lives in Melbourne, Australia with her partner and a bunch of plants.

Select Bibliography and Internet Resources

Primary Sources

Apuleius. *The Golden Ass*
Engalman, H. *The Delian Aretalogy of Sarapis*
Eusebius. *Chronicon* 32: 9-13, 40.7-9, 43.12-16
Faulkner, R.O. *The Ancient Egyptian Pyramid Texts*
Kater-Sibbes, G.J.F. *A Preliminary Catalogue of Sarapis Monuments*
Ovid. *Metamorphoses*
Plutarch. *Moralia Volume V: On Isis and Osiris*
Reardon, B.P. *The Collected Ancient Greek Novels*
Vanderlip, Vera. *The Four Greek Hymns of Isidorus and the Cult of Isis*
Von Dassow, Eva, et. al. *The Egyptian Book of the Dead: The Book of Going Forth by Day - The Complete Papyrus of Ani Featuring Integrated Text and Full-Color Images*

Secondary Sources

Almond, Jocelyn. *Egyptian Paganism for Beginners: Bring the Gods and Goddesses of Ancient Egypt into Daily Life*
Alvar, Jaime. *Romanising Oriental Gods: Myth, Salvation and Ethics in the Cults of Cybele, Isis and Mithras*
Antelme, Ruth Schumann. *Becoming Osiris: The Ancient Egyptian Death Experience*
Apostolos-Cappadona, Diane. *Dictionary of Women in Religious Art*
Brady, Thomas A. *Sarapis and Isis: The Collected Essays of Fordyce Mitchel*
Bricault, Laurent. *Nile Into Tiber: Egypt in the Roman World: Proceedings of the IIIrd International Conference of Isis Studies*
Burkert, Walter. *Ancient Mystery Cults*
Cashford, Jules, and Anne Baring. *The Myth of the Goddess: Evolution of an Image*
Cott, Jonathon. *Isis and Osiris*
De la Bedoyere, Guy. *Gods with Thunderbolts: Religion in Roman Britain*
Dill, Samuel. *Isis and Serapis in Roman Society*

Doherty, PC. *The Assassins of Isis: A Story of Ambition, Politics and Murder Set in Ancient Egypt*

Donalson, Malcolm Drew. *The Cult of Isis in the Roman Empire: Isis Invicta*

Ebers, George. *Serapis.*

Ellis, Normandi. *Dreams of Isis: A Woman's Spiritual Sojourn*

Forrest, M Isidora. *Isis Magic*

Forrest, M Isidora. *Offering to Isis: Knowing the Goddess Through Her Sacred Symbols*

Frankfurter, David. *Religion in Roman Egypt*

Graham, Jo. *Hand of Isis*

Ikram, Salima. *Divine Creatures: Animal Mummies in Ancient Egypt*

Jacq, Christian. *For the Love of Philae*

Kinsley, David. *The Goddesses' Mirror: Visions of the Divine From East and West*

Kinstler, Clysta. *The Moon Under Her Feet*

Knapp, Bettina. *Women in Myth*

LaFevers, RL. *Theodosia and the Staff of Osiris*

Lesko, Barbara. *The Great Goddesses of Egypt*

Lester, Julius. *Pharaoh's Daughter: A Novel of Ancient Egypt*

Lewis, H. Jeremiah. *Balance of the Two Lands: Writings on Greco-Egyptian Polytheism*

Limke, Jeff. *Isis and Osiris: To The Ends of the Earth*

Martin, Luther H. *Hellenistc Religions: An Introduction*

Mojsov, Bojana. *Osiris: Death and Afterlife of a God*

Muten, Burleigh, and Rebecca Guay. *Goddesses: A World of Myth and Magic*

Olson, Carl (ed.). *The Book of the Goddess, Past and Present: An Introduction to Her Religion*

Ozaniec, Naomi. *Daughter of the Goddess: The Sacred Priestess*

Pinch, Geraldine. *Egyptian Myth: A Very Short Introduction*

Reed, Ellen Cannon. *Circle of Isis: Ancient Egyptian Magic for Modern Witches*

Reitzenstein, Richard. *Hellenistic Mystery Religions: Their Basic Ideas and Significance*

Regula, deTraci. *The Mysteries of Isis: Her Worship and Magick*

Smith, Wilbur. *River God: A Novel of Ancient Egypt*

Stambaugh, John E. *Sarapis Under the Early Ptolemies*

Stone, Merlin. *When God Was a Woman*

Takacs, Sarolta. *Isis and Sarapis in the Roman World*

Trobe, Kala. *Invoke the Goddess: Visualizations of Hindu, Greek and Egyptian Deities*
Turcan, Robert. *The Cults of the Roman Empire*
Tyldesley, Joyce. *Daughters of Isis: Women of Ancient Egypt*
Versluys, M.J. *Aegyptiaca Romana: Nilotic Scenes and the Roman Views of Egypt*
Waldherr, Kris. *The Book of Goddesses: A Celebration of the Divine Feminine*
Walters, Elizabeth. *Attic Grave Reliefs that Represent Women in the Dress of Isis*
Wild, Robert A. *Water in the Cultic Worship of Isis and Sarapis*
Witt, RE. *Isis in the Ancient World*

Internet Resources

Neos Alexandria, a Greco-Egyptian polytheist group, and parent organization of Bibliotheca Alexandrina.
http://www.neosalexandria.org/

Children of Kemet discussion forums.
http://childrenofkemet.freeforums.org/portal.php

Fellowship of Isis, a multi-religious group dedicated to honoring the goddesses of the planet.
http://www.fellowshipofisis.com/

Kemetic Orthodoxy.
http://www.kemet.org/

Kemetic Traditional Religion.
http://www.per-ankh.org/

Kemet Online, a forum sponsored by Per Ankh.
http://www.kemetonline.com/

Veridical Kemetic Faith.
http://per-heh.org/

Nuhati-Am-Nutjeru Faith Community
http://www.thelivingnuhati.org/

International Network of Kemetics
http://www.inkemetic.org/

The House of Aset
http://www.philae.nu/akhet/aset.html

Isis Magic
http://www.hermeticfellowship.org/Iseum/index.html

Pagan Regeneration, by Harold R. Willoughby, [1929], Chapter VII: Isiac Initiation.
http://www.sacred-texts.com/cla/pr/pr09.htm

Temple of Isis at Philae
http://www.eyelid.co.uk/philae1.htm

Wesir.org, a site dedicated to Osiris.
http://www.wesir.org/

Martin Luther King Jr.'s article on mystery religions
http://www.stanford.edu/group/King/publications/papers/vol1/500215-The_Influence_of_the_Mystery_Religions_on_Christianity.htm

Serapis as depicted on ancient coins.
http://www.forumancientcoins.com/moonmoth/reverse_serapis.html

Appendix A – List of Divinities

Adonis: A Near Eastern deity who entered Hellenic mythology. He has been interpreted as a dying and rising god of vegetation, and is thus compared with **Osiris**.

Aion: An eastern god of time.

Ammon: An Egyptian creator deity, conflated in Egypt with **Ra** and by the Greeks with **Zeus**.

Antinous: A young male of Hellenistic origins who was the companion and probable lover of the Roman emperor Hadrian. He mysteriously drowned in the Nile. He was deified by order of Hadrian and became equated with a variety of gods, including **Osiris**. The *Ekklesia Antinoou* is a modern day queer, Graeco-Roman-Egyptian syncretist reconstructionist polytheist group dedicated to him.

Anubis: The jackal headed Egyptian god of embalming, also guide and guardian of the dead. In Isiac myth, Anubis assists **Isis** in finding the scattered remains of the dismembered **Osiris**, and then helps turn Osiris into the first mummy. Identified sometimes with the Greek **Hermes**.

Aphrodite: The Hellenic goddess of love, beauty and sea-faring. Sometimes identified by the Greeks of the Hellenistic era with **Isis**.

Apis: A bull deity worshiped very early in Egypt. He was the most important of the sacred animals in Egypt and something of a national mascot. In death he was conflated with **Osiris** as Osorapis. The basis of the Hellenistic god **Serapis**.

Asklepios: Greek god of medicine and healing. Sometimes syncretized with **Serapis**.

Atum: An Egyptian creator deity later identified with **Ra**.

Daimones: In Hellenic religion, intermediary spirits between humans and deities. The Agathos Daimon was a protective spirit of a Greek household. The city of Alexandria had an Agathos Daimon identified with **Serapis**. *Daimones* also appear prominently in magical texts of Late Antiquity.

Demeter: The Hellenic goddess of agriculture and motherhood, and from her cult center in Eleusis the presiding deity of one of the most popular mysteries in Antiquity. Identified by the Greeks of the Classical Era with **Isis**.

Dionysus: The Hellenic deity of vegetation, wine, the performing arts, and afterlife mysteries. In the Hellenistic era he is increasingly equated with **Osiris**. Known to the Romans as Bacchus.

Fate: *Fortuna* in Latin, *Tyche* in Greek. Greeks and Romans came increasingly to feel the affairs of the universe were governed by this capricious goddess. Cults whose deities promised protection from Fate, such as **Isis** and **Serapis**, became popular. Sometimes these deities were even syncretized with Fate, as in the case of the Roman era Isis-Fortuna.

Geb: The Egyptian earth god, of whom **Isis** and **Osiris** were children.

Hapi: The deification of the annual flooding of the Nile river, and thus a god linked with **Osiris** and fertility.

Harpokrates: Also known as **Horus the Younger**, the child magically conceived by **Isis** and **Osiris** after the latter's death. After a war against **Seth**, Horus ascended to the throne of Egypt, becoming the embodiment of kingly power. Iconic depictions of Isis nursing an infant Horus were common throughout the Greco-Roman world.

Hathor: An ancient Egyptian goddess who was the personification of the sky. Also a mother goddess connected with royal power, and a goddess of love and the arts. Much of her iconography and attributes were eventually taken over by **Isis**.

Helios: The Greek solar deity. *Sol* in Latin. Helios was identified with many deities in the Hellenistic era, including **Serapis**.

Herakles: Known as Hercules to the Romans, Herakles was the son of **Zeus** known for his great strength and his famous twelve labors.

Hermanubis: The syncretic formation of **Hermes** and **Anubis** from their roles as guides of the dead. Like Anubis, Hermanubis is depicted as cynocephalous (dog headed), but with Hermes' wand.

Hermes: The Greek god of travel, heraldry, and guide of the dead. Identified with **Anubis**.

Horus: A falcon headed Egyptian deity. There was an elder Horus and a younger Horus. For the latter, see **Harpokrates**.

Iao: Also known as Iao Sabaoth, Jehovah, YHWH. The Creator deity of the Hebrew tribes who eventually became *the* deity of later Judaism. Iao was worshipped in Alexandria by the Jewish population as well as some pagans, and was identified with a variety of pagan gods such as **Zeus**.

Isis: In origin, an old Egyptian goddess connected with funerary mourning and kingly power. In Egypt she was conflated with a variety of goddesses, including **Hathor**, to eventually become a popular and powerful mother and magician goddess. The Greeks and Romans further conflated her with various Mediterranean goddesses.

Ma'at: An Egyptian term for their concept of order, harmony, law, truth and justice that was opposed to chaos. Sometimes personified as a goddess, and sometimes equated with the Platonic *logos*. The souls of the dead had to recite 42 negative confessions of Ma'at to gain admittance to the afterlife.

Magna Mater: The Great Mother, known to the Greeks as Cybele. A goddess of mountaintops, wild animals and fortresses, honored with orgiastic rites by eunuch priests.

Min: An Egyptian fertility god, depicted with an erect phallus.

Mithras: A Mystery god, possibly of Indo-Iranian origins, who became popular with Roman soldiers. In some places it seems Mithras and **Serapis** were linked, due to both deities being identified with **Helios**. In the novel *The Golden Ass*, the high priest who initiates the character Lucius into the cult of Isis is named Mithras.

Nephthys: The sister of **Isis** and **Osiris**, and wife of **Seth**. She assists Isis in morning for Osiris.

Nut: The Egyptian sky goddess, of whom **Isis** and **Osiris** were children.

Osiris: From the Middle Kingdom onward, the principle Egyptian god of the dead and afterlife. Brother and husband to **Isis**, father of **Horus the Younger**, and murdered by **Seth**. In Egypt he was conflated with a variety of deities. The Greeks and Romans knew him as **Serapis**.

Pan: A goat footed Greek god of the countryside, but also a god of healing and thus linked with **Serapis**.

Poseidon: Greek god of the sea, horses and earthquakes.

Ptah: An Egyptian creator god whose chief cult was in Memphis. Important in funerary religion, he is linked with both the **Apis** bull and **Osiris**.

Ra: The Ancient Egyptian king of the gods, and the solar god par excellence who was conflated with other solar deities. Humanity was thought to be formed from the tears of Ra. In the *Contendings of Horus and Seth*, Ra initially supported **Seth**. Ra was tricked by **Isis** into revealing his true name, which gave Isis great power.

Serapis: Also **Sarapis**. The conflation of **Osiris** with the **Apis** bull, whom the Greeks also identified with other deities. Serapis was the principle god of the Ptolemies; his great temple at Alexandria was renowned throughout the ancient world. He was a god of healing, dreams, agriculture, and a benevolent savior deity. In Roman times his cult often was secondary to **Isis**.

Seth: A warrior deity and the Egyptian god of chaos. His murder of **Osiris** and the usurpation of the throne begins the *Contendings of Horus and Seth*. The Greeks equated him with Typhon, a demonic force that challenged **Zeus** and the Olympians.

Sothis: The deification of the star Sirius, the brightest star in the sky which historically appeared before the annual Nile flooding. Sothis was later identified with **Isis**.

Thoth: The Egyptian god of wisdom, writing and magic, and counselor of the gods. In Isiac myth, Thoth assists **Isis** variously with his magic, and provides the legal defense for the succession of **Horus** against the claims of **Seth**.

Zeus: The Hellenic king of the gods who presided over the home and the social order, as well as being a sky god. Equated with numerous gods, including eventually **Serapis**.

Zeus-Ammon: The conflation of **Zeus** with **Ammon**. Zeus-Ammon was an oracular deity with cult centers in Northern Africa and the Hellenic lands. His oracle at the Siwa Oasis confirmed Alexander the Great as his son, and as the legitimate Pharaoh of Egypt.

Appendix B – Glossary

Abydos: An ancient city in Upper Egypt and home to an important cult center for Osiris and Isis.

Akhu: The spirits of the dead, sometimes identified with the shining stars of the sky. Ancestor worship played a part in domestic Egyptian religion.

Alexander the Great: Son of Phillip the Great of Macedon who forcefully united Greece. Alexander overthrew the Persian Empire, becoming Pharaoh of Egypt in the process. The end of the isolation of the Greek city-states from themselves and from the Near East ends the Classical era and begins the Hellenistic Era.

Alexandria: The seat of the Ptolemaic regime, the capital of Hellenistic Egypt, and the greatest port city in the Eastern Mediterranean. The city was known for its Library and Museum, its multi-cultural and cosmopolitan make up, and the great Temple of Serapis.

Amenti: See **Duat**.

Apuleius: Lucius Apuleius Platonicus (c. 123/125–c. 180) was a Romano-African author. He wrote *The Golden Ass*, also called *Metamorphoses*. It is the only Roman novel to survive intact, and describes the bawdy adventures of a character called Lucius and his eventual initiation into the cults of Isis and Serapis.

Aretalogy: A lengthy list of attributes of a deity, told in the first person.

Bennu-bird: A creature that arose from the primordial chaos to announce the beginning of time. Sometimes seen as equated with Osiris, the *bennu* bird leads souls of the deceased through the underworld. A likely prototype for the phoenix myth.

Book of the Dead: Also known as "Going Forth By Day." Funerary hymns and spells, often written on a scroll and placed in a coffin. Derived from the earlier Pyramid Texts and Coffin Texts.

Caesars: The generic term for the Roman Emperors. The early emperors, Augustus and Tiberius, were officially conservatives opposed to the spread of Nilotic cults within Roman society. Caligula ended official opposition by building a temple to Isis in Rome. Vespasian claims to have received an oracle from Serapis proclaiming him emperor. Caracalla built a magnificent temple to Serapis.

Coffin Texts: Funerary spells found mostly on Middle Kingdom coffins. They describe an afterlife ruled by Osiris, and offer protection to souls for their journey through subterranean levels.

Contendings of Horus and Seth: Pyramid Texts and papyri depict one of the greatest mythological themes from antiquity, the struggle for the throne of Egypt between Seth and Horus the Younger after the murder of Osiris. The most complete account of this myth is recorded by Plutarch.

Cult: From the Latin *cultus*. Everything associated with the worship of a particular god. The ancient use of the word has none of the sinister connotations of modern usage.

Diodorus Siculus: A Greek historian in the 1st century BCE. His writings on Egypt and Alexander the Great are invaluable primary texts.

Djed: An Egyptian pillar symbol linked with Osiris.

Duat: The Egyptian underworld, where souls of the dead go to be judged. Also called **Amenti**.

Duumvir: In a Roman town, one of the two chief elected magistrates.

Eleusinian Mysteries: Mysteries practiced annually at Eleusis near Athens in honor of Demeter and Persephone.

Empyrean: The highest heaven. In savior cults such as those involving Isis, it was thought the soul would ascend to this blessed place, and be beyond the reach of the ravaging effects of **Fate**.

Fellowship of Isis (FOI): A multi-religious neopagan organization founded in 1976. It is dedicated to honoring the religions of all goddesses.

Gellabiya: Traditional Arab garment worn for casual and evening wear.

Greco-Egyptian: An adjective referring to the historical fusion of Greek and Egyptian cultures and religions that transpired under the Ptolemaic dynasty.

Haides: Also spelled Hades. The Greek underworld where the souls of the dead reside. Sometimes equated with the Egyptian **Duat**.

Hall of Two Truths: In Egyptian mythology, the place where souls in the afterlife are judged. Thoth pronounces the deeds of each soul, and Osiris weighs their hearts.

Hellenic: Of or having to do with Hellas (Ancient Greece).

Hellenismos: One of the names for Hellenic Reconstructionism, though different groups may employ other terms. Hellenic groups honor the major Greek deities (Olympians) and usually minor deities as well. Reverence for ancestors, nature spirits and deified local spirits called Heroes are widespread. Hellenismos has various festivals throughout the year, often based on the Athenian lunar calendar.

Hennu: A complicated ritualistic gesture performed by Egyptians during religious ceremonies as a sign of respect toward deities.

Herodotus: A Greek historian of the 5th century BCE. He wrote extensively on Egypt, though sometimes his veracity is in debate.

Iseum: A temple to Isis. Unlike most religious structures in the Greco-Roman world, an Iseum was closed off from the surrounding street, and had a sanctuary where only clergy and the duly initiated could enter. In the morning and early afternoon, clergy led cult adherents for public ceremonies to Isis, which involved the singing of hymns, and rituals of fire and water.

Kemet: The native Ancient Egyptian term for their country. It means "Black Land," in reference to the life giving silt deposited on the banks of the Nile after the river's yearly inundation. People practicing the reconstruction of Ancient Egyptian religion tend to call themselves Kemetic rather than Egyptian.

Kemetic Orthodoxy: A modern organized religion based on the beliefs of Ancient Egypt, as taught by the Rev. Tamara Siuda. Kemetic Orthodoxy emphasizes upholding Ma'at in one's life.

Khernips: The water used for purifying one's hands in Hellenic rituals.

Kouros (pl: Kouroi): A statue depicting a standing male youth.

Mithraeum: A ritualistic meeting place for the cultic adherents of Mithras. These were designed to resemble caves. There were various altars, statues and iconography dedicated to Mithras and other deities. The centerpiece of worship culminated in a shared meal among the adherents.

Modius: The vessel used for storing and measuring grain, also in some cults a symbol of fertility and of resurrection after death. Serapis was depicted with a modius as a crown.

Mysteries: In the Greco-Roman world, some cults had private initiations of individuals, which contrasted with the more communal, public affairs of Greco-Roman polytheism. The initiated were sworn to secrecy about the sacred rites, images and mythologies they were shown. Mystery religions promised secret knowledge about a deity that engendered a spiritual rebirth and/or a better afterlife for the initiate. The cults of Isis and Serapis were among the most popular mystery religions of antiquity.

Naos: The inner most shrine in a temple. Alternatively, box-like shrines in modern domestic worship.

Natron: A salt mixture that occurs naturally in dry lake beds. Ancient Egyptians used it to purify their mouths for religious rituals.

Nemes: The striped head cloth worn by pharaohs in ancient Egypt.

Neopaganism: An umbrella term for a very wide array of pagan faiths and magical paths, the largest of which is Wicca. Neopaganism is a modern movement, though it may have antecedents stretching back several generations.

Neos Alexandria: A multi-faith organization dedicated to Greco-Egyptian religion. Its publishing arm is the Bibliotheca Alexandria.

Netjer: The Kemetic word for god or divine power.

Nilotic: Of, or having to do with Ancient Egypt. "Nilotic cults" refers to Egyptian cults, especially Isis and Serapis.

Oracle: In Greek and Egyptian religions, the cults of certain deities offered to foretell the future through divination by clergy or seers.

Pastophoros (pl: Pastophoroi): A lesser order of Egyptian clergy. In the Isaic cult they were connected with liturgy and processions.

Pax Romana: The relative peace and unity imposed on the classical world by the Roman Empire. The Roman Peace facilitated the spread of universal religions, from the savior cult of Isis to Christianity.

Pharaoh: The Greek term for Egyptian rulers. Pharaohs were the heads of Egyptian government, army and religion. They were considered embodiments of the god Horus, and were the chief mediators between the world of men and the gods. Pharaonic Egypt began before 3000 BCE, and ended in 30 BCE when Rome annexed Egypt as an imperial possession.

Phyle: A Greek wording meaning "tribe." Lower orders of priests in Egypt were divided into such tribes, and served on a rotating basis.

Plutarch: A Greek writer in the Roman era. His *De Iside et Osiride* is a valuable primary text on Egyptian religious rites and mythology.

Proskynesis: The act of venerating a god or ruler by bowing and other means of submission.

Ptolemies: The dynasty founded by Ptolemy Soter, a general to Alexander the Great, and ending with Cleopatra VII. The Ptolemies ruled Hellenistic Egypt from 305 BCE to 30 BCE from their great port city of Alexandria. The Ptolemies had many notable cultural achievements, and under their rule the cults of Isis and Serapis spread throughout the Mediterranean.

Pyramid Texts: Spells dating from the Old Kingdom that were carved on Pyramid walls and sarcophagi. Mentioning the god Osiris, they are concerned with preserving the Pharaoh's remains and ushering him into the afterlife.

Reconstructionism: A belief that ancient religions should be practiced as closely as possible on historical models according to literary and archaeological findings.

Rhakotis: A small fishing village on the northern coast of Egypt. Later rebuilt into Alexandria by Alexander the Great.

Senut: What modern Kemetics term the daily religious rite performed before their domestic shrine.

Serapeum: A temple to Serapis. The largest was in Alexandria; it was famous throughout antiquity.

Sinope: A city on the Black Sea in Asia Minor. Plutarch says Ptolemy stole a statue of an unknown god from this city that was later proclaimed as Serapis.

Sistrum (pl: Sistra): A percussion device consisting of a handle and metal frames that produces a distinct sound when shaken. Sistra were cultic instruments for Isis and other Egyptian goddesses.

Stygian: Having to do with the river Styx, the waterway to the Greek underworld.

Syncretism: Syncretic deities are two previously separate, though similar, deities whose identities are conflated. This can occur within a culture (e.g., between Isis and Hathor in Ancient Egypt), or more often between different cultures (e.g., between Isis and Aphrodite). Isis became the most syncretized deity in the ancient world, eventually conflated by her cult adherents with every important Mediterranean goddess.

Tamera: Means "Beloved Land," another native term for Ancient Egypt. There are circles of Egyptian Wicca that call themselves Tameran.

Triclinium: A Roman dining room, containing three couches seated around a low table.

The Two Lands: Another term the Ancient Egyptians gave to their country. It can refer either to the union of Upper and Lower Egypt, or the dichotomy of the Black Land (fertile land along the Nile) and Red Land (barren desert beyond the Nile).

Wabu: In Egypt, the wab priests were the lowest order of clergy who oversaw the cleanliness of the temple.

Wicca: While definitions vary, in general a group of Neopagan religions either directly descended or inspired by a faith popularized by Gerald Gardner. Most Wiccans honor a god and goddess, practice ritualistic magic, and celebrate eight holidays throughout the year.

Zep Tepi: In Egyptian mythology, the First Time, the point when the mound of creation arose from the waters of chaos.

Appendix C – Historical Eras

Ancient Egypt:

Predynastic Period (c. 5000 – 3100 BCE): The ancient districts, or nomes, of Egypt coalesce into the Two Lands of Upper and Lower Egypt.

Archaic Period (c. 3100 – 2686 BCE): The Two Lands are unified with a capital at Memphis.

Old Kingdom (c. 2686 – c. 2181 BCE): Increasing centralization of government. Construction of the first Pyramids. The afterlife cult centers around the Pharaoh.

First Intermediate Period (c. 2181 – 1991 BCE): Collapse of the central government. Social chaos.

Middle Kingdom (1991 – 1786 BCE): Reemergence of central government with a new capital at It-towy. Osiris and Isis gain popularity with the common people and their afterlife hopes.

Second Intermediate Period (1786 – 1567 BCE): Foreign invasion by the Hyksos, a nomadic Asiatic peoples.

New Kingdom (1567 – 1085 BCE): Rulers from the city of Thebes expel the Hyksos. Egypt is reunited and forms an empire.

Third Intermediate Period (1089 – 525 BCE): Collapse of central authority.

Late Period (525 – 332 BCE): Egypt is ruled by the Persian Empire.

Ptolemaic Egypt (305 – 30 BCE): Alexander the Great overthrows the Persian Empire and becomes Pharaoh of Egypt. After his death, his general Ptolemy founds a dynasty and rules from Alexandria. The Hellenistic cults of Isis and Serapis spread throughout Greek lands, and eventually into Roman ones as well.

Roman Egypt (30 BCE – c. AD 600): Cleopatra VII, the last Ptolemaic ruler, dies. Egypt is annexed by the Roman Empire. The cults of Isis and Serapis are eventually recognized by the emperors until their eclipse by Christianity. When the Roman Empire splits between east and west, Egypt becomes part of the Eastern Empire under Constantinople. Roman Egypt later falls to invading Islamic armies.

Ancient Greece:

- **Minoan-Mycenaean Age** (c.3300 – c.1500 BCE): Proto-Hellenic civilizations centered around palaces and citadels form on the islands and mainland of Greece. After reaching a high point, they quickly collapse from natural disaster or invasions.
- **Dark Age** (c. 1050 – c. 750 BCE): Dorian and Ionian Greeks settle the mainland and islands.
- **Archaic Age** (c. 750 – 479 BCE): The formation of the Greek city-states. The Persian Empire attempts to invade Greece twice and both times is ultimately repelled.
- **Classical Age** (479 – 336 BCE): The period of Ancient Greek history from the end of the Persian wars to the rise of Alexander the Great. Defined by competition between Greek city-states, especially between Athens and Sparta. This is an amazing century of Western cultural achievements, especially in the city-state of Athens.
- **Hellenistic Age** (336 BCE – 30 BCE): The period of ancient history from Alexander the Great's death to Cleopatra VII's death in 30 BCE. It marks the spread, and to some degree the fusion, of Hellenic culture with the culture of non-Greek peoples in the wake of Alexander's conquests. The cultural center of the Greek world shifts from Athens to the Ptolemaic capitol at Alexandria. The savior cults of Isis and Serapis spread throughout the Greek speaking world.
- **Roman Age** (30 BCE – 330 CE): The Romans conquer all of the Hellenistic kingdoms bordering the Mediterranean. In turn, Hellenistic culture infiltrates Roman lands. Hellenistic religions become popular with the Roman masses. Christianity is introduced and later becomes the state religion. The Roman Empire is split between East and West, and the Hellenistic lands in the east are ruled from the new capital at Constantinople. The Eastern Empire eventually evolves into what is now known as the Byzantine Empire.

Ancient Rome:

- **The Monarchy** (753 BCE – 509 BCE): According to myth, Rome is founded by Romulus and Remus, sons of Mars. A line of kings rule, the last of whom are Etruscans. The monarchy is expelled by a conspiracy of Roman nobles in conjunction with the waning of Etruscan power in Italy. Rome is subject to Greek influences from the beginning via trade with Greek colonies in the south of Italy.

Early Republic (509 BCE – 264 BCE): Rome is ruled by a republican government with strong oligarchic tendencies. Rome contends with its immediate neighbors for dominance. Celtic tribes sack Rome itself, but Rome recovers to eventually conquer the Italian peninsula.

Middle Republic (264 BCE – 146 BCE): Rome fights its three Punic Wars with Carthage for control of the Western Mediterranean. It also begins its conquest of the Hellenistic East, and Hellenistic culture and religion begin to penetrate Rome.

Late Republic (146 BCE – 27 BCE): Gaul is conquered, as is the rest of the Hellenistic Mediterranean. Ambitious Roman generals begin a series of civil wars which will topple the Republic. Hellenism continues to influence Roman culture.

The Principate (27 BCE – 235 CE): After generations of bloody civil wars at the hands of ambitious generals, Augustus Caesar effectively concentrates all power in one person, ending the Republic. The Empire enjoys a period of relative peace and stability, despite occasional civil wars and deranged emperors. Romano-Hellenistic culture and religions flourish.

Crisis of the Third Century (235 CE – 284 CE): A period of constant civil war and military anarchy ensues. The Empire splits into three parts, and is attacked by foreign foes. The empire is reunited and the invaders driven out only with great effort.

The Dominate (284 CE – 476 CE): Diocletian and Constantine reorganize the empire into a more centralized and authoritarian state. Constantine is the first emperor to recognize Christianity, and it eventually becomes the state religion. In 394 CE the empire splits between East and West. The West slowly disintegrates until its last emperor is deposed in 476 CE.

Appendix D – Chronology of Important Events

BCE

c. 3100: Upper and Lower Egypt are unified with a capital at Memphis.
c. 2500: First written mention of Isis.
c. 2400: The Pyramid Texts mention Osiris.
c. 2890 – 2686: The cult of Apis is established under the 2nd Dynasty.
c. 2589 – 2566: The Great Pyramid is built.
c. 1991 – c. 1786: The Middle Kingdom of Egypt. The cults of Osiris and Isis gain popularity.
c. 5th century: Isis is honored by Egyptian metics (resident aliens) at Piraeus, the port of Athens.
332: Alexander the Great conquers Egypt, founds Alexandria.
305 – 283: Ptolemy I founds the Ptolemaic dynasty, promotes the cult of Serapis and Isis.
246 – 222: Ptolemy III oversees the construction of the great Serapeum at Alexandria.
c. 2nd century: Isis receives a sanctuary on the slope of the Athenian acropolis.
69 – 30: Cleopatra VII Philopator. The last Ptolemy has affairs with Julius Caesar and Marc Antony. She declares herself Isis incarnate, while Marc Antony is likened to Osiris.
58: Isiac militants disturb a sacrifice of a Roman consul, claiming Rome had done nothing on behalf of Isis. Private Isiac sanctuaries and altars within Rome are ordered destroyed by the Senate. They are quickly rebuilt by the cult followers.
53: The Roman Senate orders destruction of private chapels to Egyptian gods.
50: The Roman Senate again orders demolition of private chapels to Isis. The demolition workers refuse to carry out the orders, prompting the Consul to grab an axe and do the deed himself.
48: Another Senatorial decree to destroy private chapels to Isis and Serapis.
43: Roman triumvirs Octavian, Marc Antony and Lepidus vow an official temple to Isis on Roman soil: this never materializes. A Roman magistrate proscribed to death by the Triumvirs escapes by disguising

himself in a cultic festival to Isis. Antony legitimizes Isis worship in Rome.
30: Cleopatra VII, who considered herself the living incarnation of Isis, commits suicide after a failed war with Rome. Egypt annexed as a Roman territory.
28: Egyptian cults prohibited within the city of Rome by the Augustan regime. The order is largely ignored.
c. 25 BCE - 8 CE: Roman poets Propertius, Tibullus and Ovid mention the growing Isiac faith in their writings.
21: Agrippa takes action against Egyptian cults in Rome.
14 BCE - 37 CE: Reign of Tiberius. After a sexual scandal involving a Roman knight, an aristocratic woman, and the cult of Isis, Tiberius has a temple to Isis destroyed and her cultic image throne into the river.

CE

37 - 41: Reign of Caligula. Caligula builds a temple to Isis on the Field of Mars. Isis becomes an official part of Roman religion.
46 - 120: Life of Plutarch, who writes *De Iside et Osiride*.
69: The Roman general Vespasian performs a healing "miracle" in the Serapeum in Alexandria. An Oracle of Serapis proclaims him the next emperor. Meanwhile, his son, Domitian, flees from political opponents by disguising himself in the garb of an Isiac cult adherent.
80: After a fire burns the temple of Isis, Emperor Domitian has it rebuilt and embellished, and adds an Egyptian style obelisk to it.
117 - 138: Reign of Emperor Hadrian. Hadrian visits Egypt. Builds a villa which contains strong Egyptian themes.
180 - 192: Reign of Emperor Commodus. Commodus was wont to dress up like an Isiac cultic adherent; he beats those around him with a cultic mask of Anubis.
c: late 2nd century: Apuleius writes *The Golden Ass*.
212: Roman Emperor Caracalla pledges a special cult to Serapis as a healing god. Later builds a giant temple to Serapis.
284 - 305: Reign of Diocletian. He builds a new sanctuary to Isis and Serapis somewhere in Rome.
313: Constantine the Great proclaims the Edict of Milan, reversing sporadic persecution of Christians. Constantine and his successors become patrons of the Church.
360 - 363: Julian the Apostate fights the increasing Christian influence on the Roman state. He shows special favor to Serapis-Helios.

380: Emperor Theodosius I declares all subjects of the empire should profess the faith upheld by the Bishops of Rome and Alexandria (Nicene Christianity).

391 – 392: Theodosius issues a series of decrees banning the practice of paganism on pain of death. Almost all temples are destroyed or confiscated.

391: The Serapeum at Alexandria is destroyed following a bitter clash between pagans and militant Christians.

c. 540: The Emperor Justinian closes the last temple to Isis on the island of Philae in the Nile River.

About the Bibliotheca Alexandrina

Ptolemy Soter, the first Makedonian ruler of Egypt, established the library at Alexandria to collect all of the world's learning in a single place. His scholars compiled definitive editions of the Classics, translated important foreign texts into Greek, and made monumental strides in science, mathematics, philosophy and literature. By some accounts over a million scrolls were housed in the famed library, and though it has long since perished due to the ravages of war, fire, and human ignorance, the image of this great institution has remained as a powerful inspiration down through the centuries.

To help promote the revival of traditional polytheistic religions we have launched a series of books dedicated to the ancient gods of Greece and Egypt. The library is a collaborative effort drawing on the combined resources of the different elements within the modern Hellenic and Kemetic communities, in the hope that we can come together to praise our gods and share our diverse understandings, experiences and approaches to the divine.

A list of our current and forthcoming titles can be found on the following page. For more information on the Bibliotheca, our submission requirements for upcoming devotionals, or to learn about our organization, please visit us at *www.neosalexandria.org*.

Sincerely,

The Editorial Board of the Library of Neos Alexandria

Current Titles from the Bibliotheca Alexandrina:

Written in Wine: A Devotional Anthology for Dionysos
Dancing God: Poetry of Myths and Magicks by Diotima
Gods and Mortals: New Stories of Hellenic Polytheism by
   H. Jeremiah Lewis
Goat Foot God by Diotima
Longing for Wisdom: The Message of the Maxims by Allyson Szabo
The Phillupic Hymns by P. Sufenas Virius Lupus
Unbound: A Devotional Anthology for Artemis
The Balance of the Two Lands: Writings on Greco-Egyptian Polytheism
   by H. Jeremiah Lewis
Echoes of Alexandria: Poems and Stories
   by H. Jeremiah Lewis
Waters of Life: A Devotional Anthology for Isis and Serapis

Forthcoming Titles from the Bibliotheca Alexandrina:

Words of Power: A Collection of Modern Greek- and Egyptian-Themed
   Fiction in Honor of Thoth
Queen of the Great Below: An Ereshkigal Devotional
Bearing Torches: A Devotional Anthology for Hekate

Made in United States
North Haven, CT
17 June 2022